INSPIRE / PLAN / DISCOVER / EXPERIENCE

KRAKÓW

KRAKÓW

CONTENTS

DISCOVER 6

EXPERIENCE 58

NEED TO KNOW 202

Left: Magnets depicting iconic symbols of the city
Previous page: Wawel Cathedral on a winter's day
Front cover: St Mary's Basilica, seen through the
arches of the Cloth Hall

DISCOVER

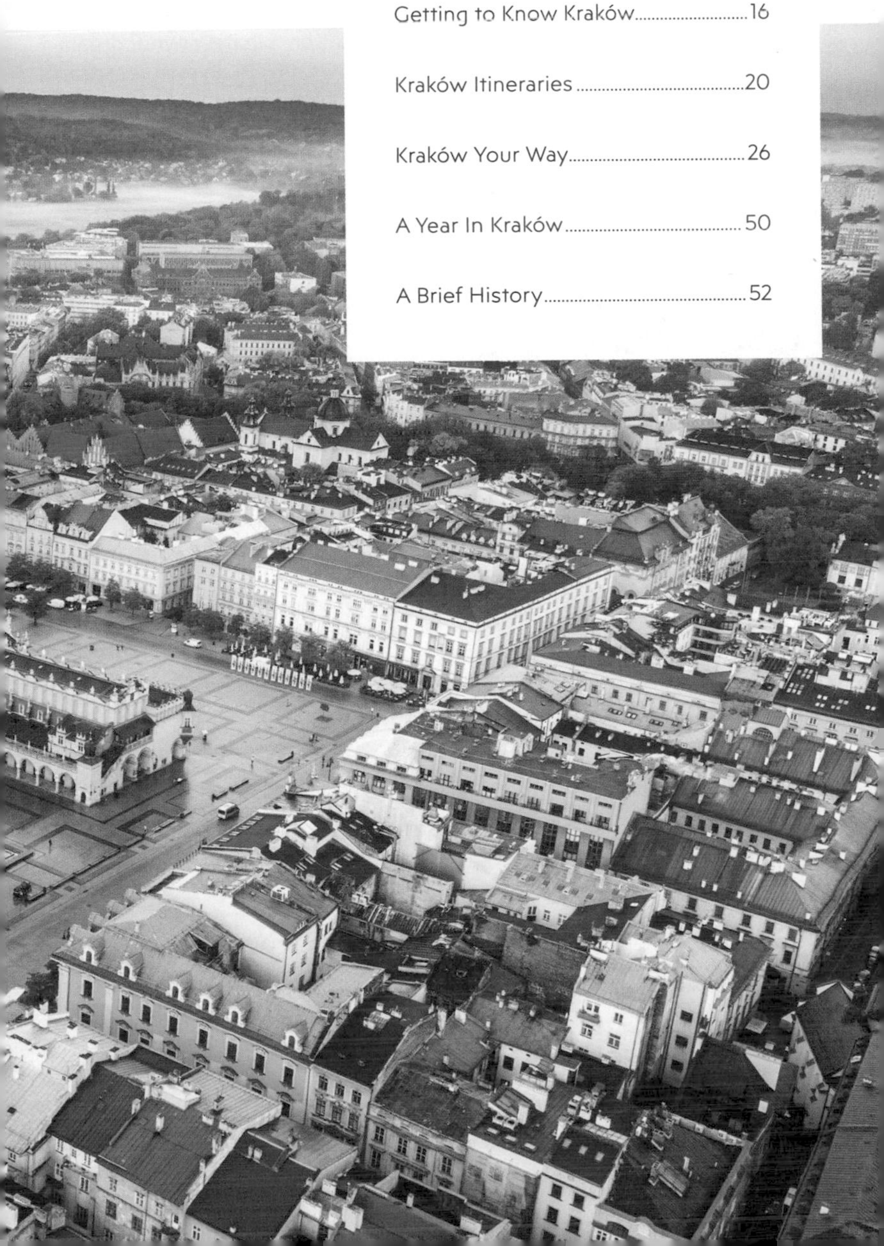

WELCOME TO
KRAKÓW

Fairy-tale spires and winding medieval streets. Masterpiece-filled art galleries and compelling museums. Traditional restaurants serving moreish pierogi and candle-lit bars buzzing with late-night conversation. Whatever your dream trip to Kraków entails, this DK Eyewitness travel guide is the perfect companion.

1 A plate of mouthwatering and moreish pierogi.

2 Snow-covered statues in Planty Park.

3 A stained-glass window in St Mary's Basilica.

4 Kraków's spectacular Main Market Square.

Fairy-tale Kraków could have stepped straight out of a storybook. Once Poland's royal capital, this historic city has managed to hold fast to its medieval character. At the city's heart lies the magical Old Town, home to the vast Main Market Square, and sprinkled with sumptuous palaces, awe-inspiring churches and historic monuments. Surrounding this central core are a variety of vibrant areas, from ancient Wawel Hill, previously the seat of the Polish monarchy, to bohemian Kazimierz, Kraków's former Jewish quarter. The city is also the perfect place to feast, whether you're devouring plates of pierogi, snacking on mouthwatering *zapakeni* or sating your sweet tooth with a serving of classic *szorlota* (apple pie). As night falls, the city's many watering holes come to life, from atmospheric, old-world pubs to candlelit wine bars housed in hidden cellars.

Beyond the centre, you'll find historic mounds, a scattering of impressive abbeys and the lush green of Wolski Forest. Further afield lies the sparkling Wieliczka Salt Mine, spectacular national parks, and an array of picturesque villages and charming towns. There's also the Auschwitz–Birkenau Memorial and Museum, today a major site of remembrance.

Kraków is filled with such a variety of sights that it can be hard to know where to start. We've broken the city down into easily navigable chapters, with detailed itineraries, expert local knowledge and colourful, comprehensive maps to help you plan the perfect visit. Whether you're staying for a weekend, a week or longer, this DK Eyewitness guide will ensure that you see the best this magical city has to offer. Enjoy the book and enjoy Kraków.

REASONS TO
KRAKÓW

This former royal capital is brimming with awe-inspiring architecture, captivating art galleries and achingly cool jazz bars. There are so many reasons to love Kraków; here are some of our favourites.

1 ART NOUVEAU
Kraków is peppered with stunning examples of Młoda Polska (p49) – Poland's version of Art Nouveau – including the Franciscan Church's (p108) arresting stained glass.

MYSTIC MOUNDS 2
Clamber up one of the artificial mounds built to honour famous Poles: Kościuszko Mound (p174) offers epic views and Krakus Mound (p141) is said to hold the remains of the city's founder.

3 JEWISH HISTORY
Traces of the city's rich Jewish heritage survive in Kazimierz's synagogues and cemeteries, while Schindler's Factory tells the tragic story of the city's Jews during World War II (p136).

GOING UNDERGROUND 4
Some of Kraków's most riveting history lies down below. Unearth vampire graves at the Rynek Underground (p72) or explore Wieliczka's incredible sculpted salt mines (p190).

MAIN MARKET SQUARE 5
The city's undisputed heart, this vast square (p64) is home to some of Kraków's most iconic sights, including the striking St Mary's Basilica (p68) and Renaissance Cloth Hall (p70).

COMFORT FOOD 6
There's no shortage of tummy-lining food here, whether it's eat-till-you-pop pierogi, those irresistible pockets of stuffed dough, or addictive *obwarzanek*, a seed-sprinkled bread ring.

KAZIMIERZ NIGHTS 7

While the city is packed with atmospheric bars and pubs, the quintessential Kraków crawl undoubtedly begins and ends in the candle-lit clubs of the former Jewish quarter.

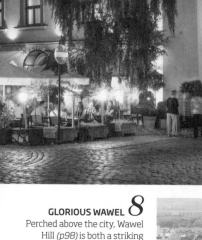

GLORIOUS WAWEL 8

Perched above the city, Wawel Hill *(p98)* is both a striking symbol of Polish statehood and a powerful reminder of the city's former role as the country's capital.

9 LIVE JAZZ

Poles have always been jazz aficionados, and you can still sample those cool 1950s and 60s beats in the Old Town's cellar bars, such as legendary Jazz Club U Muniaka *(p86)*.

THE PLANTY *10*

A leafy belt of green encircling the Old Town, the Planty *(p92)* is the perfect place to escape the city's hustle and bustle. Dotted with trees, flowers and benches, it's great for a picnic.

SZARLOTKA *11*

Cracovians love their cafés and patisseries, so you're never far from something sweet. Sample to your stomach's content, and don't leave town without trying delicious *szarlotka* (apple pie).

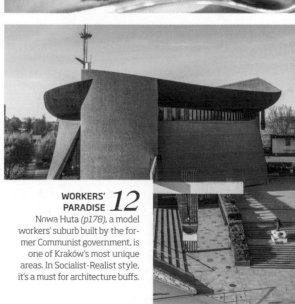

WORKERS' PARADISE *12*

Nowa Huta *(p178)*, a model workers' suburb built by the former Communist government, is one of Kraków's most unique areas. In Socialist-Realist style, it's a must for architecture buffs.

ŁOBZÓW

NOWA WIEŚ

Park Krakowski

Convent of the Nuns of the Visitation

KLEPARZ

Carmelite Church

Planty

Czartoryski Museum

PIASEK

THE OLD TOWN
p60

Park Jordana

PIASEK AND NOWY ŚWIAT
p154

Church of St Anne

Market Square

Cloth Hall

St Mary's Basilica

Planty

National Museum in Kraków

Dominican Church

Błonia Fields

NOWY ŚWIAT

Philharmonic Hall

OKÓŁ

Planty

WAWEL HILL AND AROUND
p94

STRADOM

Wawel Hill

WAWEL

Vistula

DĘBNIKI

Corpus Christi Church

Plac Wolnica

KAZIMIERZ
p118

LUDWINÓW

EXPLORE
KRAKÓW

This guide divides Kraków into six colour-coded sightseeing areas, as shown on this map, plus two areas beyond the city. Get to know each area on the following pages.

WARSZAWSKIE

Museum of the
Home Army

ESOŁA, KLEPARZ
AND BISKUPIE
p142

Former Main
Railway
Station

WESOŁA

Church of the
Sacred Heart
of Jesus

Jagiellonian
University
Botanical
Gardens

GRZEGÓRZKI

New Jewish
Cemetery

Remuh
Synagogue

Vistula

Old Synagogue

AZIMIERZ

Museum of
Contemporary Art
(MOCAK)

PODGÓRZE
p132

Schindler's
Factory

PODGÓRZE

ZAGUMNIE

Rynek
Podgórski

St Benedict
Fort

Park
Bednarskiego

Krakus
Mound

Liban
Quarry

Płaszów
Concentration Camp

EASTERN EUROPE

SWEDEN

DENMARK

LITHUANIA

Gdańsk

Poznań

Warsaw

BELARUS

GERMANY

POLAND

CZECH
REPUBLIC

KRAKÓW

UKRAINE

SLOVAKIA

SWITZ.

AUSTRIA

HUNGARY

ITALY

CROATIA

ROMANIA

SERBIA

0 metres   600
0 yards   600

N

GETTING TO KNOW
KRAKÓW

Enchanting Kraków expands outwards from the Old Town, its medieval heart. Encircling it are a number of unique areas, each with their own distinctive character, from regal Wawel Hill to bohemian Kazimierz. Beyond the centre lie subterranean cities, lofty mountains and poignant sites of remembrance.

PAGE 60

THE OLD TOWN

Dominated by the magical Main Market Square, this area is Kraków's historic heart. A UNESCO World Heritage Site, the Old Town has charming medieval streets and some of the city's most renowned sights, including the magnificent Renaissance Cloth Hall and iconic St Mary's Basilica.

Best for
Old-world charm and medieval streets

Home to
Main Market Square, Collegium Maius, Church of St Anne, Czartoryski Museum, Dominican Church

Experience
Spying vampires at the Rynek Underground

PAGE 94

WAWEL HILL AND AROUND

Overlooking the city, Wawel Hill is an impressive fortified complex home to the city's royal castle and cathedral. Surrounding the hill to the north, east and south are two picturesque areas, historic Okol and verdant Stradom, offering winding, cobbled streets, quaint churches and captivating museums.

Best for
Royal pomp and pageantry

Home to
Wawel Hill, Church of Saints Peter and Paul, Franciscan Church

Experience
Exploring the castle's opulent interior

KAZIMIERZ

Found to the south of the Old Town and Wawel Hill, Kazimierz is the city's former Jewish Quarter. This historic suburb, nestled on the banks of the Vistula river, is peppered with an array of spectacular synagogues that were refurbished following World War II; highlights include the historic Old Synagogue, and the beautifully decorated Tempel and Remuh synagogues. Engaging museums are also found here, including the evocative Galicia Jewish Museum and hands-on Museum of Municipal Engineering. Sprinkled throughout Kazimierz are innumerable old-world bars and cafés that ooze bohemian atmosphere.

Best for
Jewish heritage

Home to
Old Synagogue

Experience
A night out in one of the area's candle-lit bars

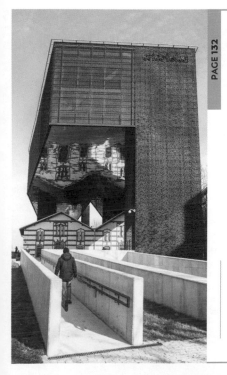

PODGÓRZE

Sitting opposite Kazimierz on the other side of the Vistula river is Podgórze, the former Jewish ghetto. This now-verdant area contains many memorials to its harrowing past, including the compelling Schindler's Factory and poignant Eagle Pharmacy, as well as the remains of the old Ghetto Wall. Also found within Podgórze is the striking Cricoteka, a museum filled with theatre paraphernalia, and the excellent Galeria Starmach, one of the country's best art galleries. Outside the area's central core you'll find the lush green expanse of Bednarski Park and the majestic Krakus Mound – the latter is thought to be the burial site of the city's founder, King Krakus.

Best for
World War II memorials and museums

Home to
Schindler's Factory and MOCAK

Experience
Learning about life under the Nazi regime at Schindler's Factory

→

PAGE 142

WESOŁA, KLEPARZ AND BISKUPIE

Extending to the north and east of the Old Town, these three neighbourhoods are ranged around Kraków Główny, the city's main train station. While a little off the beaten track, they're nevertheless home to a number of fascinating sights, from the wonderfully eclectic and exquisitely decorated Church of the Sacred Heart of Jesus to the utterly engaging Museum of the Home Army. Sprinkled across the area is a wealth of striking Art Nouveau architecture, including the renowned Globe House.

Best for
Awesome Art Nouveau architecture

Home to
Church of the Sacred Heart of Jesus, Museum of the Home Army

Experience
Escaping the city in the Jagiellonian University Botanical Gardens

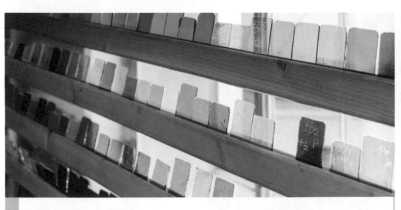

PAGE 154

PIASEK AND NOWY ŚWIAT

Stretching west of the Old Town, both of these delightful areas are criss-crossed by pretty, tree-lined streets and dotted with a number of charming churches. The main draw here is the museums, whether it's the vast, art-filled National Museum or the mind-boggling Museum of Illusions. Other cultural highlights include the intriguing Stained Glass Museum and, further west, the Błonia Fields, an expansive green oasis.

Best for
Enthralling museums and galleries

Home to
National Museum in Kraków

Experience
Eating apple pie at beloved book shop, Massolit

BEYOND THE CENTRE

Countless attractions are located just beyond Kraków's city centre. Dominating the area to the west of the city is the leafy district of Zwierzyniec, best known for its collection of churches, convents and monasteries, as well as for the leafy expanse of Wolski Forest. Further west you'll find the impressive Benedictine Abbey in Tyniec, while to the east lies the sprawling suburb of Nowa Huta, built to be a model Communist town.

Best for
Parks and forests

Home to
Kościuszko Mound, Wolski Forest, Nowa Huta

Experience
Scaling the heights of Kościuszko Mound

DAYS OUT FROM KRAKÓW

A diverse collection of sights lie beyond the city boundary of Kraków, which are ideal for day or overnight trips. South of the city you'll find the Auschwitz-Birkenau Memorial and Museum, the site of some of World War II's most heinous crimes and today an important symbol of remembrance. Also found to the south are the spectacularly sculpted Wieliczka Salt Mine and the majestic Tatra Mountains. Elsewhere you'll find imposing castles, picture-postcard towns and pretty villages scattered across the bucolic landscape.

Best for
National parks and subterranean cities

Home to
Auschwitz-Birkenau Memorial and Museum, Wieliczka Salt Mine, Zakopane and Tatra National Park

Experience
Bearing witness at Auschwitz-Birkenau Memorial and Museum

←

1 Picturesque Grodska Street.

2 The striking interior of St Mary's Basilica.

3 The Hejnał, Kraków's famous trumpet call.

4 The pretty arcades of the Renaissance Cloth Hall.

With its bewitching medieval Old Town, awe-inspiring galleries, enthralling museums and offbeat bars, Kraków is brimming with exciting things to see and do. These itineraries will help you make the most of your visit.

24 HOURS

Morning

Get an early start and make a beeline for the Main Market Square (p64), nestled in the heart of the Old Town. Stroll around this vast marketplace, dominated by the splendid Renaissance Cloth Hall (p70), to take in its harmonious proportions – it's almost a perfect square. Next, pop into the landmark St Mary's Basilica (p68), which towers over the square, and admire its dazzling interior, home to the magnificent Gothic altarpiece of Veit Stoss. Don't miss the Hejnał, the city's famous trumpet call, which sounds from the church's tallest tower. Spend the rest of the morning in the Rynek Underground (p72), located below the Main Market Square: wander through its ancient tunnels, unearth vampire graves and learn all about the city's fascinating history from the interactive, multimedia displays. For lunch, splurge on some elegant Polish fare at Szara Gęś (p89), perched on the edge of the square.

Afternoon

Walk off your lunch with a stroll through some of the Old Town's pretty side streets before wandering south along the former Royal Route, Grodzka Street (p110). Pop in to the Franciscan Church (p108) to admire the Art Nouveau stained-glass windows, the work of the celebrated Polish artist Stanisław Wyspiański (p49). Continue along Grodzka Street to reach Wawel Hill (p98), a fortified complex containing a castle and cathedral that was once home to Poland's royalty. Admire the eclectic architecture of Wawel Cathedral (p102), then delve inside to discover its many chapels and imposing tombs. Next, explore Wawel Royal Castle's (p104) arcaded courtyard and then, if you have time to spare, take a tour of the castle's opulent state rooms and royal apartments. Once you're done, pop into Słodki Wawel (p100) for a chocolate-fuelled late-afternoon pick-me-up.

Evening

Begin the evening with a walk around the Planty (p92), the leafy park surrounding Old Town, then return to the now beautifully illuminated Main Market Square for a decadent dinner in regal Wierzynek (p89), thought to be Kraków's oldest restaurant. After, grab a drink in one of the area's many watering holes – the Old Town reputedly has more pubs and bars per square metre than any other place in Europe, so you'll be spoilt for choice. Fancy a beer? You can't go wrong with Multi Qlti Tap Bar (p86). Or, for a taste of the city's legendary jazz scene, head to iconic Jazz Club U Muniaka (p86).

←

1 Exploring the courtyard of the Collegium Maius.

2 Charming Floriańska Street.

3 The wall found in Remuh Synagogue's cemetery.

4 A serving of *zapiekanki,* a delicious Polish snack.

2 DAYS

Day 1

Morning Start your day with a healthy breakfast and aromatic espresso at Tektura *(p171)*, a specialist coffee shop. Fuelled up, amble towards the imposing Collegium Maius *(p74)*, the alma mater of renowned astronomer Nicolaus Copernicus. Admire its impressive Gothic architecture before taking a guided tour of its elegant courtyard and artifact-filled rooms – remember to book in advance. It's only a short walk from here to Wentzl *(p89)*, found on the Main Market Square, to enjoy a filling lunch of traditional Polish fare.

Afternoon Stroll north of the square along charming Floriańska Street *(p86)*, one of Kraków's prettiest thoroughfares, heading for the Czartoryski Museum *(p78)*. Here, you can admire an incredible array of art, including the city's (and country's) most important artwork: Leonardo da Vinci's *Lady with an Ermine*. After, walk beneath St Florian's Gate *(p86)* towards the imposing Barbican *(p87)* – both were once part of the city's defensive fortifications.

Evening As the sun sinks, set your sights on Tytano *(p160)*; this former tobacco factory is packed with some of Kraków's coolest restaurants, bars and clubs. Sample creative veggie dishes such as butternut squash lasagne and tofu dumplings, at Veganic *(www.veganic.restaurant)*, then sip on local craft beers at Weźże Krafta *(www.wezze-krafta.ontap.pl)*.

Day 2

Morning Today begins with a trip to the Museum of the Home Army *(p148)* – this engrossing museum tells the compelling story of Poland's underground resistance movement during World War II. If you're not quite ready for lunch after this, take a stroll through the verdant Jagiellonian University Botanical Gardens *(p150)*, keeping an eye out for its half-a-millennium-old oak tree. Your tummy rumbling now, take a tram to New Square *(p129)*, known to locals as Plac Nowy, in Kazimierz, the city's former Jewish quarter. Sate your hunger at one of the food stalls found here that sell mouthwatering *zapiekanki*, open baguettes piled high with toppings like cheese and mushrooms.

Afternoon Spend the first part of this afternoon admiring the area's preserved synagogues – the red-brick Old Synagogue *(p122)* has displays dedicated to the history and culture of the city's Jews, while Remuh Synagogue's poignant cemetery is home to a wall made up of tombstone fragments *(p124)*.

Evening It's been a long day, so stay put in Kazimierz for some nighttime fun. Found in the centre of Kazimierz, Ariel *(www.ariel-krakow.pl)* is a great place to sample traditional Jewish food. After, enjoy a late-night drink in candle-lit Alchemia's *(p125)*, a bohemian bar that sometimes hosts jazz concerts.

5 DAYS

Day 1

Morning Begin your day walking the Old Town's cobbled streets, ending up in the monumental Main Market Square *(p64)*. Stop by the magnificent Cloth Hall *(p70)* to peruse works by famous artists in the Gallery of 19th-Century Polish Art. Have a bite to eat in Café Szal *(p71)* on the hall's second floor – it offers epic views.

Afternoon Take the tram to Podgórze, the site of the Jewish ghetto built by the Nazis during World War II. Spend the afternoon in Schindler's Factory *(p136)*, where moving exhibits tell the story of life for the city's Polish and Jewish inhabitants under the Nazi regime.

Evening Wander over the Father Bernatek Bridge *(p129)* to Kazimierz for a dinner of freshly made pizzas at Nolio *(www.nolio.pl)*.

Day 2

Morning An hour or so outside the city is the UNESCO-protected Wieliczka Salt Mine *(p190)*. Take a tour of this fascinating subterranean city, painstakingly carved from the sparkling rock salt by generations of miners.

Afternoon Back in Kraków , enjoy a well-deserved lunch of locally sourced Polish fare at Pod Nosem *(p113)*, then amble north up picturesque Kanonicza Street *(p112)*. Take a detour to the Church of Saints Peter and Paul *(p106)*; the railings in front are guarded by beautifully sculpted statues of the 12 apostles.

Evening Grab dinner at cosy Café Camelot *(p89)*; make sure to save room for some of its famous *szarlotka* (apple pie).

Day 3

Morning Steel yourself for an emotional journey to Oświęcim, site of the Auschwitz-Birkenau Memorial and Museum *(p186)*. This extermination camp, set up and run by the Nazis, is a harrowing reminder of the horrors inflicted during World War II.

1 One of the Old Town's charming medieval streets.

2 The incredible Chapel of St Kinga in Wieliczka Salt Mine.

3 Alfresco drinking at Tytano.

4 A temporary exhibition in the National Museum in Kraków.

5 Aerial view over Nowa Huta.

Afternoon Return to the Old Town for a late lunch at at Milkbar Tomasza *(ulica Świętego Tomasza 24)*, then take a reflective stroll along the tree-shaded paths of the Planty *(p92)*.

Evening Savour a quiet dinner of classic Polish food at intimate spot Copernicus *(p113)*, then have a relaxed nightcap at one of the Tytano complex's many bars *(p160)*.

Day 4

Morning Pass a leisurely morning at the main branch of the arty National Museum in Kraków *(p158)*. The most spectacular of its three galleries is dedicated to a collection of 20th- and 21st-century art, including Art Nouveau works by Józef Mehoffer *(p166)* and Stanisław Wyspiański *(p49)*.

Afternoon Walk or bus to the impressive Kościuszko Mound *(p174)*, found just outside the city centre. Scale this artifical monument, dedicated to national hero Kościuszko, for picture-perfect views.

Evening Make for Dynia Resto Bar *(www.dynia.krakow.pl)*, a laid-back restaurant offering a delicious array of pumpkin dishes *(dynia* means pumpkin in Polish).

Day 5

Morning It's an hour by tram out to Nowa Huta *(p178)*, a huge industrial suburb built by the Communists to be a model proletarian city. Be awestruck by its Socialist-Realist architecture – don't miss the Lord's Ark Church, designed to resemble Noah's Ark.

Afternoon Grab a sandwich at Lajkonik *(www.lajkonik-pik.pl)*, a café offering melt-in-the-mouth bread. It's a 15-minute walk from here to the Stained Glass Museum *(p160)*, where you can learn all about how this eye-catching art form is made. You can also take a two-hour course and create your own stained-glass masterpiece.

Evening Take a last stroll through the Old Town and splurge for dinner at the award-winning Art Restauracja *(p113)*.

Early Christian

Awe-inspiring sacral art abounds here, whether it's the simple yet exquisite icons in the Bishop Erazm Ciołek Palace (p113) or the rich murals that adorn the Franciscan Church (p108). Don't miss the breathtaking interior of St Mary's Basilica (p68), with its stunning stained glass and magnificent Gothic altarpiece.

$\rightarrow$

The arresting interior of St Mary's Basilica, decorated with Gothic art

 INSIDER TIP
On the Street

Kazimierz is home to incredible street art. A highlight is the Judah mural (ulica Świętego Wawrzyńca 16), which speaks to the survival of the Jewish spirit.

KRAKÓW FOR
ART LOVERS

Kraków is awash with incredible artworks. While the city's museums and galleries are undoubtedly strongest on Polish art, especially the Art Nouveau splendour of the Młoda Polska ("Young Poland") movement, you'll find works from all epochs, from early Christian art through to contemporary pieces.

Modern Masters

Kraków's home-grown talent isn't well known outside of Poland but is worth tracking down at galleries around town. The National Museum in Kraków (p158) is home to works by famed painter Maria Jarema (1908-58), known for her jazzy abstractions. It also contains arresting pieces by the multitalented Tadeusz Kantor, a celebrated theatre director; spy some of the costumes he designed at the Cricoteka (p139).

$\leftarrow$

The abstract *Sitting Woman* by contemporary artist Maria Jarema

Royal Renaissance

The Renaissance signalled a high point in Kraków's history. To see some of the best art from this time, head to Wawel Royal Castle (p104), itself a Renaissance marvel: the opulent state rooms are filled with intricate tapestries from Flemish masters, while the private royal apartments are filled with enchanting Renaissance furniture.

→ The Renaissance courtyard of Wawel Royal Castle

TOP 4 **ART GALLERIES**

Gallery of 19th-Century Polish Art
An impressive collection that's strongest on portraits, landscapes and historic scenes (p70).

MOCAK
This striking space is dedicated to the best of Polish contemporary art (p136).

National Museum in Kraków
Strong on the Młoda Polska movement (p49) and great for visiting exhibitions (p158).

Bishop Erazm Ciołek Palace
A 16th century palace filled with splendid sacral artworks (p113).

National Treasures

On the hunt for Polish masterpieces? Don't miss the grand historical paintings of Jan Matejko at the Gallery of 19th-Century Polish Art (p70) or the work of Art Nouveau master Stanisław Wyspiański at the National Museum (p158). You can also spy the city's most valuable work of art, Leonardo Da Vinci's *Lady With An Ermine*, at the Czartoryski Museum (p78), also home to Rembrant van Rijn's *The Good Samaritan*.

↑ A collection of artworks found in the Gallery of 19th-Century Polish Art

27

Planes, Trams and Automobiles

When it comes to fast cars and flying machines, Kraków has more to offer than you might think. The whole family will be inspired by the Polish Aviation Museum *(p178)*, which is home to over 200 aircraft and an array of awesome interactive exhibits. There's also the fun-filled Museum of Municipal Engineering *(p125)*, jam-packed with automobiles through the ages, including a shed full of historic trams, and hands-on displays that are perfect for kids.

→

One of the many aircraft on display at the Polish Aviation Museum

KRAKÓW FOR
FAMILIES

Kraków is a great place for families to explore. Whether it's interactive museums, imaginative puppet shows or the city's legendary creatures, there's plenty to keep young ones occupied. Plus, Kraków has plenty of outdoor spaces where energetic kids can burn off steam.

Outdoor Fun

Pockets of green are peppered across the city. Błonia Fields *(p166)* is a vast park where kids can run wild, while Jordan Park *(Aleja 3 Maja 11)* has a great play area and boating lake. In the Stanisław Lem Garden of Experiences *(p178)*, there are countless scientific instruments that can be investigated by young explorers.

→

A scientific instrument in the Stanisław Lem Garden of Experiences

 INSIDER TIP
See a Show

Kraków's Groteska Theatre *(www.groteska. pl)* is famous for the imagination-kindling wonder of its children's shows, which usually feature a mixture of live action and puppetry.

Unusual Attractions

Scattered across the city are an array of weird and wacky experiences that children will love. The mind-boggling Museum of Illusions *(p170)* is filled with awesome visual tricks, incredible holograms and bizarre upside-down rooms, as well as a variety of hands-on puzzles that little (and big) kids will enjoy figuring out. Rather more hair-raising are the horrors on offer at Lost Souls Alley *(p89)*, an immersive haunted-house experience that might appeal to spook-seeking teenagers; note that kids need to be over 14 years old to be able to participate.

← Having fun with an optical illusion at the Museum of Illusions

TOP 3 **INDOOR PLAY CENTRES**

Akukuu Play Centre
🏠 Bratysławska 4, Prądnik Biały 🌐 akukuu.pl
Well-equipped centre with designated areas for all age groups.

Gibon
🏠 Ulica Dobrego Pasterza 126, Prądnik Czerwony 🌐 gibon.pl
With loads of things to scramble around on, it's great for younger kids.

GOKidz!
🏠 Ulica Rzemieślnica 20G Podgórze 🌐 gokidz.pl
Indoor adventure park for kids who want to climb, bounce and play.

↑ A fire-breathing statue of Kraków's legendary dragon, found below Wawel Hill

Legendary Creatures

Kraków will forever be associated with its fire-breathing dragon. Kids can spy a statue of this ferocious creature below Wawel Hill *(p98)*; if they hang around long enough, they'll even see him breathe fire. There's also the Dragon's Lair *(p100)*, a series of atmospheric caves beneath Wawel Royal Castle *(p104)* where this winged beast supposedly lived. Older children will be fascinated by the rather more ghoulish "vampire" burials preserved in the Rynek Underground *(p72)*. Here, so-called vampires were buried with their decapitated heads set between their legs.

Perfect Pierogi

Think of Polish food and you'll probably think of pierogi. These little parcels of dough are stuffed with a variety of fillings, from minced meat and onion to cottage cheese and potato; they can even be filled with blueberries and cream for a decadent dessert. Sample this national snack in one of the city's cheap-and-cheerful cafeterias, such as Milkbar Tomasza *(ulica Świętego Tomasza 24)*, or visit in August to see stall after stall selling these tasty pastry pockets appear on the city's streets for the Pierogi Festival *(p51)*.

→

A bustling stall at the annual Pierogi Festival in August

KRAKÓW FOR
FOODIES

Forget all preconceptions about Polish cuisine being simple and stodgy. The country – and Kraków – serves up an amazing variety of dishes, including perfect pierogi and ruby-red borscht. Get ready to sample celebratory platters of roast fowl, messy-yet-moreish street food and delectable desserts.

Festive Fowl

Here, it's not a celebration unless roast fowl and game are on the menu. Tender meats are frequently served with sweet fruit-based sauces: roast duck often comes with apples, while wild boar is usually teamed up with forest berries.

> INSIDER TIP
> **Perfect Pork**
>
> Poland is famous for its *kiełbasa* (sausages), with "Krakowska" (smoked pork seasoned with garlic and caraway seed) one of the most popular types. Find it at delis and on restaurant menus.

↑ Mouthwatering roasted duck served with pickled plum and dumplings

TOP 3 STREET FOODS

Zapiekanki
Half a baguette, toasted, smothered in tomato sauce, and topped with mushrooms and cheese.

Obwarzanek
Crunchier than a bagel and chewier than a pretzel, these twisted bread rings are sprinkled with salt, poppy seed or sesame seed.

Oscypek
Rounds of sheep's cheese, sliced and grilled, and served with a dollop of cranberry.

Beautiful Beetroot

The whole of Poland is head over heels in love with beetroot, and Kraków is no different. This mineral-rich vegetable is used in countless dishes, the most famous being "borscht" (*barszcz* in Polish), a heart-warming soup which is sure to feature on the menu of every restaurant. Classic borscht is usually light and clear, although other variations can come with meat and chunky vegetables.

←

A steaming bowl of *barszcz* (borscht) made from beetroot

Sweet Treats

Often served alongside a rich, aromatic cup of coffee, cakes and pastries are at the heart of Polish life. Mouthwatering *szarlotka* (apple pie with crumbly pastry) often takes the prize for the nation's favourite dessert – sample some of the best in the city at either Café Camelot (*p89*) or Massolit (*p162*). Be sure to leave room for a dose of *lody* (ice cream) from the legendary Good Lood (*p129*) in Kazimierz.

→

Several cones piled high with deliciously creamy *lody*

Gothic Grandeur

It was in the Gothic epoch that Kraków began to take shape as a grand city of architectural set pieces. The city's majestic Dominican Church *(p80)*, with its stepped gable, vaulted ceiling and quiet cloisters, will show you just how ambitious and awe-inspiring medieval buildings could be. More discreet in style but oozing period charm is the Late-Gothic Collegium Maius *(p74)*, with its delicate brickwork and graceful arcades.

→

The spectacular Gothic interior of the Dominican Church

KRAKÓW FOR
ARCHITECTURE

Sprinkled with splendid buildings from myriad historical periods, Kraków is like an open-air museum of European architecture. Strolling through the city leads to endless architectural discoveries, with Renaissance elegance rubbing shoulders with red-brick Gothic and elegant Baroque.

Renaissance Marvels

Renaissance architecture flourished in 16th-century Kraków, with a host of Italian architects invited to the then Polish capital by an ambitious court. For many, the most spectacular building in this style is the Cloth Hall *(p70)*, its graceful colonnades overlooked by playfully grotesque faces known as mascarones. For even more Renaissance marvels, admire the arcaded courtyard and sumptuous furnishings of Wawel Royal Castle *(p104)*. Next door in Wawel Cathedral *(p102)* is the gilded Zygmunt Chapel, widely considered to be a Renaissance masterpiece.

←

The majestic golden dome of the Renaissance Zygmunt Chapel

Beautiful Baroque

Baroque architecture was brought to Kraków by the Jesuits, whose magnificent 17th-century Church of Saints Peter and Paul *(p106)* was the city's first Baroque church. Visit to admire its elegant interior, keeping an eye out for the exquisite stuccowork above the high altar, which depicts scenes from the lives of Saints Peter and Paul. The city's love of the Baroque style reached its high point with the striking exterior and richly decorated interior of the Church of St Anne *(p76)*. Take a peek inside to spy both beautiful stuccowork and arresting trompe-l'oeil paintings.

One of the sculptures adorning the Church of St Anne's Baroque façade

INSIDER TIP
Ice Ice Baby

Explore the uber-modern interior of the spaceship-like ICE Congress Centre by attending one of its cultural performances. Choose from a menu of classical concerts, opera, theatre and ballet performances.

Modern Masterpieces

In a city known for historic architecture, there's a surprising number of modern gems. Fans of Classic Brutalism will want to visit the Bunker of Art *(p84)*, a minimalist block of concrete intended as an architectural riposte to conservative opinion. Those after a taste of Socialist Baroque should head for Nowa Huta *(p178)*. Founded as a working-class stronghold, this vast suburb features wide tree-lined boulevards spreading out from a monumental central square, generous green spaces and the Lord's Ark Church, a magnificent example of modern sacral architecture. One of the most recent contributions to Kraków's architectural avant-garde is the Cricoteka *(p139)*, whose geometric form seems to hover above the Vistula river.

→

The utterly striking exterior of the Cricoteka, found in Podgórze

Scaling Mounds

Climbing one of Kraków's memorial mounds is a great way to combine sightseeing with a decent workout. The Kościuszko Mound (p174), honouring Polish military hero Tadeusz Kościuszko, offers great views over the city, as does the mysterious Krakus Mound (p141), which legend tells is the burial site of the city's founder, Prince Krak.

→

Looking over Kraków from atop Krakus Mound

KRAKÓW FOR THE
GREAT OUTDOORS

In a city that's best known for its magnificent market square, dramatic royal castle and grand churches, Kraków's green spaces are quite often overlooked. Yet there are countless verdant oases to discover, including pretty parks, landscaped gardens and vast stretches of lush forest.

WHAT'S THE WEATHER LIKE?

Kraków has a continental climate with four seasons. Expect cold winters from December to March – there's a high chance the city will be blanketed in snow come Christmas. Trees start to blossom in April, with spring stretching into June. Peak summer heat usually hits during July and August. The autumn chill often arrives in September, though sunshine and warm days can last through October.

On Yer Bike!

Kraków is surprisingly bike-friendly, with well-tended bike paths lining both sides of the Vistula. The Planty (p92) is great for a quick spin around the Old Town, while the vast green space of Wolski Forest (p176) is home to mountain-biking paths. Wavelo (https://en.wavelo.pl) is great for short-term rentals.

→

Cycling along the tree-shaded paths of the Planty

Horticultural Wonderland

Spend a day exploring one of Kraków's lush green gardens. The Jagiellonian University Botanical Gardens (p150) has thousands of different plant species, including some rare tropical and carnivorous plants. The curators have also come up with some inspired themes for presenting the greenery, including a section on plants found in the bible. Just outside the city centre is the beautifully landscaped Deciusz Park (p176), complete with sweeping lawns, colourful flower-beds, and ancient hornbeam and lime trees.

← A waterlily in the city's botanic gardens

TOP 4 **BEST PICNIC SPOTS**

Banks of the Vistula
A comfy spot on the riverbank is a perfect perch to watch the world sail by.

Błonia Fields
A massive meadow with plenty of room to spread a blanket and soak up some rays (p166).

The Planty
Enjoy a taste of local life with an impromptu brown-bag lunch on a Planty bench (p92).

Wolski Forest
Pack a sandwich and take a hike along the trails of this protected nature reserve (p176).

Take to the Water

Leave time for a leisurely stroll along the Vistula and take in fetching views of the fortified Wawel Hill (p98) from below. Several boating companies, including Kapitan Victor (www.kapitanvictor.pl), offer cruises on the river; these range from short spins to longer jaunts out to the Benedictine Abbey in Tyniec (p179).

↑ The riverside path next to Wawel Hill

Musical Mayhem

As you might expect from the country of Chopin, there's a lot of classical music on offer in Kraków, with the fantastic Days of Bach *(p51)* festival one of the highlights. But the city also celebrates a wide variety of other genres, from sea-faring songs at the Shanties festival *(www.shanties.pl)*, to headline R&B and hip-hop acts at Kraków Live *(p51)*. Both Unsound *(p50)* and Sacrum Profanum *(p50)* shatter genres by blending traditional and experimental sounds.

→

Śląsk, a Polish folk ensemble, perform with pop artist Felicita at Unsound

KRAKÓW FOR
FESTIVALS

Kraków's mind-boggling calendar of festivals covers an endless variety of art forms and activities. The city's love of performing arts means that many events revolve around music and theatre, though Cracovians will find just about any reason to celebrate.

Foodie Fests

Scrumptious food is one of Poland's strong points, and gourmet events are a great way to tickle your taste buds. The country's fabled stuffed dumplings, pierogi, take centre stage in August at the city's annual Pierogi Festival *(p51)*. On Fat Thursday, the last Thursday before Lent, Cracovians celebrate by queuing in droves at bakeries to feast on *pączki* (doughnuts).

→

A tray of delicious *pączki* (doughnuts)

 INSIDER TIP
You Have to Bee There

In September, Wolnica Square in Kazimierz *(p118)* hosts the Kraków Honey Harvest. There are stalls selling a wide selection of honeys, plus lectures on beekeeping.

In the Limelight

Poles take their cinema seriously, so expect an A-list selection at the annual Kraków Film Festival *(p50)* in late May. The inventive Film Music Festival *(www.fmf.fm)*, held around the same time, focuses on the magic of film scores. In July, see the city's streets come alive with theatre and dance performances, thanks to the International Festival of Street Theatre *(www.teatrkto.pl)*.

←

A performance at the
city's Film Music Festival

Did You Know?

At the Lajkonik procession, the horseman taps spectators with his "mace" for good luck.

Totally Traditional

Traditional celebrations draw upon centuries of pagan and Christian heritage. In June the Lajkonik procession sees a colourfully attired horseman recall the Tartar invasions of the 13th century *(p175)*, while at the *szopki* (Christmas crib) competition, elaborate nativity scenes are displayed in the Main Market Square *(p64)*. Don't miss the midsummer Wianki festival *(www.wianki. krakow.pl)* to spy wreaths float down the Vistula.

Nativity scenes being taken to the Main Market Square for the *szopki* ↑

Kazimierz By Candlelight

Rejuvenated Kazimierz is home to a wealth of intimate, candle-lit bars that are decorated with antique furniture and embroidered tablecloths. Singer *(p125)*, filled with kooky sewing-machine tables, is a local favourite, as is bohemian Alchemia *(p125)*. Eszeweria *(ulica Józefa 9)*, meanwhile, has an eclectic vibe and a magical, seasonal garden.

→

The pretty seasonal garden at Eszeweria in Kazimierz

KRAKÓW
AFTER DARK

As you might expect from a city with thousands of students – and lots of other residents who simply like to party – Kraków has an awesome nightlife scene. Whether you're looking to dance until dawn at a live music show or simply kick back with a beer, Kraków has got you covered.

Live Music

Kraków has a thriving music scene, with rock, alternative and jazz vying for the crowds. The Old Town is a hotspot for legendary jazz clubs, including Jazz Club u Muniaka *(p86)* and Harris Piano Jazz Bar *(www.harris.krakow.pl)*. Kwadrat *(www.klubkwadrat.pl)* hosts rock acts, while Szpitalna 1 *(ulica Szpitalna 1)* does electronica.

A performance at the Old Town's legendary Harris Piano Jazz Bar ↑

Basement Bars

Kraków's Old Town (p60) is home to plenty of deep Gothic cellars, many of which today house cool and quirky bars. Klub Społem (ulica Świętego Tomasza 4), a sprawling cellar space filled with inspired Communist kitsch, is a great place to hunker down for the evening, while candle-lit Klub Awarja (ulica Mikołajska 9) offers delicious cocktails and occasional live blues shows.

If you fancy a pint then head to CK Browar (www. ckbrowar.pl), a microbrewey that harkens back to the days of the Austro-Hungarian Empire with schnitzels and freshly made beer.

← The effortlessly cool interior of Klub Spolem

WONDERFUL WÓDKA

Meeting locals for the first time? Be prepared to down a *wódka* shot – in fact, once a bottle is opened, it's the norm to finish the whole thing. Drunk neat, in one gulp and with a call of "Na Zdrowie!" ("Cheers!"), you might be surprised to hear that Poland's national tipple comes in many forms, not just the pure transparent version. Dabble with pale yellow Żubrówka, flavoured with bison grass; sample dark-red Wiśniówka, made with cherries; or sip on the amber, herb-infused Żołądkowa Gorzka.

INSIDER TIP
Kraków Cabaret

Cabaret is still popular in Kraków and can be enjoyed in a couple of places. Catch a show at legendary Piwnica pod Baranami *(Rynek Główny 27)* or iconic Loch Camelot *(www. lochcamelot.com.pl)*.

Industrial Chic

The former Tytano tobacco factory (p160) has been renovated and now features a cluster of bars and clubs to rival spots in Kazimierz and the Old Town. Bars here have a contemporary hipster vibe: think exposed brick and concrete, and light bulbs dangling from a wire. Weźże Krafta (www.wezze-krafta.ontap.pl), with its tantalizing menu of craft beers, is a popular haunt.

→ Outdoor area at Weźże Krafta, a popular bar in the renovated Tytano complex

Polish Design

Find a string of boutiques specializing in Polish fashion, art and design along Józefa Street in Kazimierz (p118). Highlights include Mapaya (ulica Józefa 3) and Eclectic Idea Fix (www.ideafix.pl), both of which offer cutting-edge contemporary clothes and accessories. Don't miss the Cracow Poster Gallery (www.cracowpostergallery.com), in the Old Town (p60), which offers spectacular, high-quality Polish poster art.

↑ One of the boutique design shops lining Jozefa Street

KRAKÓW FOR
SHOPPING

Kraków is a great place for picking up classic souvenirs and handmade crafts, as well as cool and quirky Polish design pieces. The city also has a strong market culture, from stalls selling antiques and collectables, to regular markets that offer up fresh, seasonal produce.

Souvenir shopping inside the Cloth Hall and (inset) the hall's impressive exterior ↑

Cracovian Crafts

For something quintessentially Cracovian, take a peek inside the Cloth Hall (p70). Here you'll find stalls selling charming crafts – including lace and carved wooden items – as well as more kitsch souvenirs. Traditional gift shops are also scattered around the Old Town, such as festive Calik Christmas Baubles (p86) and historical Kacper Ryx (plac Mariacki 3).

Awesome Antiques

The Old Town has dozens of high-end antique shops, stuffed floor-to-ceiling with treasures– try Salon Antyków *(www.antykwariat-pasja.pl)* for furniture and Kosek *(www.kosek.krakow.pl)* for jewellery. Kazimierz's New Square *(p129)* hosts a great antiques market on a Saturday, while the Sunday morning flea market at Plac Targowy Unitarg sees stalls offering everything from World War II memorabilia to 1980s Polish pop on vinyl.

Military memorabilia on sale at Plac Targowy Unitarg's flea market

SHOP

Several shops specialize in high-quality, daintily wrapped Polish foods, including preserves, oils, honey and sausages, that make for thoughtful gifts.

Krakowski Kredens

This impossibly cute local chain sells its own branded coffee, leaf teas, chocolates and liqueurs (and lots of other goodies as well). It has seven stores across Kraków.

**◘ N3 ◘ Ulica Grodzka 7
◘ krakowskikredens.pl**

Produkty Benedyktyńskie

Located inside the Benedictine Abbey in Tyniec *(p179)* and run by its monks, this shop offers local cheeses, meats and jams.

◘ produkty benedyktynskie.com

↑ One of the stalls at Stary Kleparz, overflowing with tasty snacks

Foodie Markets

Gastronomes have no fear – Kraków is home to a number of great food markets. For fresh, locally sourced food, head north of the Old Town to Stary Kleparz *(p153)*, a bustling market whose packed stalls sell a fantastic array of fruits, vegetables, meats and cheeses. The open-air market at Plac Targowy Unitarg – known locally as Hala Targowa – is home to some excellent street food stalls selling things like *oscypek (p31)* and grilled sausages.

Literary Cafés

The link between caffeine and literature is well documented, and Kraków is blessed with several literary cafés where you can enjoy a coffee alongside your next read. Two of the best are Cytat Café *(ulica Miodowa 23)*, home to an epic book-arch, and Kawiarnia Literacka *(www.kawiarnia-literacka.pl)*, with its stylish interior. De Revolutionibus Books & Café *(ulica Bracka 14)*, meanwhile, sells philosophical tomes along with espresso, while the city's beloved Massolit *(p162)*, a specialist English-language bookshop, is a great place to lounge with a new novel, coffee in hand.

→

The effortlessly styish literary café Kawiarnia Literacka

KRAKÓW FOR
BOOKWORMS

Kraków has a rich literary heritage – something you might expect from a university town and cultural centre that has played host to many famous writers. A UNESCO "City of Literature", the city is peppered with literary cafés, cosy bookshops and monuments to award-winning authors.

Feeling Festive

Literary events are a regular feature of the city's cultural calendar. Attracting the big names of international literature is the Conrad Festival *(p50)*, named after the Polish-born novelist Joseph Conrad. Held every October, it boasts a packed programme of lectures and workshops. There's also the Miłosz Festival *(www.miloszfestival.pl)*, in June, which celebrates the work of Polish-American Nobel poet Czesław Miłosz.

←

One of the events at Kraków's annual Conrad Festival

TOP 3

BOOKS ABOUT KRAKÓW

Schindler's Ark
Thomas Keneally's uplifting novel tells the story of Oskar Schindler *(p136)*, who saved over a thousand Jewish lives.

The Trumpeter of Kraków
Eric Kelly's fantasy tale of medieval Kraków popularized the legend of the city's Hejnał *(p69)*.

The Dollmaker of Kraków
The story of Nazi war-time occupation, viewed through the lens of fantasy and folklore, by R M Romero.

Planty Park
Nowhere better sums up Poland's love affair with literature than the Planty *(p92)*, a park where each bench has a plaque honouring one of the city's famous writers. Sit and share a sandwich with Nobel Laureate Wysława Szymborska, sip a coffee with prize-winning Olga Tokarczuk, or contemplate human nature with Anglo-Polish writer Joseph Conrad.

Reading books on the benches in the Planty

Best Bookshops
Alongside the abundance of literary cafés dotted across the city are a number of truly excellent bookshops. The Old Town's Pod Globusem (www.liberglob.pl) – an expansive bookshop perched below a giant, iconic orb – is great for grabbing maps, guides and train reads, while the shelves at charming Lokator (ulica Mostowa 1), in Kazimierz, are heaving with hard-to-find works.

$\rightarrow$
A display of books at Pod Globusem in the Old Town

Moving Museums

Kazimierz (p118) and the neighbouring district of Podgórze (p132), across the river, are home to several museums that illustrate both the richness of the city's Jewish culture and its wartime destruction. Schindler's Factory (p136) has been converted into a museum dedicated to life under the Nazi occupation, while displays at the Eagle Pharmacy (p138) tells the story of a gentile Pole who helped save many residents of the Jewish ghetto. The Galicia Jewish Museum (p124), meanwhile, artfully uses powerful photography to highlight the once-thriving Jewish culture of southern and eastern Poland.

↑ One of the fascinating displays found at the Eagle Pharmacy in Kazimierz

KRAKÓW FOR
JEWISH HERITAGE

Kraków – particularly Kazimierz – was a leading centre of Jewish life from the Middle Ages until World War II, when the Nazi occupation led to the destruction of this vibrant community. After decades of neglect, restored synagogues and new museums show a renewed appreciation of the city's Jewish heritage.

Bearing Witness

Memorial sites dedicated to the victims of the Holocaust can be found around Kraków. The most harrowing of these is the Auschwitz-Birkenau Memorial and Museum (p186), where an estimated 1.1 million people died – most were Jewish. Today, the bleak remains of the camp and the mountain of suvivor testimony stand as a memorial to and a record of the Holocaust. Płaszów Concentration Camp (p140), in Podgórze, was a forced labour camp for the city's Jews; today it is marked by several moving memorials.

←

One of the many memorials in Płaszów Concentration Camp dedicated to Kraków's Jews

↑ The spectacular interior of Remuh Synagogue, with its colourful ceiling

💬 INSIDER TIP
Celebrating Jewish Culture

Every summer, the streets of Kazimierz come alive with song, dance, food and theatre to celebrate Jewish heritage at the Festival of Jewish Culture *(p50)*.

Striking Synagogues

No visit to the city would be complete without a stroll through the former Jewish quarter of Kazimierz to discover the city's surviving synagogues. To learn all about Jewish culture, head to the historic Old Synagogue *(p122)*, which holds a permanent exhibition on Jewish rites and rituals. Don't miss Tempel *(p123)* and Kupa *(p125)* synagogues, both of which have exquisitely decorated interiors, as does Remuh Synagogue *(p124)*, with its eye-catching, colourful ceiling. Remuh is also home to an evocative cemetery, unusual both for its abundance of carved gravestones and for its Wailing Wall; here, fragments of tombstones damaged in World War II have been built into the cemetery wall.

Klezmer Sounds

Traditional Jewish *klezmer* – a lively form of folk music – is performed at several Jewish restaurants along Kazimierz's Szeroka Street – Ariel *(www. ariel-krakow.pl)* is one of the best. Kraków has spawned some great modern *klezmer* bands, including the Bester Quartet, who host shows here *(www.besterquartet.com)*.

→

A musician playing a trumpet during a *klezmer* performance

World War II

Extraordinarily moving accounts of life during the Nazi occupation can be found across the city. The displays at Schindler's Factory *(p136)* focus on the sufferings of ordinary citizens, both gentile and Jewish, while the Eagle Pharmacy *(p138)* tells the heartbreaking story of those forced to live in the city's ghetto. Head to the Museum of the Home Army *(p148)* for an inspirational account of Polish resistance to Nazi rule, told using weaponry, photos and personal recollections.

$\longrightarrow$

A photographic display found inside Schindler's Factory

KRAKÓW FOR
HISTORY BUFFS

As you might expect from the former royal capital of Poland, Kraków has a wealth of stories to tell. Even after the court moved to Warsaw in 1596, the city continued to be the focus of patriotic tradition, and today is regarded by many Poles as the spiritual and cultural home of the country.

The impressive Kościuszki Mound, rising above the surrounding landscape ↑

Hills for Heroes

You need only scale the Kościuszki Mound *(p174)* to see how Kraków holds its heroes in high esteem. This emerald-green hill was erected in honour of the patriot Tadeusz Kościuszki *(p55)*. Near here is another grassy mound, this time dedicated to freedom fighter and interwar leader Józef Piłsudski *(p176)*.

Did You Know?

Thousands of patriotic volunteers helped to construct the Piłsudski Mound.

Postwar Poland

Poland's Communist regime left an indelible mark on the city. Using photographs and audio recordings, exhibits at the People of Kraków in Times of Terror 1939–1945–1956 (p170) reveal the suffering of ordinary citizens under the Stalinist regime. One of the era's most striking remnants is the suburb of Nowa Huta (p178). Visit this so-called "model Communist town" to admire its Socialist-Realist architecture.

← The impressive Lord's Ark Church, one of the buildings found in the suburb of Nowa Huta

A Royal Capital

The Polish capital for over 500 years, Kraków has a strong regal heritage. Nowhere is this more evocative than at Wawel Hill (p98), where Poland's royalty once lived. Here you'll find Wawel Royal Castle (p104); take a tour of its lavish state rooms to see something of the splendour in which Poland's monarchs once lived. Just next door, Wawel Cathedral (p102) is filled with the sculptured sarcophagi of Poland's monarchs.

↑ Looking towards Wawel Cathedral, the resting place of Poland's royals

Creative Arts and Crafts

The best possible introduction to the art of Młoda Polska is a visit to the National Museum *(p158)*, which displays the work of pretty much everyone associated with the movement; it's here you'll find most of Stanisław Wyspiański's exquisite pastels. The Józef Mehoffer House *(p166)* is another essential stop-off, offering fascinating insights into Young Poland's passion for interior design.

→

One of Stanisław Wyspiański's beautiful pastel drawings

KRAKÓW FOR
ART NOUVEAU

Few cities are as closely associated with Art Nouveau as Kraków, whose art and architecture stand as testimony to this period of frenzied creativity. Examples of Kraków's unique take on this ornamental style, brought to life by the Młoda Polska ("Young Poland") movement, can be found across the city

Cultural Cafés

Some of the city's most gorgeous Art Nouveau interiors can be enjoyed with coffee and cake at historic cafés like Noworolski *(www.noworolski. com.pl)*, whose luxuriant furnishings, wall-coverings and chandeliers have been beautifully preserved. Many Młoda Polska artists congregated at the Jama Michalika Café *(p86)*, today famous for its original stained glass and upholstery.

←

The spectacular Art Nouveau interior of Noworolski café

Arresting Architecture

Examples of eye-catching Art Nouveau architecture are peppered across the city. If the Młoda Polska epoch has a single signature building it is Globe House (p153), the dazzlingly unorthodox corner house that combines an asymetrical design with striking brickwork and a soaring, pyramidal tower, atop which sits an eye-catching globe. Its renowned architect Franciszek Mączyński was much in demand, working on the equally original and beautifully decorated Church of the Sacred Heart of Jesus (p146), as well as the dreamily charming Palace of Art (p84).

Other architectural highlights include the spectacular Old Theatre (p85), decorated with an impressive stucco frieze.

←

The beautiful Place of Art, one of the city's most spectacular Art Nouveau buildings

↑ The eye-catching *God the Father*, found in the Franciscan Church

WYSPIAŃSKI AND MŁODA POLSKA

Around 1900 there was a cultural upsurge known as Młoda Polska ("Young Poland"). This creative movement believed that Polish art could be regenerated through renewed contact with its folk roots. The movement took inspiration from Parisian Art Nouveau, Viennese Secession and the graphic art of Japan. The movement's central figure was the multitalented Stanisław Wyspiański (1869-1907), Poland's leading post-Impressionist painter. Wyspiański was also a great dramatist, writing plays such as *Wescle* ("The Wedding") which knitted together historical obsessions and patriotic myth. Examples of his work adorn multiple buildings and art galleries across Kraków.

Spectacular Stained Glass

Placing modern art at the service of an ancient craft, Stanisław Wyspiański designed a striking series of stained-glass windows for Kraków's churches. Spy some of the most famous in the Franciscan Church (p108), including the incandescent *God the Father*. Don't miss the artist's dramatic designs for Wawel Cathedral, now on display in the Wyspiański Pavilion (p115).

A YEAR IN
KRAKÓW

JANUARY

New Years Day *(1 Jan)*. Carol singers and well-wishers visit neighbourhood houses.

△ **Epiphany** *(6 Jan)*. The three kings of the nativity are celebrated with processions. The initials "K + M + B" (Kaspar, Melchior and Balthazar) are chalked above doorways to ensure good fortune in the coming year.

FEBRUARY

△ **Fat Thursday** *(Feb or Mar)*. The last Thursday before Lent is marked by the eating of *paczki* (Polish doughnuts). There are massive queues outside bakeries throughout the city.

Materia Prima *(mid- to late Feb)*. Spectacular festival of puppetry and theatre, with shows that will suit children as well as drama for grown-ups.

MAY

△ **Juvenalia** *(mid-May)*. High-school and college students mark the end of the academic year by flooding through the streets in chaotic procession, singing and blowing whistles.

Kraków Film Festival *(May–Jun)*. A packed programme of international features, shorts, documentaries and cartoons.

JUNE

△ **Dragon Parade** *(early Jun)*. Youth groups build huge dragon models which are paraded around the Main Market Square, then a dragon-themed son-et-lumière takes place on the banks of the Vistula.

Festival of Jewish Culture *(late Jun)*. A week of film, music, theatre, discussions and outdoor klezmer concerts in the former Jewish quarter of Kazimierz.

SEPTEMBER

△ **March of the Dachshunds** *(mid-Sep)*. A popular annual event in which dachshund owners parade their pooches down Floriańska Street to the Main Market Square.

Sacrum Profanum *(mid-Sep)*. A contemporary music festival embracing everything from string quartets to DJ culture, with performances in spaces around the city.

OCTOBER

△ **Unsound** *(early to mid-Oct)*. An international festival of electronic, experimental and avant-garde music held in unusual and atmospheric venues around the city.

Conrad Festival *(mid- to late Oct)*. Featuring readings and discussions, this week-long festival is Poland's largest literary event.

MARCH

△ **Palm Sunday** *(late Mar to early Apr)*. Processions and masses are held at churches, while traditional Easter Palms made from dried flowers and grasses provide a riot of colour on the city's streets.

Days of Bach *(end Mar)*. Featuring works both by the Bach family and by other composers from the same period, this festival is a leading celebration of Baroque music.

APRIL

△ **Easter Monday** Boys douse girls in water in a spring fertility rite that dates back centuries.

Mistera Paschalia *(early to mid-Apr)*. This festival celebrates religious music, from medieval to modern.

Beethoven Easter Festival *(early to mid-Apr)*. Orchestral and chamber recitals of Beethoven's music, including shows on the Main Market Square.

JULY

Crossroads *(early Jul)*. Performances of traditional folk music from around the world, with shows often spilling out onto the city's Main Market Square.

△ **Ulica Festival of Street Theatre** *(mid-Jul)*. Street performers, puppet shows and a wealth of children's entertainment in outdoor locations throughout the city.

AUGUST

△ **Pierogi Festival** *(mid-Aug)*. Poland's favourite dish is celebrated with row upon row of stalls selling a mouthwatering variety of these stuffed pastry pockets.

Kraków Live *(mid-Aug)*. An open-air festival attracting the big names of rock and pop, held in fields near the Polish Aviation Museum.

Feast of the Assumption *(15 Aug)*. Masses are held in churches throughout the city.

NOVEMBER

All Saints' Day *(1 Nov)*. Cemeteries throughout the city are lit up with candles as Polish families honour their dead.

△ **All Souls' Jazz Festival** *(2 Nov)*. The oldest jazz festival in Poland, this one-night-only event sees the best local musicians perform.

Polish Independence Day *(11 Nov)*. A mass is held at Wawel Cathedral and wreaths are laid at the Grunwald Monument found on Matejko Square.

DECEMBER

△ **Advent Fair** *(throughout Dec)*. A huge festive market takes over the Main Market Square, with stalls selling Christmas crafts and delicatessen products as well as sausages and mulled wine.

St Barbara's Day *(4 Dec)*. The feast day of St Barbara, the patron saint of miners, is celebrated with processions and street parties in the historic salt-mining towns of Wieliczka and Bochnia, located just outside of Kraków.

A BRIEF
HISTORY

Supposedly founded following the slaughter of a ferocious dragon, Kraków has been at the centre of Polish life for much of its history. Having served as a royal capital for over five centuries, the city remains a constant focus of national pride, as well as an inspiration to Polish artists and writers.

Kraków's Origins

The Kraków area has been occupied since prehistoric times, with hills such as Wawel and the Krakus Mound serving as major sites for a succession of different groups. A flourishing market town began to take shape on this site in the 7th century, when it became the capital of a Slav group known as the Vistulans (Wiślane). The town became part of the Greater Moravian Empire around the 9th century, then the Kingdom of Bohemia in the 10th. Mieszko I (r 960-992), ruler of the Polonians (another Slav group who settled in today's Wielkopolska) took control of the city around 990.

Did You Know?

The bones of Kraków's legendary dragon allegedly hang above Wawel Cathedral's entrance.

Timeline of events

c 200,000 BC
First evidence of human settlement in the Kraków area

c 500 AD
The Vistulans settle in Kraków

885 AD
Kraków becomes part of the Greater Moravian Empire

1042
Kazimierz the Restorer makes Kraków the capital of Poland

1079
Bishop (later Saint) Stanisław is killed by Bolesław the Bold

Medieval Kraków

Kraków became the Polish capital under Mieszko's great-grandson, Kazimierz the Restorer (r 1034-1058). His son, Bolesław the Bold (r 1076–79), was involved in a power struggle with Bishop Stanisław of Kraków, and had him murdered in 1079. The city's importance increased under the rule of Władysław the Elbow-High (r 1260-1333), the first Polish king to be crowned in Wawel Cathedral. After being sacked twice by Mongols during the 13th century, an elaborate system of fortifications was constructed around the city. It later flourished under Kazimierz the Great (r 1333-1370), who convened a glittering court here and also guaranteed Jewish rights.

Jagiellonian Kraków

On the death of Kazimierz the Great, the Polish crown passed to Louis of Anjou and then to his daughter Jadwiga. The country's first female monarch and a major donor to Kraków's university, she reigned alongside her husband, the Grand Duke Jogaila of Lithuania, Władysław II Jagiełło. The resulting Jagiellonian dynasty ruled Poland for the next 185 years; during this time, Kraków became one of Europe's major cultural centres.

1 Historic map showing the city of Kraków.

2 A 19th-century print of Bolesław the Bold.

3 Painting depicting Kazimierz the Restorer.

4 Artwork showing King Władysław II Jagiełło surrounded by some of his subjects.

1241
Kraków is destroyed by the Mongols

1173
Bolesław the Curly is the first Piast to be buried at Wawel

1334
Kazimierz the Great grants privileges to the Jews

1364
Kazimierz the Great founds the Academy of Kraków

1386
Queen Jadwiga marries Grand Duke Jogaila of Lithuania

1

2

Renaissance Kraków

At the beginning of the 16th century, Kraków was opening up to Italian Renaissance culture, with Italian architects reconstructing Wawel Royal Castle in the Renaissance style. The pace of artistic change increased in 1517 when Sigismund the Old (r 1506-1548) married Bona Sforza, daughter of the Duke of Milan. Under her son, Sigismund Augustus (r 1548-1572), the Zygmunt Chapel, a Renaissance masterpiece, was built in Wawel Cathedral.

The Commonwealth of the Two Nations

Poland and Lithuania signed the Union of Lublin in 1569, creating the Commonwealth of the Two Nations. The geographical extent of the Commonwealth, and the fact that many of its powerful nobles lived in the northeast, persuaded King Sigismund III Waza to move the capital to Warsaw in 1596. As a result, noble families ceased to spend time in Kraków and the city entered a period of decline. Things were made worse by an outbreak of plague in 1651, and a sacking by Swedish armies in 1655. Despite this, Baroque culture left a profound mark on the city, with a number of magnificent buildings built, including the Church of St Anne.

BONA SFORZA (1494-1557)

Kraków's cultural upsurge during the Renaissance owes a lot to Bona Sforza. As the daughter of the Duke of Milan, she had been surrounded by fine art and architecture since birth. She brought an Italianate sense of style to Wawel Castle, ordering tapestries and laying out gardens. Bona passed on her refined tastes to her son, Sigismund Augustus.

Timeline of events

1400
Nawojka becomes the first female student at Kraków's Jagiellonian University by dressing as a man

1491
Nicolaus Copernicus begins his studies at the Jagiellonian University

1495
King Jan I Olbracht has Kraków's Jews resettled in the suburb of Kazimierz

1517
King Sigismund the Old marries Bona Sforza of Milan

Kraków Under the Partitions

The Commonwealth came to an end in the late 18th century when Poland was partitioned by three neighbouring empires – Prussia, Austria and Tsarist Russia. In 1794, patriotic Poles led by Tadeusz Kościuszko attempted to overturn the partitions by staging a revolt centred on Kraków; they were defeated and the city fell under Austrian control. Kraków was allowed partial autonomy as a free city from 1815 to 1846, when another uprising persuaded the Austrians to place the city under tighter control.

Fin-de-Siècle Kraków

Despite the Austrian occupation, a lively cultural scene emerged in Kraków, with the city becoming the unofficial cultural capital of a divided Poland in the years before World War I. The city's proximity to Vienna meant that revolutionary ideas in the arts were taken up quickly; as a result, around 1900, Młoda Polska ("Young Poland") was born in Kraków. Inspired by Art Nouveau in France and the Secession in Austria, this creative movement, led by Kraków-born artists Stanisław Wyspiański, resulted in a flurry of artistic expression in the city.

1 A 16th-century portrait of Queen Bona Sforza.

2 A statue of King Sigismund III Waza

3 The spectacular Baroque altar found inside the Church of St Anne

4 A painting depicting the 1794 uprising led by Tadeusz Kosciuszko.

5 A self-portrait of Stanisław Wyspiański with his wife.

1655-57
Kraków is occupied by an army of Swedes and Transylvanians

1794
The Second Partition provokes an armed uprising led by Tadeusz Kościuszko

1850
The Kraków Fire destroys large sections of the Old Town

1596
The capital is moved from Kraków to Warsaw

1734
Coronation of Augustus III Wettin, the last to take place in Kraków

Kraków 1914-1939

With Germany and Austria-Hungary lined up against Britain, France and Russia in World War I, Kraków found itself near the front line. Patriots under Józef Piłsudski met in Kraków to form a Polish Legion that would fight with the Austrians against the Russians, in return for a promise of Polish autonomy. Too independent-minded for the Central Powers, Piłsudski was imprisoned, emerging in 1918 to lead a newly independent Poland. Kraków went through a period of renewal after World War I, with buildings like the National Museum and the Jagiellonian Library testifying to its cultural importance.

Kraków in World War II

In August 1939 the Molotov-Ribbentrop pact between the Soviet Union and Nazi Germany divided Poland into spheres of conquest. Kraków endured over four years of German occupation, with Nazi governor Hans Frank taking up residence in the city's castle. In 1941, the city's Jewish population was either crowded into a ghetto built in Podgórze or deported to work in camps elsewhere. The ghetto was brutally cleared in March 1943 – some of its inhabitants were murdered on the spot, others were sent to Auschwitz-Birkenau.

1 Photograph of Józef Piłsudski surrounded by government ministers. ↑

2 Polish Jews being forced to work in the city's ghetto.

3 The Communist suburb of Nowa Huta, designed in Socialist-Realist style

4 A collection of Polish and EU flags

Timeline of events

1934
Construction begins on the main building of the National Museum

1941
Jewish Ghetto established in Podgórze

1949
Construction of Nowa Huta starts

1921
Church of the Sacred Heart of Jesus in Wesoła consecrated

1945
Soviet troops enter Kraków on 18 January

4

Communist Kraków

Kraków came under Soviet control following the end of World War II. The Communist authorities, eager to provide a counter-weight to a city they saw as bourgeois, began the construction of Nowa Huta in 1949. This vast suburb was intended to house a working-class community that would be loyal to the new regime. Things turned out differently, with Nowa Huta instead providing support for anti-Communist movements, such as the Solidarity trade union, formed in 1980. Kraków and Nowa Huta were also bastions of the Catholic Church, a bond strengthened by Kraków Archbishop Karol Wojtyła's election as Pope John Paul II in 1978.

Kraków Today

After the collapse of Communism in 1989, Kraków developed further as both a centre for new technologies and as a major university city. Poland's entry into the EU in 2004 led to a surge of investment in the city. Tourism has become a key industry in Kraków, with the city today receiving over nine million visitors a year. Kraków has also been named a UNESCO City of Literature, reinforcing its position as an important cultural hub.

POPE JOHN PAUL II

Born Karol Wojtyła in Wadowice in 1920, the future pope studied at Kraków's university before entering the priesthood; he became Archbishop of Kraków in 1964. His election as Pope in 1978 had an immediate impact on Communist Poland, encouraging opposition activists and strength-ening the church's moral authority. He died in 2005 but is still a source of inspiration.

1956
Piwnica pod Baranami cabaret established

1968
Construction of the Lord's Ark Church begins in Nowa Huta

1993
Steven Spielberg films *Schindler's List* in Kraków

2014
Opening of impressive, ultra-modern congress centre ICE

2019
Kraków named European Capital of Gastronomic Culture

EXPERIENCE

Lunching on the Main Market Square

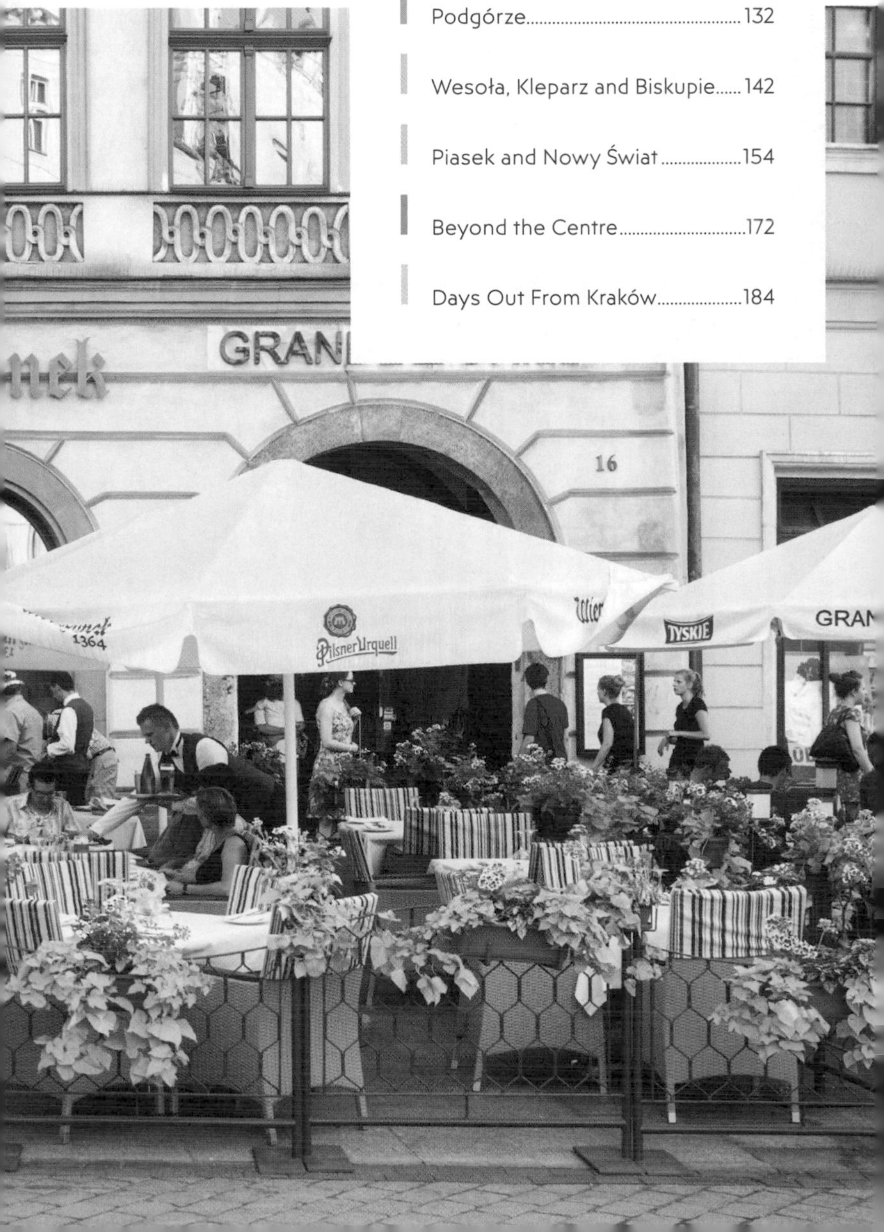

GRAN
16
Pilsner Urquell
TYSKIE

THE OLD TOWN

This area has been a centre of regional trade from at least the 10th century. Its position as a trading hub was further developed when, in 1257, Duke Bolesław the Chaste gave Kraków a charter. Alongside awarding trade privileges to merchants, this document also regulated town planning, providing for a centrally located square surrounded by a regular grid of streets – thus, the city's Main Market Square (Rynek Główny) was born, with the Old Town growing up around it. Over the following centuries, the area thrived, with merchants from all over Central Europe building grand houses on the Main Market Square, each with backyards and cellars for storing goods. The university (founded in 1364 and re-founded in 1400) turned the Old Town's southwest quarter into a bustling student quarter. The area also became the centre of social life for the nobles of southern Poland, who built opulent town houses around the square. Gothic, Renaissance and Baroque styles flourished over the ensuing centuries, each generation adding to the buildings bequeathed by their predecessors. The Old Town escaped significant damage during the two world wars and has managed to retain its medieval atmosphere. It remains the undisputed heart of Kraków.

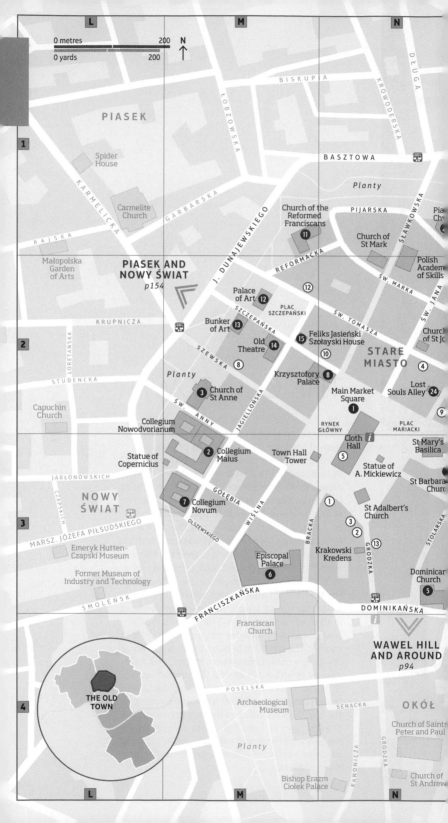

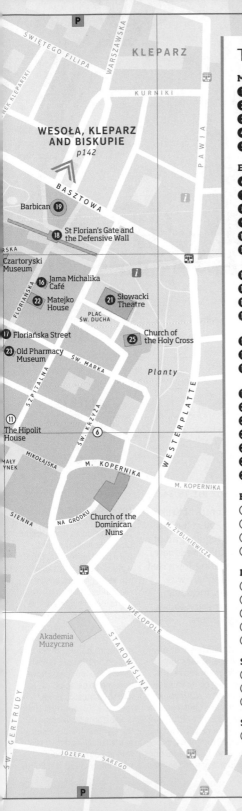

THE OLD TOWN

Must Sees

1. Main Market Square
2. Collegium Maius
3. Church of St Anne
4. Czartoryski Museum
5. Dominican Church

Experience

6. Episcopal Palace
7. Collegium Novum
8. Krzysztofory Palace
9. The Hipolit House
10. St Barbara's Church
11. Church of the Reformed Franciscans
12. Palace of Art
13. Bunker of Art
14. Old Theatre
15. Feliks Jasieński Szołayski House
16. Jama Michalika Café
17. Floriańska Street
18. St Florian's Gate and the Defensive Wall
19. Barbican
20. Piarist Church
21. Słowacki Theatre
22. Matejko House
23. Old Pharmacy Museum
24. Lost Souls Alley
25. Church of the Holy Cross

Eat

1. Wentzl
2. Wierzynek
3. Szara Gęś
4. Café Camelot

Drink

5. Café Szal
6. House of Beer
7. Viva la Pinta
8. Multi Qlti Tap Bar
9. Jazz Club U Muniaka

Stay

10. Hotel Stary
11. Tango House
12. Globtroter

Shop

13. Calik Christmas Baubles

St Mary's Basilica seen from beneath the arches of the Cloth Hall ↑

①

MAIN MARKET SQUARE
RYNEK GŁÓWNY

📍N2 🏠Rynek Główny 🚌124, 152, 424, 502 🚊1, 18, 24, 52

This magnificent square has been the centre of Kraków since medieval times. Measuring some 200 m (660 ft) by 200 m (660 ft), it is surrounded by a regular grid of streets. Several buildings are found within the square, including the magnificent Cloth Hall, soaring Town Hall Tower and iconic St Mary's Basilica. The square was once a venue for many important events, including the coronation ceremonies of Poland's royalty; today, it is the first taste of Kraków for many visitors.

Did You Know?

In 1794 the square was the starting point for a patriotic revolt, led by Tadeusz Kościuszko.

①

St Adalbert's Church
Kościół św. Wojciecha

🏠 Rynek Główny 3
🕐 10am–3pm daily
🌐 wojciechnarynku.pl

The diminutive church of St Adalbert dates from around the 11th century and is one of the oldest churches in all of Kraków. A legend tells that St Adalbert preached here before leaving on his missionary journey to try to convert the Prussians to Christianity in 997. He was killed by Prussian pagans the same year and his bones were brought back to Poland, where he became one of the nation's patron saints.

The architecture of the church amalgamates several different styles, including Romanesque, Gothic, Renaissance and Baroque. This mixture reflects various stages in the development of the square, an exhibition on which is located in the Rynek Underground (p72). To the north side of the church you can view the remnants of a Romanesque wall, dating from the 12th century. Etched on the right is what looks like a four-petal flower, believed to be a sign carved into the sandstone by a medieval stonemason. There is also a small exhibition in the crypt on the the history of the church and the Main Market Square, although most information is in Polish.

Masses are celebrated in the church between 8pm and 10pm every day; the church is open during this time, although visitors should be respectful of worshippers. The church also hosts classical music concerts by the Royal Chamber Orchestra.

---

②

Town Hall Tower
Wieża Ratuszowa

🏛 Rynek Główny 1 🕐 Mar-Oct: 10:30am-6pm Tue-Sun, 10:30am-2pm Mon; Nov-Dec: 11am-5pm Tue-Sun, 11am-2pm Mon
🌐 muzeumkrakowa.pl

Crowned by a Baroque cupola, this Gothic tower dominates the Main Market Square. It is the only remaining vestige of the City Hall, built in the 14th century and pulled down in the first half of the 19th century. The tower is now a branch of the Historical Museum of the City of Kraków (Muzeum Historyczne Miasta Krakowa or MHK) dedicated to the history of the city from

the Middle Ages to the present day; it is also a venue for the Ludowy Theatre.

Found just next to the tower is *Eros Bendato*, a giant bronze head by Polish artist Igor Mitoraj. Known locally as "The Head", it is one of the city's most famous sculptures.

---

③

International Cultural Centre
Międzynarodowe Centrum Kultury

🏛 Rynek Główny 25
🕐 11am-7pm Tue-Sun
🌐 mck.krakow.pl

Housed on the upper floors of the "House Under the Raven", found on the south side of the Main Market Square, this centre was founded in 1991 to promote the heritage of Central Europe. It publishes a range of books as well as the quarterly English-Polish magazine *Herito*. The centre also organizes some of the city's most compelling exhibitions on history and culture. Recent exhibitions have been dedicated to such diverse topics as Hungarian Art Nouveau, Polish contemporary design, and works by the renowned Surrealist artist Max Ernst.

LEGENDS OF THE SQUARE

Many unusual stories are told about the Main Market Square. One says the square's pigeons are the enchanted knights of Duke Henryk Probus, who agreed to the metamorphosis in exchange for gold that he needed to secure papal acceptance for his coronation. The knights were supposed to regain human form after the coronation but the duke lost the gold and his knights remained pigeons. A different legend concerns the brothers who built the towers of St Mary's Basilica. When the older mason completed the taller tower, he killed his younger sibling to prevent him surpassing his work but then, full of remorse, killed himself.

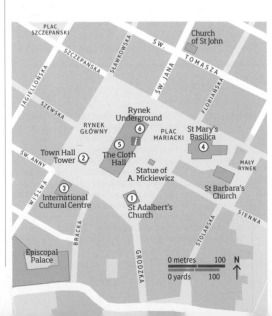

MAIN MARKET SQUARE ARCHITECTURE

Kraków's magnificent Main Market Square was first laid out in the 13th century, although the square has since been renovated and updated countless times over the centuries. Many of its principal buildings date not from the 1400s but from various subsequent epochs – with the Renaissance, Mannerist and Neo-Classical eras particularly well represented. In fact, many of the buildings which surround the square are an eclectic blend of different styles, such as Renaissance buildings with Gothic cellars.

Did You Know?

The 11th-century St Adalbert's Church is the only surviving Romanesque building in the square.

The sloping buttresses at the base of the building give it an asymmetrical, fortress-like charm. It also has graceful arches at ground level.

The house features an undulating parapet.

The 16th-century Mannerist attic floor is distinguished by an ornate scrolled parapet and reliefs known as Herms, head-and-torso sculptures of Greek gods and spirits.

Timeline

Renaissance: The Grey House

Although the most attention-grabbing example of Renaissance architecture on the square is the magnificent Cloth Hall *(p70)*, there are many more examples of this style ranged around the sides. Renaissance architecture brought a new sense of proportion and harmony which emphasized straight lines, clean forms and simple elegance. One of the most handsome examples of the style is the Grey House *(Kamienica Szara)* on the east side of the square. The house is currently home to the award-winning Szara Gęś *(p89)* restaurant.

Mannerist: The Boner House

The towering Boner House *(Kamienica Bonerowska)* on the east side of the square was built by Jan Boner, a wealthy merchant who became a noble. Constructed on the foundations of a Gothic structure, this house is like many buildings of the Late-Renaissance in that it displays ever more frivolous decorative flourishes, creating a hybrid architectural style that eventually became known as Mannerist. Its best feature is the beautifully decorated attic floor.

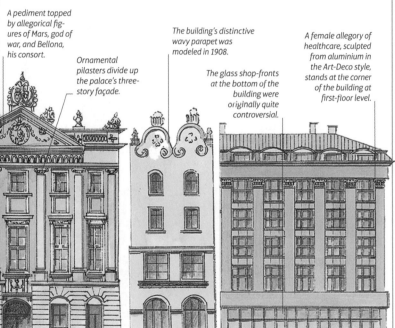

A pediment topped by allegorical figures of Mars, god of war, and Bellona, his consort.

Ornamental pilasters divide up the palace's three-story façade.

The building's distinctive wavy parapet was modeled in 1908.

The glass shop-fronts at the bottom of the building were originally quite controversial.

A female allegory of healthcare, sculpted from aluminium in the Art-Deco style, stands at the corner of the building at first-floor level.

Neo-Classical: The Potocki Palace

One of the most imposing buildings on the south side of the square is the Potocki Palace *(Pałac Potockich)*, an ancient structure rebuilt in French Neo-Classical style in the 1770s by its then owner Eliasz Wodzicki. Neo-Classicism looked to the architecture of ancient Greece and Rome for inspiration, producing buildings that frequently had the magnificence of ancient temples.

Art Nouveau: Rynek Główny 4

Known in Poland as Młoda Polska ("Young Poland"), Art Nouveau *(p48)* combined a modernist enthusiasm for geometrical shapes with a no-holds-barred attitude to decorative detail, using motifs which were taken from a wide range of sources, from classical Greece to local folk art. The tall, narrow mansion at Rynek Główny 4 is one of the only houses on the square with Art Nouveau decoration.

Art Deco: The Phoenix Building

One of the few examples of 20th-century architecture on the square is the Phoenix Building *(Budynek Feniksa)*. Built for the Feniks insurance company in 1928, it embodies the Art Deco characteristics of symmetry, simplicity and repetition. Featuring glass shop-fronts at street level and angular bay windows further up, it was considered shockingly avant-garde – even controversial – when first built.

ST MARY'S BASILICA
KOŚCIÓŁ MARIACKI

🏠 Plac Mariacki 5 🕐 11:30am-6pm Mon-Sat, 2-6pm Sun
ⓦ mariacki.com

Occuping the western edge of the Main Market Square, St Mary's is instantly recognizable thanks to its two contrasting towers. The church's exquistely decorated interior is one of the most breathtaking in the world.

Construction of St Mary's, a Gothic church began in the late 13th century, but work on the vaulting and chapels continued until the mid-15th century. The taller tower, which acted as Kraków's watchtower, was extended in the early 15th century; the lower tower was not completed until the early 16th century.

The spectacular interior is adorned with eye-catching wall paintings, including a sky-blue ceiling dotted with stars, and jewel-bright stained-glass windows, many made by the celebrated Polish artists Stanisław Wyspiański (*p49*) and Józef Mehoffer (*p166*). The church's crowning glory is the magnificent high altar by famed German sculptor Veit Stoss. This intricately carved and gilded masterpiece is the world's largest Gothic altar. It is currently undergoing restoration and so some sections may not be on display.

↑ The striking façade of St Mary's Basilica, with its unidentical twin towers

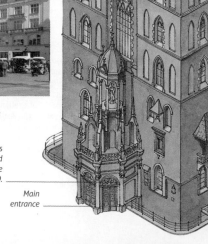

Hejnał Tower

This Late-Baroque porch was built in the 18th century. Carved busts of the Apostles and saints were added to the door panels in 1929.

Main entrance

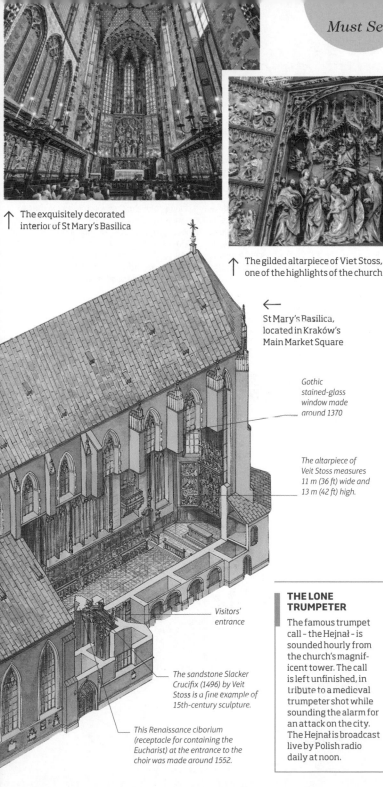

↑ The exquisitely decorated interior of St Mary's Basilica

↑ The gilded altarpiece of Viet Stoss, one of the highlights of the church

← St Mary's Basilica, located in Kraków's Main Market Square

Gothic stained-glass window made around 1370

The altarpiece of Veit Stoss measures 11 m (36 ft) wide and 13 m (42 ft) high.

Visitors' entrance

The sandstone Slacker Crucifix (1496) by Veit Stoss is a fine example of 15th-century sculpture.

This Renaissance ciborium (receptacle for containing the Eucharist) at the entrance to the choir was made around 1552.

THE LONE TRUMPETER

The famous trumpet call – the Hejnał – is sounded hourly from the church's magnificent tower. The call is left unfinished, in tribute to a medieval trumpeter shot while sounding the alarm for an attack on the city. The Hejnał is broadcast live by Polish radio daily at noon.

⑤ 🖋 🚊 🖥 🛍

THE CLOTH HALL
SUKIENNICE

📍 Rynek Główny 1-3 🕐 Stalls: 10am-8pm daily; gallery: 10am-6pm Tue-Sat, 10am-4pm Sun 🌐 mnk.pl

The enchanting Cloth Hall dominates the centre of the Main Market Square. A place of trade for over 700 years, this bustling hall is sometimes referred to as "Europe's oldest shopping centre".

This elaborate structure has evolved over time, transforming from simple stone trading stalls in the 12th century to a spectacular Renaissance building in 1555. The hall was remodelled again in 1875, when the building's now-characteristic exterior arcades were added. On the ground floor is a shopping arcade, lined with stalls selling colourful Cracovian crafts. On the top floor is the compelling Gallery of 19th-Century Polish Art, part of the National Museum (p158). Spread over four rooms, it contains a magnificent collection of works by some of Poland's best artists, including Jan Matejko – his dramatic painting *Prussian Homage* is a highlight.

↑ Stalls selling handicrafts and souvenirs inside the Cloth Hall

The Gallery of 19th-Century Polish Art

Roof with sunken rafters

The Renaissance parapet is not only decorative but also offers protection from fire.

Entrance to stalls

The side arcades and oriels were added during the rebuilding in 1875. The arcades echo the medieval architecture of Venice.

Did You Know?

Salt from the now-famous Wieliczka Salt Mine used to be sold at the Cloth Hall.

↑ The Adam Mickiewicz Monument standing in front of the Cloth Hall

Renaissance parapet

← Illustration of the Cloth Hall, found in the Main Market Square

Entrance to the Rynek Underground (p72)

Entrance to gallery

DRINK

Café Szal
On the second floor of the Cloth Hall, this excellent café serves delicious coffee and cake along with epic views of the square - especially of the lofty towers of St Mary's Basilica.

📍N3 🏛Rynek Główny 1-3 ☎695 602 774

ⓩⓩⓩ

→ One of the rooms in the Gallery of 19th-Century Polish Art

⑥ 🖼️ Ⓜ️

RYNEK UNDERGROUND

PODZIEMIA RYNKU

📍 Rynek Główny 1 🕐 Apr–Oct: 10am–10pm daily (to 8pm Mon, to 4pm Tue); Nov–Mar: 10am–8pm daily (to 4pm Tue) 📅 2nd Mon of month 🌐 muzeumkrakowa.pl; podziemiarynku.com

Concealed beneath Kraków's magical Main Market Square, the Rynek Underground is part archaeological treasure trove, part high-tech museum. A variety of fascinating exhibits will take you on a whirlwind ride through the city's compelling history, from the time of the first settlers all the way to modern day.

Opened in September 2010, this museum is composed of an underground route that winds through the remnants of medieval streets, market stalls and a variety of other subterranean rooms. Along the way you'll unearth a wealth of archaeological finds, including everyday objects such as ancient coins and clothing. Among the highlights are the remains of an 11th-century cemetery, containing the graves of those suspected to be vampires. The museum brings its archaeological discoveries spectacularly to life with interactive multimedia exhibits, as well as lasers, smoke machines and holograms.

As the museum is so popular and there are only 300 visitors allowed in at a time, it's a good idea to book your tickets in advance.

> 💬 INSIDER TIP
> ### Keep the Kids Entertained
>
> Alongside a wealth of youngster-friendly multimedia content, the Rynek Underground also has a designated children's area featuring interactive puzzles and a mechanical puppet show acting out scenes from the history of Kraków.

→

A skull, one of the many archaeological finds on display at the Rynek Underground

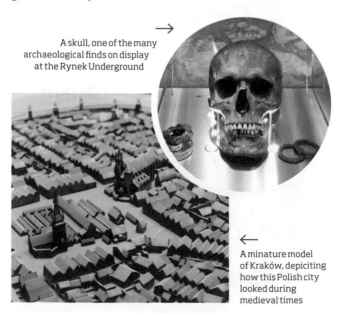

←

A miniature model of Kraków, depicting how this Polish city looked during medieval times

Did You Know?

In Poland, supected vampires were buried with their heads cut off to stop them from rising again.

↑ One of the museum's walkways going past archaeological remains

2️⃣ 🚇 Ⓜ️

COLLEGIUM MAIUS
COLLEGIUM MAIUS

📍M3 🏛️Ulica Jagiellońska 15 🚌504 🚋2, 8, 13, 18, 20 🕐Apr–Oct: 10am–2:20pm Mon, Wed & Fri, 10am–5:20pm Tue & Thu, 10am–1:30pm Sat; Nov–Mar: 10am– 2:20pm Mon–Fri, 10am–1:30pm Sat 🌐maius.uj.edu.pl

Best known for being the alma mater of Nicolaus Copernicus, one of the world's greatest astronomers, the Collegium Maius is filled with a cornucopia of fascinating historic artifacts.

The Collegium Maius is the oldest building within the Academy of Kraków (now the Jagiellonian University). It was constructed during the 15th century by amalgamating a number of town houses. Lecture rooms and accommodation for professors were originally located here. Between 1840 and 1870 the college was rebuilt in the Neo-Gothic style. After World War II the University Museum, established in 1867, was moved here.

The only way to explore this historic sight is on a guided tour, which take place every 20 minutes (it's best to book in advance). These fascinating tours take in the building's expansive courtyard, as well as a variety of rooms, including the treasury filled with artifacts and the breathtaking library with its beautifully painted ceiling. As you explore you'll get to admire scientific instruments and historic manuscripts.

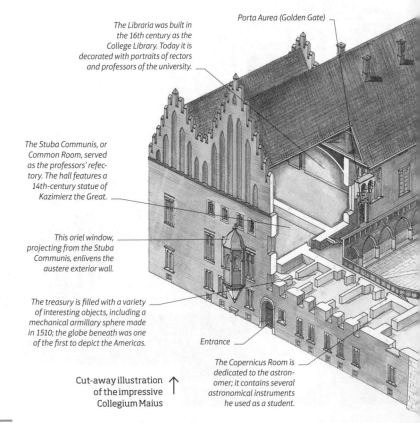

The Libraria was built in the 16th century as the College Library. Today it is decorated with portraits of rectors and professors of the university.

Porta Aurea (Golden Gate)

The Stuba Communis, or Common Room, served as the professors' refectory. The hall features a 14th-century statue of Kazimierz the Great.

This oriel window, projecting from the Stuba Communis, enlivens the austere exterior wall.

The treasury is filled with a variety of interesting objects, including a mechanical armillary sphere made in 1510; the globe beneath was one of the first to depict the Americas.

Entrance

The Copernicus Room is dedicated to the astronomer; it contains several astronomical instruments he used as a student.

Cut-away illustration ↑ of the impressive Collegium Maius

Charming Chimes

Time your visit to the Collegium Maius to coincide with the chiming of the mechanical clock found on the south side. The clock sounds at 9am, 11am, 1pm, 3pm and 5pm daily, with its tinkling peals signalling the arrival of a procession of wooden statuettes, including Queen Jadwiga and other figures.

The columns of the Gothic cloister have a cut crystal-like decoration.

1 The library, adorned with an eye-catching painted ceiling of blue sky and white clouds.

2 The expansive courtyard of the Collegium Maius, encircled by a Gothic cloister

3 The dramatic Neo-Gothic exterior of the Collegium Maius

A collection of national memorabilia, including the piano that Frédéric Chopin played, can be visited by prior arrangement in the Green Hall.

Rector's Stairs

This lavishly inlaid door was originally in the old Town Hall.

The former apartment of John of Kęty, the professor of theology who became the university's patron saint; it was converted into a chapel.

The Great Hall features stalls used by the senate during the ceremonies at which honorary degrees are conferred.

COPERNICUS

Kraków's Jagiellonian University owes much of its renown to the fact that revolutionary astronomer Nicolaus Copernicus studied here between 1491 and 1495. Born in Toruń in 1473, his greatest contribution to science was the discovery in 1543 that the earth revolved around the sun – and not the sun around the earth, as had been taught previously by the medieval church.

③

CHURCH OF ST ANNE

KOŚCIÓŁ ŚW. ANNY

📍 M2 🏛 Ulica Świętej Anny 11 🚌 124, 152, 502, 352, 424 🚃 2, 8, 13 18, 20 🕐 1:30-7pm Tue-Fri, 9am-7pm Sat, 2-7pm Sun 🌐 kolegiata-anna.pl

St Anne's, with its sumptuous interior, is considered to be a leading example of Baroque architecture in Poland. Attached to the Jagiellonian University, it is the resting place of many university professors.

This church was first built in the Gothic style during the 14th century. One of the most renowned professors of the Academy of Kraków (later known as the Jagiellonian University), John of Kęty was buried here after his death in 1473; at the time he was already considered a saint. Following his beatification, the senate of the academy commissioned the popular architect Tylman van Gameren to build a beautiful new church to house his tomb. This new Baroque church was erected at the end of the 17th century; the tomb of St John of Kęty is to the right of the transept.

The interior of the church is exquisitely decorated with both ornate stuccowork by Italian sculptor Baldassare Fontana and eye-catching trompe-l'œil paintings.

The 17th-century Baroque Church of St Anne

↑ The striking Baroque exterior of the Church of St Anne

The main entrance's "scenographic" effect is due to the superimposition of three portals.

TYLMAN VAN GAMEREN

Greatest of all the architects working in 17th-century Poland was Tylman van Gameren (1632-1706), a Dutchman who came to work in the country at the age of 28. He built grand palaces all over Poland for some of the greatest aristocratic families of the age, including for the Czartoryskis in Puławy, the Krasińskis in Warsaw and the Branickis in Białystok.

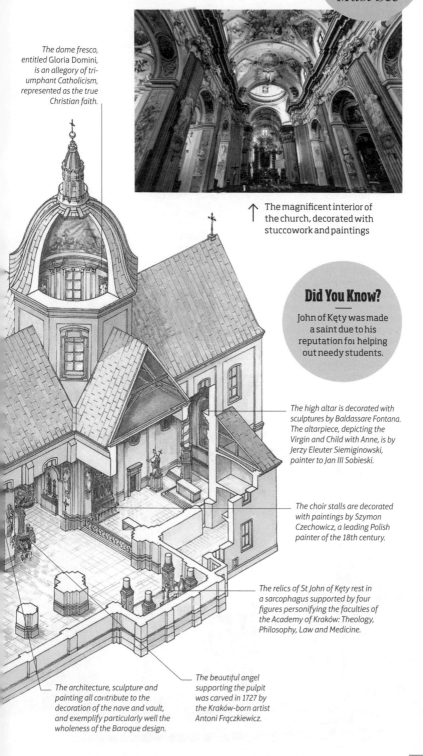

The dome fresco, entitled Gloria Domini, is an allegory of triumphant Catholicism, represented as the true Christian faith.

↑ The magnificent interior of the church, decorated with stuccowork and paintings

Did You Know?

John of Kęty was made a saint due to his reputation for helping out needy students.

The high altar is decorated with sculptures by Baldassare Fontana. The altarpiece, depicting the Virgin and Child with Anne, is by Jerzy Eleuter Siemiginowski, painter to Jan III Sobieski.

The choir stalls are decorated with paintings by Szymon Czechowicz, a leading Polish painter of the 18th century.

The relics of St John of Kęty rest in a sarcophagus supported by four figures personifying the faculties of the Academy of Kraków: Theology, Philosophy, Law and Medicine.

The architecture, sculpture and painting all contribute to the decoration of the nave and vault, and exemplify particularly well the wholeness of the Baroque design.

The beautiful angel supporting the pulpit was carved in 1727 by the Kraków-born artist Antoni Frączkiewicz.

4

CZARTORYSKI MUSEUM

MUZEUM CZARTORYSKICH

🗺 N2 🏠 Ulica Pijarska 15 🚊 2, 4, 18, 20, 24 🚌 124, 152, 424, 502, 512 🕐 9am-7pm Tue-Fri, 10am-8pm Sat, 10am-6pm Sun 🌐 mnk.pl

The Czartoryski Museum contains one of the most magnificent collections of art in Poland. An artistic treasure trove, its most prized possession is the 15th-century masterpiece *Lady With an Ermine* by Leonardo Da Vinci.

This impressive collection, established by Princess Izabella Czartoryska, encompasses an astounding variety of artworks. Spread over two floors and 26 rooms, the museum's exhibits include displays on ancient, medieval and Renaissance works, as well as both Northern European and Asian art. While the undisputed star of the collection is Da Vinci's masterpiece, the museum contains many other highlights, among them a display of works by the Dutch Old Masters, including *The Good Samaritan* by Rembrant van Rijn. Two further must-sees are the exhibit devoted to the Czartoryski family and a series of rooms tracing Poland's history through works of art and historical objects.

1 This armoured casket, once owned by King Augustus II, is just one of many historical objects found in the museum.

2 An eye-catching piece of medieval art on display in the Czartoryski Museum.

3 The striking *Lady with an Ermine* by the renowned Old Master Leonardo da Vinci is the highlight of the Czartoryski Museum's art collection.

THE HISTORY OF THE CZARTORYSKI ART COLLECTION

This collection was established by Izabela Czartoryska in 1796, to be displayed in her so-called "Temple of Memory" in the grounds of the family palace in Puławy. Intended to preserve cultural heritage for future generations, the collection grew to include a staggering number of Old Masters, including Da Vinci's spectacular *Lady With an Ermine*, purchased by Izabela's son Adam in 1798. Exiled to France in 1830 following the November Uprising, the family and their collection returned to Kraków in 1878; the artworks were put on public display soon after. The collection was sold to the Polish Government in 2016.

↑ The striking exterior of the Czartoryski Museum

⑤

DOMINICAN CHURCH

KOŚCIÓŁ DOMINIKAŃSKI

⑨ N3 **🏠 Ulica Stolarska 12** **🚌 1, 3, 6, 8, 10, 13, 18, 20, 24, 52**
🕐 6:30am–8pm daily **🌐 krakow.dominikanie.pl**

Twice destroyed by fire, the Dominican Church has managed to rise from the ashes and remains one of Kraków's most impressive churches. Its peaceful interior is home to grand tombs and exquisite altars.

The Dominicans began the construction of a new church in 1250. It contained the shrine of St Jacek and so was a place of mass pilgrimage. The church was badly damaged by fire in 1462 and had to be rebuilt. In the 17th century, opulent mausolea, modelled on the Zygmunt Chapel at Wawel Hill (p98), were added by noble families, and in the 18th century the church was furnished with Late-Baroque altars. The Kraków Fire of 1850 almost destroyed the church. It was reconstructed by 1872 and today is an important evangelical centre which attracts the faithful.

🔍 HIDDEN GEM
Leszek the Black

In the chancel is the tombstone of Leszek Czarny, or Leszek II the Black, who became High Duke of Poland in 1279. A fantastic example of Gothic stone carving, it shows a Polish eagle on Leszek's shield.

The Gothic cloister was a burial place of burghers whose memorial plaques and tombs can still be seen here.

The carved tomb of General Jan Skrzynecki commemorates the hero of the November Uprising of 1830.

Crowstep gable

The fine decoration of the Zbaraski Chapel, built in 1627–33, is in sharp contrast with the monumental forms of the altar and tombs in black marble.

The Lubomirski Chapel displays lovely paintings and sculptures.

THE GREAT FIRE

The Dominican Church was substantially damaged by a huge fire that broke out on 18 July 1850. The fire started at a mill on Krupnicza Street, over 0.5 km (0.3 miles) northwest of the church, but its sparks were carried across town by the wind. Many of the city's buildings were made of wood at this time and the fire raged for days before being put out with the help of the army. Around one tenth of the city was destroyed.

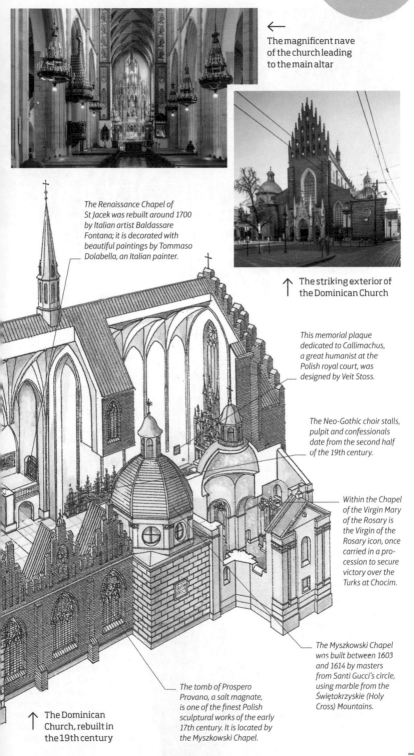

← The magnificent nave of the church leading to the main altar

↑ The striking exterior of the Dominican Church

The Renaissance Chapel of St Jacek was rebuilt around 1700 by Italian artist Baldassare Fontana; it is decorated with beautiful paintings by Tommaso Dolabella, an Italian painter.

This memorial plaque dedicated to Callimachus, a great humanist at the Polish royal court, was designed by Veit Stoss.

The Neo-Gothic choir stalls, pulpit and confessionals date from the second half of the 19th century.

Within the Chapel of the Virgin Mary of the Rosary is the Virgin of the Rosary icon, once carried in a procession to secure victory over the Turks at Chocim.

The Myszkowski Chapel was built between 1603 and 1614 by masters from Santi Gucci's circle, using marble from the Świętokrzyskie (Holy Cross) Mountains.

The tomb of Prospero Provano, a salt magnate, is one of the finest Polish sculptural works of the early 17th century. It is located by the Myszkowski Chapel.

↑ The Dominican Church, rebuilt in the 19th century

The imposing façade ↑
of the Neo-Gothic
Collegium Novum

EXPERIENCE MORE

6

Episcopal Palace

Pałac Biskupi

Q M3 **Q** Ulica
Franciszkańska 3
🚌 1, 6, 8, 13, 18, 20
🔒 To the public

The first record of this palace dates from the 13th century, making it one of Kraków's oldest buildings. Damaged by fire in the 15th century, the palace gained its current appearance in the 17th century when it was reconstructed by Bishop Piotr Gembicki. In 1850, a second fire caused extensive damage, but the splendid furnishings have partly survived.

Pope John Paul II lived here between 1964 and 1978, when he was Archbishop of Kraków. A striking mosaic of this beloved pope adorns the building's exterior and there's also a statue of him in the courtyard. Note that while the interior of the palace is not open to the public, the courtyard is.

7

Collegium Novum

Q M3 **Q** Ulica Gołębia 24
📞 12 422 10 33 🚌 2, 8, 13, 18 🔒 To the public

Today the Collegium Novum (Latin for "New College") is the main building of Kraków's Jagiellonian University. It was built to replace the Jerusalem College after it was destroyed by fire in the 19th century. It was constructed with funds from the city's then Austrian rulers, something which meant its official opening turned into a patriotic demonstration. The architect of the new building, Feliks Księłarski, intended to emulate the vernacular architecture of the Collegium Maius (p74), especially the crystal vaults and decoration, but in fact he imitated German and Austrian models.

Close by is a statue of the famous astronomer Nicolaus Copernicus, an alumnus of the university. He is depicted as a scholar holding an astrolabe.

POPE JOHN PAUL II

Karol Wojtyła was born in 1920 in Wadowice, but lived in Kraków for years. He arrived here in 1938 to read Polish philology at the Jagiellonian University, but the outbreak of World War II put a stop to his studies. He entered the underground theological Seminary in 1942. Despite his election to the Apostolic See in 1978 his links with Kraków remained as close as ever.

INSIDER TIP
Away in a Manger

During Advent, head to Krzysztofory Palace to see its annual *szopki* (nativity crib) competition take place. Here, locals compete to create the most ornate and festive nativity scene.

8

Krzysztofory Palace
Pałac Krzysztofory

📍 N2 🏛 Rynek Główny 35
🕙 10am-5:30pm Tue-Sun
🌐 muzeumkrakowa.pl

This, the main branch of the Kraków Museum (*Muzeum Krakowa*), is located in the Krzysztofory Palace, one of the oldest and most beautiful palaces in the whole city. It was remodelled between 1682 and 1685 by Jacopo Solari for Kazimierz Wodzicki, a rich nobleman.

The palace is named after St Christopher, whose 14th-century statue decorates the building. The top floor holds the fascinating exhibition Cyberteka, which tells the history of the city through a combination of models and interactive touch-screens. In the basement is a spectacular display devoted to the art of the *szopka* or nativity crib, something which is an important expression of Kraków's folk art.

9

The Hipolit House
Kamienica Hipolitów

📍 N2 🏛 Plac Mariacki 3
🚊 3, 10, 24, 52 🕙 10am-5.30pm Wed-Sun
🌐 muzeumkrakowa.pl

A handsome 14th-century mansion, the Hipolit House holds a fascinating display of period interiors. The house gets its name from the Hipoliti, an Italian merchant family who lived here in the 17th century. Rococo stuccowork survives in some of the rooms, with furniture, paintings and clocks reflecting the domestic tastes of Kraków's wealthier families. There is a sequence of 19th-century interiors on the top floor, which features an elegant sitting room with piano and chaise-longue, as well as a fascinating "collector's room" packed with objets d'art.

10

St Barbara's Church
Kościół św. Barbary

📍 N3 🏛 Mały Rynek 8
📞 12 428 15 00 🕙 9am-6pm Mon-Sat, 2-3:30pm Sun

According to a local legend this church was built using the bricks that were left over from the construction of the city's famed St Mary's Basilica (*p68*). St Barbara's actually dates from 1394 to 1399, which coincides with one of the stages in the construction of St Mary's. Between 1415 and 1536 sermons in this church were delivered in Polish, while those at St Mary's Basilica were done in German; the noblemen of Kraków were mostly German at this time and it was only much later that they became a minority among the Polish population. In 1586 the church was taken over by the Jesuits. The militant Jesuit Piotr Skarga preached at St Barbara's Church and Jakub Wujek, the translator of the Bible, is buried here. Added from 1488 to 1518 is a late Gothic chapel with a porch decorated with sculptures made by Veit Stoss's workshop. Furnishings date mostly from the 18th century but there is also a 15th-century crucifix on the high altar.

↑ The striking Baroque interior of the 14th-century St Barbara's Church

↑ Interior of the Church of the Reformed Franciscans and *(inset)* mummified bodies in the crypt of the church

Church of the Reformed Franciscans

Kościół Reformatów

📍M1 🏛Ulica Reformacka 4
📞 12 422 29 66 🚌124, 152, 502 🚊2, 4, 14, 18, 24
🕐During services only

The Church of the Reformed Franciscans was built between 1666 and 1672. The architecture and modest furnishings conform to the strict rule of the order. The altarpiece on the left that depicts St Kazimierz is an outstanding example of 17th-century work.

The specific microclimate within the crypt beneath the church causes the reposing corpses to undergo mummification. Those visitors seeking a macabre experience may request access to the crypt, which is open on 2 and 3 November every year.

12

Palace of Art

Pałac Sztuki

📍M2 🏛Plac Szczepański 4
🚊2, 4, 14, 18, 24 🚌124, 152, 352, 424, 502 🕐8:15am-6pm Mon-Fri, 10am-6pm Sat & Sun 🌐palac-sztuki.krakow.pl

In 1854 the Friends of the Fine Arts Society was established in Kraków to encourage the development of Polish art. The society embarked upon the organization of exhibitions by living artists, the acquisition of paintings and sculptures, and the setting up of a records office that would contain documents relating to the history of Polish art in the 19th and early 20th centuries.

In 1901, the Palace of Art was built to be the society's headquarters. Modelled on the famous Secession Pavilion in Vienna, it was Kraków's first Art Nouveau building. The finest local artists worked on the decoration, including

Jacek Malczewski who designed the frieze depicting the vicissitudes of fortune and the struggle of artistic genius. Sculptors, including Antoni Madeyski, contributed busts of great Polish artists. A portico on the façade is topped with a statue of Apollo. Today the palace hosts temporary exhibitions of 19th-century and contemporary art.

13

Bunker of Art

Bunkier Sztuki

📍M2 🏛Plac Szczepański 3a
🚊2, 4, 14, 18, 24 🚌124, 152, 352, 424, 502 🕐11am-7pm Tue-Sun 🌐bunkier.art.pl

This modern grey concrete building, facing the Planty, is one of the few examples of mid-1960s Brutalist architecture in Poland. It is the venue for interesting exhibitions of contemporary art, by both Polish and foreign artists. The Bunker of Art is also home to a popular café with floor-to-ceiling windows.

→

The brightly coloured façade of Kraków's legendary Old Theatre

Old Theatre
Teatr Stary

📍M2 🏛Ulica Jagiellońska 5 🚊2, 4, 14, 18, 24 🚌124, 152, 352, 424, 502 🕐For performances 🌐stary.pl

This theatre is also known as the Modrzejewska theatre after the renowned Polish actress Helena Modrzejewska. The oldest theatre building in Poland, it has been in use continuously since 1798. It was remodelled in the Neo-Renaissance style between 1830 and 1843. The next major rebuilding was undertaken from 1903 to 1905; the reinforced concrete construction applied to the interior, and the exterior Art Nouveau decoration, both date from this time. The spectacular stucco frieze which adorns the outside of the building was made in 1906 by the famous Art Nouveau sculptor Józef Gardecki. The plaques on the Jagiellońska Street side commemorate the composer Władysław Żeleński, the director Konrad Swinarski and the actor Wiktor Sadecki.

Did You Know?

Oscar-winner Andrzej Wajda directed plays at the Old Theatre throughout the 1970s.

The Old Theatre is regarded as one of the best in Poland. Many outstanding directors have worked here, including the famous Polish director Zygmunt Hübner.

Feliks Jasieński Szołayski House
Kamienica Szołayskich

📍M2 🏛Plac Szczepański 9 🚌124, 152, 304, 424, 502 🚊2, 4, 8, 13, 14, 18, 24 🕐10am–4pm Tue–Fri & Sun; 10am–6pm Sat 🌐mnk.pl

The oldest parts of the Feliks Jasieński Szołayski House date from the 15th century. Since then this building has served as a private residence, part of a monastery and a newspaper office. Since 1934, it has been an exhibition space, except for a period during World War II when it was occupied by the Nazis. The house is now home to a branch of the National Museum in Kraków (*Muzeum Narodowe w Krakowie*) and showcases visiting art exhibitions from abroad, as well as themed exhibitions celebrating prominent cultural figures from Poland. There is also a permanent display of memorabilia relating to the museum's namesake, Felix Jasieński (1861–1929), an art collector who popularized Japanese art in Poland. The house also offers lectures, plays and art classes for children. Entrance is free on Sundays.

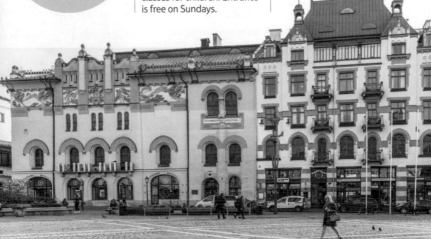

DRINK

House of Beer

A welcoming pub with a dizzying array of bottled beers from around the world, plus a changing selection of Polish brews on tap.

📍P2 📍Ulica Świętego Tomasza 35 🌐houseofbeer krakow.com

Viva la Pinta

Nestled in the Old Town, this friendly bar has a fabulous range of local craft beers and an inviting beer garden.

📍N2 📍Ulica Floriańska 13 📞12 421 0590

Multi Qlti Tap Bar

A huge choice of beers on tap and by the bottle are backed up by a mouthwatering menu of pizzas and burgers.

📍M2 📍Ulica Szewska 21 📞12 341 5847

Jazz Club U Muniaka

Housed in an historic cellar just steps away from St Mary's Basilica, this legendary jazz bar offers great cocktails and regular concerts.

📍N2 📍Ulica Floriańska 3 🌐jazzumuniaka.club

SHOP

Calik Christmas Baubles

An array of colourful festive baubles, including some painted with Kraków scenes.

📍N3 📍Rynek Główny 7/3 🌐calik.pl

16

Jama Michalika Café
Jama Michalika

📍P2 📍Ulica Floriańska 45 🚊2, 4, 7, 14, 24 🚌124, 152, 304, 502 🕐9am–10pm Mon–Thu & Sun, 9am–11pm Fri & Sat 🌐jamamichalika.pl

Found close to the Main Market Square (p64), this now-famous café was established in 1895. It was popular with both students of the Fine Arts School, and with poets, writers and artists. The café quickly became a hotbed of artistic creativity. Poland's Art Nouveau movement, Młoda Polska (p49), was born here; the renowned cabaret Zielony Balonik (The Green Balloon) was also established in the café in 1905.

The café's interior was given an Art Nouveau makeover in 1910, including the addition of colourful stained-glass windows. The decoration has hardly changed since then, so visiting this fin-de-siècle café feels like stepping back in time. As well as offering mouthwatering Polish food, the café also hosts folk shows where dancers and musicians in colourful costumes perform traditional dances and songs.

17

Floriańska Street
Ulica Floriańska

📍P2 🚊2, 3, 4, 8, 10, 14, 19, 20, 24, 52 🚌124, 152, 304, 424, 502

This street, leading from St Florian's Gate to the Main Market Square, formed part of the Royal Route. This route was often used by a sovereign arriving for a coronation, and again when their body was taken in procession for the funeral at Wawel. In the 19th century Floriańska was the busiest street in Kraków, with trams introduced in 1881. Medieval walls have survived in most houses, but much of the original architecture has been lost

through later remodelling. More storeys and new eclectic façades were added to most buildings early in the 20th century, when the street gained its present appearance.

18

St Florian's Gate and the Defensive Wall
Brama Floriańska i Mury Obronny

📍P1 📍Ulica Pijarska 30 🚌124, 152, 502 🚊2, 4, 7, 14, 24 🕐Apr–Oct: 10:30am–6pm daily 🌐muzeum krakowa.pl

In 1285 Duke Leszek the Black gave Kraków the right to have the city surrounded by walls. These fortifications developed during the following centuries, finally consisting of a series of inner and outer moated walls and 47 towers. Eight fortified gates lead into the city. With the introduction of artillery, the defence system became redundant; it fell into disrepair by the end of the 18th century. The walls were dismantled in the 19th century and later replaced by the Planty gardens.

↑ St Florian's Gate, a remnant of Kraków's military fortifications

Looking towards the imposing Barbican through St Florian's Gate ↑

St Florian's Gate, dating from the end of the 13th century, and a small stretch of the adjoining walls have been saved. East of this gate is the Haberdashers' Tower, while the towers of the Joiners and Carpenters are to the west.

You can purchase tickets to explore the tower online via the Museum of Kraków's website or at its Visitors' Office (*Rynek Główny 1*).

 19

Barbican
Barbakan

⦿ P1 **⌂ Ulica Basztowa** **🚋 2, 4, 7, 14, 24** **🚌 124, 152, 304, 502** **⏰ Apr–Oct: 10:30am– 6pm daily** **🌐 muzeumkrakowa.pl**

This round bastion was built in 1498–99 after King Jan Olbracht was defeated by the Turks in Bukowina, and further Turkish incursions were feared. It shows the changes to military architecture as a result of the rapid development of artillery. The bastion was originally surrounded by a moat and linked

Did You Know?

Originally surrounded by a moat, the Barbican was only accessible by a bridge from St Florian's Gate.

to St Florian's Gate by a corridor over the water. Over 100 arrow-slits enabled the defenders to fire at the enemy while being protected. It is the best preserved barbican in Europe.

Tickets for the Barbican are available via the Museum of Kraków's website or at the Visitors' Office (*Rynek Główny 1*).

 20

Piarist Church
Kościół Pijarów

⦿ N1 **⌂ Ulica Pijarska 2** **🚌 124, 152, 502** **🚋 2, 4, 14, 18, 24** **⏰ During services only** **🌐 pijarzy.pl**

This Baroque church was built between 1718 and 1728.

The Rococo façade was added later between 1759 and 1761. Inside, the church is decorated with frescoes by a master of illusion, Franz Eckstein. The high altar painted on the wall is by the same artist, as is the fresco in the nave vault that glorifies the name of the Virgin Mary. The altars in the aisles feature 18th-century paintings by the well-known Polish Baroque painter Szymon Czechowicz.

The crypt located under the church is known for the decoration of Christ's Tomb, which usually alludes symbolically to patriotic themes, and is set up every year during Holy Week.

 INSIDER TIP
Keeping it Classical

One of the most atmospheric places to catch classical concerts in the Old Town is the Piarist Church. Choral and chamber music events take place here throughout the year.

㉑ Słowacki Theatre
Teatr im. Juliusza Słowackiego

♥P2 ♨Plac Świętego Ducha 1 🚋2, 4, 7, 14, 24 🚌124, 152, 424, 502 ⊘For performances only ⊕teatrwkrakowie.pl

The proposal for a new theatre in Kraków, one which would replace the small Old Theatre *(p85)*, was put forward in 1872. Polish architect Jan Zawiejski designed the building, which was based on the Paris Opera House, and the theatre opened in 1893. Zawiejski designed an opulent building in which vernacular elements, such as the parapet inspired by the Cloth Hall, and foreign influences were blended into an eclectic whole.

The sumptuous interior features a grand staircase decorated with stuccowork. The four-tiered auditorium can seat up to 900 people. Its stage curtain is one of the theatre's major attractions: it depicts Apollo striking an accord between Beauty and Love, surrounded by muses and other allegorical figures.

The theatre puts on a range of performances, all with English subtitles; past plays have included *Hamlet* and *The Name of the Rose*.

JAN MATEJKO (1838-1893)
Few Polish artists are as widely celebrated as Kraków's Jan Matejko, whose vast canvases hang in galleries across the country. Matejko specialized in huge narrative paintings that illustrate key events in Polish history. They served as a rich source of popular inspiration at a time when Poland was under the rule of foreign powers. His vivid crowd scenes are filled with drama.

㉒
Matejko House
Dom Matejki

♥P2 ♨Ulica Floriańska 41 🚋2, 4, 8, 10, 14, 19, 20, 24, 52 🚌124, 152, 304, 424, 502 ⏰10am–4pm Tue–Fri & Sun, 10am–6pm Sat ⊕mnk.pl

The artist Jan Matejko was born here in 1838, and in 1873 returned to live with his family. He rebuilt the house adding a new façade designed in the Neo-Baroque style. After he died in 1893, the house was turned into a museum. The private rooms on the first floor remain unchanged, while the second floor displays the artist's works, including sketches for the murals that are in St Mary's Basilica *(p68)*. His studio on the third floor is full of props and curiosities he collected: look out for pieces of old armour and instruments of torture. Audiotours of the house are available.

㉓
Old Pharmacy Museum
Muzeum Farmacji

♥P2 ♨Ulica Floriańska 25 🚋2, 4, 7, 14, 24 🚌64, 69 ⏰12-6.30pm Tue, 9.30am-3pm Wed-Sat ⊕museum. farmacja.uj.edu.pl

Set up by the Jagiellonian University's medical faculty, the Pharmacy Museum

The Słowacki Theatre and, right, the Church of the Holy Cross ↑

(*Muzeum Farmacji*) takes a fascinating look at the history of drugs and pharmacies. It also offers a visually compelling display of flasks, bottles and apothecary equipment throughout the ages.

Exhibits cover five floors of a 14th-century town house, beginning with a display of bulbous glass flasks in the Gothic cellars. Fascinating recreations of pharmacy interiors over the centuries reveal changing fashions in furnishing styles from Baroque through to Biedermeier. On the top floor, rafters are hung with dried herbs which still play a significant role in traditional medicine.

 🥽

Lost Souls Alley

📍N2 🏠 Ulica Floriańska 6 🚊 2, 4, 7, 14, 24 🚌 64, 69 🌐 lostsoulsalley.com

Lost Souls Alley is an interactive experience that allows small groups of visitors to enter a haunted-house environment where they might be startled, chased or challenged to find their way out of a dark room. With actors playing the parts of villains and victims, it's a bit like being in a movie.

There is a choice of tours offering different levels of theatrical shock. Participants must be at least 14 years old to enter and there are higher age limits on some of the scarier tours.

Church of the Holy Cross
Kościół św. Krzyża

📍P2 🏠 Ulica Świętego Krzyża 23 🚊 2, 4, 7, 14, 24 🚌 124, 152, 424, 502 🕐 During services only 🌐 krzyzkrakow.pl

The Gothic church of the Order of the Holy Cross was erected in two stages. The construction of the choir began immediately after 1300. The main nave and tower date from the first half of the 14th century. The interior is extremely well preserved and the nave impresses with its intricate pattern of vaulting ribs, supported on a single, round pillar. Among its ornate furnishings, the Gothic font made in 1423 and the Late-Renaissance triptych in the Węgrzyn Chapel (next to the porch) are of particular interest. There are also various Baroque altars and stalls, as well as a number of memorial plaques of famous sculptors, active at the end of the 19th century, which are worth seeing.

EAT

Wentzl
This atmospheric restaurant serves traditional Polish fare with a French twist in an elegant 19th-century setting.

📍N3 🏠 Rynek Główny 19 🌐 restauracja wentzl.pl

ⓩ ⓩ ⓩ

Wierzynek
Dating from the 14th century, this restaurant is said to be the oldest in Kraków. Expect delicious Polish cuisine and walls adorned in opulent oil paintings and tapestries.

📍N3 🏠 Rynek Główny 16 🌐 wierzynek.pl

ⓩ ⓩ ⓩ

Szara Gęś
In the heart of the Old Town, this exclusive restaurant offers eye-catching interiors and a mouthwatering menu, including delicious roast goose and venison.

📍N3 🏠 Rynek Główny 17 🌐 szarages.com

ⓩ ⓩ ⓩ

Café Camelot
This cosy café, filled with old furniture and statues of angels, dishes up a great choice of main meals and salads. It also has some of the best *szarlotka* (apple pie) in the city.

📍N2 🏠 Ulica Świętego Tomasza 15 📞 12 421 0123

ⓩ ⓩ ⓩ

A SHORT WALK
MAIN MARKET SQUARE

Distance 600 m (655 yd) **Nearest bus stop** Kraków
Główny **Time** 10 minutes

The expansive Main Market Square (Rynek Główny) is the
heart of Kraków's historic Old Town. A stroll around it will
allow you to take in some of the city's most iconic sights,
including the magnificent Renaissance Cloth Hall and striking St Mary's Basilica. The buildings surrounding the square
are a wonderful mix of architectural styles *(p66)* and house
charming cafés, restaurants and bars. Lively throughout
the year, the square is home to flower stalls and street musicians in summer, and to a festive Christmas market in winter.

The **Rynek Underground**
*museum (p72) offers
tours of the maze of
medieval tunnels and
chambers beneath
the square.*

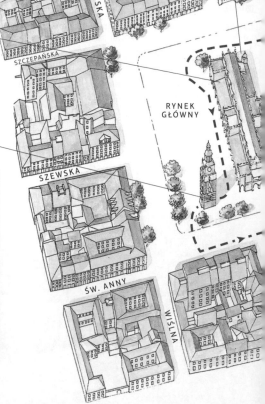

The Renaissance **Cloth
Hall** (p70) *replaced an
earlier Gothic market hall;
today its upper floor houses
the renowned Gallery of
19th-Century Polish Art.*

The Gothic **Town Hall Tower**
(p65) *is the only remaining
part of the former Town Hall,
which was pulled down in the
first half of the 19th century.*

↑ Kraków's striking Town
   Hall Tower in the Main
   Market Square

↑ The awe-inspiring interior
of St Mary's Basilica

Locator Map
For more detail see p62

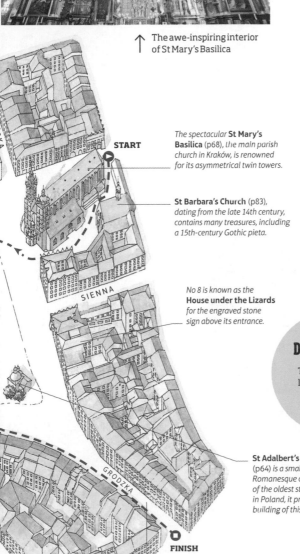

START

The spectacular **St Mary's
Basilica** (p68), *the main parish
church in Kraków, is renowned
for its asymmetrical twin towers.*

St Barbara's Church (p83),
*dating from the late 14th century,
contains many treasures, including
a 15th-century Gothic pieta.*

No 8 is known as the
House under the Lizards
*for the engraved stone
sign above its entrance.*

Did You Know?

The square is the
largest medieval
market square
in Europe.

St Adalbert's Church
(p64) *is a small yet splendid
Romanesque church. One
of the oldest stone churches
in Poland, it predates the
building of this vast square.*

FINISH

*Cafés and shops line the
length of pretty Grodzka
Street, which leads to*
Wawel Hill (p98).

| 0 metres | 80 |
| 0 yards | 80 |

N

A LONG WALK
PLANTY

Distance 3.5 km (2.2 miles) **Walking time** 50 minutes
Terrain Largely easy strolling along well-maintained
paths **Nearest tram stop** Jubilat

The Planty, a leafy belt encircling Kraków's Old Town, is
wonderfully lush. This tranquil green oasis replaced the
city's medieval fortifications, which had been built between
the late 13th and 15th centuries. The fortifications were demolished early in the 19th century; the only fragment to have
survived is the small stretch of wall by Floriańska Street *(p86)*.
The gardens of Planty were landscaped to include a network
of radiating lanes and beautiful vistas. In the second half
of the 19th century the well-kept Planty became a popular
venue for socializing. After a period of regeneration the
Planty now features period fencing, benches and street
lamps. A relaxing stroll along the park's tree-lined paths
will take you past pretty ponds and beautiful statues.

*Sitting to the left of the Collegium
Novum, the statue of the astronomer
Nicolaus Copernicus (p75) is
surrounded by trees.*

↑ The statue of Lilla Veneda found
within the lush green of the Planty

*Carry on until you reach a tiny
square where there is a 19th-century
statue of Grażyna and Litawor,
two characters from a poem
by Adam Mickiewicz.*

*Enter the
Planty and stroll
north along its
tree-lined paths.*

*Start your walk at the
impressive Coat of Arms
gate at **Wawel Hill** (p98).*

*Stroll towards the **statue
of Lilla Veneda**, the leading character in a play by
the renowned Polish poet
Juliusz Słowacki.*

Statue of
Lilla Veneda

REFORMA

Statue of Artur
Grottger

PLAC
SZCZEPAŃSKA

KRUPNICZA

J. DUNAJEWSKIEGO

SZEWSKA

JAGIELLOŃSKA

SZCZE

PODWALE

ŚW. ANNY

Church of
St Anne

N

Collegium
Maius

C
H

Statue of
Nicolaus Copernicus

Collegium
Novum

WIŚLNA

BRACKA

F. STRASZEWSKIEGO

Planty

Episcopal
Palace

FRANCISZKA

SMOLEŃSK

Philharmonic
Hall

Statue of Grażyna
and Litawora

Francisc
Church

FELICIANEK

ZWIERZYNIECKA

POSELS

Archaeol
Muse

Planty

POWIŚLE

START
Coat of
Arms Gate

Wawel
Hill

V i s t u l a

BERNARD

The next monument you will notice is that of Poland's beloved **Queen Jadwiga** and her husband, King Władysław II Jagiełło (p53).

After crossing Sławkowska Street, you'll spy a **large pond** where in summer swans can be seen. Cross the bridge over the pond and head towards the **statue of the Harpist**.

Locator Map
For more detail see p62

Planty
THE OLD TOWN

Queen Jadwiga and King Władysław Jagiełło Monument

● Statue of the Harpist

● Barbican

PLAC KOLEJOWY

St Florian's Gate

ℹ Straszewski Obelisk

Słowacki Theatre

SW. JANA
SW. MARKA
FLORIAŃSKA
SW. TOMASZA

Statue of Michał Bałucki

WESTERPLATTE

RADZIWIŁŁOWSKA

Pass by **St Florian's Gate** (p86) and the remains of the city's defensive wall to reach the imposing **Barbican** (p87).

Continue through the park until you reach the **Straszewski Obelisk**. This monument is dedicated to Florian Straszewski, the man who laid out the Planty.

STARE MIASTO

SZPITALNA
SW. KRZYŻA

St Mary's Basilica

Church of the Dominican Nuns

M. KOPERNIKA

STOLARSKA
SIENNA

Planty

Dominican Church

M. ŻYBLIKIEWICZA

MINIKAŃSKA

Statue of Colonol Narcyz Wiatr-Zawojny

STAROWIŚLNA

Before you cross Sienna Street, take a moment to admire the **Church of the Dominican Nuns** on your right.

Keep strolling and you'll soon spy the spectacular **Dominican Church** (p80) on your right. Further on you'll pass an unusual **statue of Colonel Narcyz Wiatr-Zawojny**, *who was shot dead in 1946 by the secret police.*

FINISH 🅾
Stradom Gardens

OKÓŁ

JÓZEFA SAREGO

Church of St Andrew

Royal Arsenal

...SKA

Wander another 500 m (0.3 mile) downhill to enter what are known as the **Stradom Gardens**, *where you'll end your walk.*

0 metres   300   N
0 yards   300   ↑

↑ One of the pretty tree-lined paths that wind through the Planty

WAWEL HILL AND AROUND

One of Kraków's – and Poland's – most important sites, Wawel Hill has a chequered history that dates back to ancient times. Once inhabited by a Slavic group, the Vistulanians, it was first designated the seat of political power by Kazimierz the Restorer. A cathedral was built here in the 12th century and, after the hill became the official residence for Polish royalty in the 14th century, a castle was also erected. In the late 16th century, the capital was moved from Kraków to Warsaw and the site entered a period of decline. From 1795, it was home to the military: the Austrian army were garrisoned here until the early 20th century and during World War II it became the headquarters of the Nazi Governor General. In the 20th century, substantial restoration saw Wawel regain its former magnificence.

Just north, the area known as Okół was probably the earliest settlement to develop at the foot of the hill. Timber houses and a palisade enclosure were already here in the 10th century. The settlement expanded along the "Salt Route" which led from Hungary to Greater Poland. It became an elite quarter because of its proximity to the Royal Castle and the cathedral. In the 19th century, Ulica Grodzka, the main street linking Wawel Hill with the Main Market Square, became a popular shopping street, a role it retains to this day. Meanwhile, the development of Stradom, an area to the east of the hill, was hindered by its location on peat marshes. However, the 19th century saw it become a residential area characterized by handsome apartment blocks. Nowadays Okół and Stradom are two of Kraków's busiest areas, with a constant stream of visitors strolling between the Old Town and Wawel Hill.

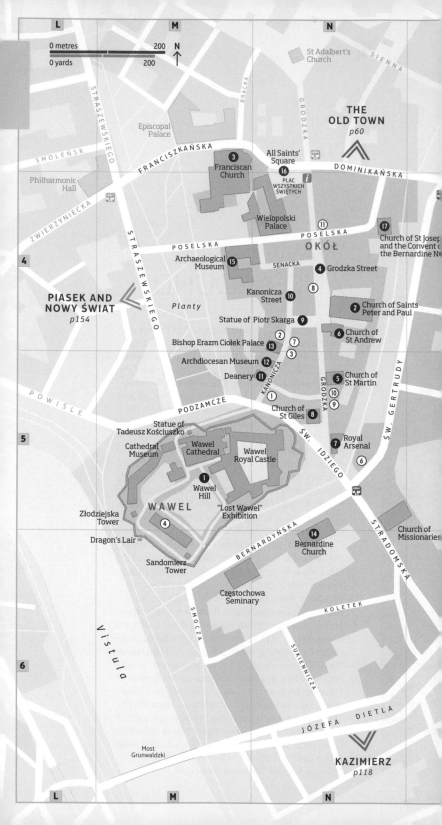

WAWEL

0 metres 200
0 yards 200

N

St Adalbert's Church

SIENNA

THE OLD TOWN
p60

Episcopal Palace

FRANCISZKAŃSKA

BRACKA

GRODZKA

DOMINIKAŃSKA

SMOLEŃSK

Philharmonic Hall

③ Franciscan Church

All Saints' Square

⑯

PLAC WSZYSTKICH ŚWIĘTYCH

i

ZWIERZYNIECKA

STRASZEWSKIEGO

Wielopolski Palace

POSELSKA

⑪

OKÓŁ

⑰

Church of St Joseph and the Convent of the Bernardine Nu

4

POSELSKA

Archaeological Museum ⑮

SENACKA

❹ Grodzka Street

PIASEK AND NOWY ŚWIAT
p154

Planty

Kanonicza Street ⑩

⑧

Statue of Piotr Skarga ⑨

❷ Church of Saints Peter and Paul

POWIŚLE

Bishop Erazm Ciołek Palace ⑬

② ⑦
③

❻ Church of St Andrew

Archdiocesan Museum ⑫

GRODZKA

❺ Church of St Martin

Deanery ⑪

KANONICZA

① ⑩
⑨

ŚW. GERTRUDY

PODZAMCZE

Church of St Giles ⑧

Statue of Tadeusz Kościuszko

Cathedral Museum

Wawel Cathedral

Wawel Royal Castle

❼ Royal Arsenal

ŚW. IDZIEGO

❶

5

Wawel Hill

⑥

Złodziejska Tower

WAWEL

"Lost Wawel" Exhibition

STRADOMSKA

Church of Missionaries

Dragon's Lair

❹

BERNARDYŃSKA

❶⑭ Bernardine Church

Sandomierz Tower

Częstochowa Seminary

KOLETEK

SMOCZA

SUKIENNICA

Vistula

6

JÓZEFA DIETLA

Most Grunwaldzki

KAZIMIERZ
p118

L   M   N

WAWEL HILL AND AROUND

WAWEL HILL AND AROUND

Must Sees
1 Wawel Hill
2 Church of Saints Peter and Paul
3 Franciscan Church

Experience More
4 Grodzka Street
5 Church of St Martin
6 Church of St Andrew
7 Royal Arsenal
8 Church of St Giles
9 Statue of Piotr Skarga
10 Kanonicza Street
11 Deanery
12 Archdiocesan Museum
13 Bishop Erazm Ciołek Palace
14 Bernardine Church
15 Archaeological Museum
16 All Saints' Square
17 Church of St Joseph and the Convent of the Bernardine Nuns

Eat
1 Pod Nosem
2 Art Restauracja
3 Copernicus

Drink
4 Słódki Wawel

Stay
5 Mundo Hostel
6 Hotel Royal
7 Hotel Copernicus
8 Hotel Senacki

Shop
9 Kobalt Pottery
10 Bajo Wooden Toys
11 Ciuciu Cukier Artist

The expansive royal complex perched atop Wawel Hill ↑

WAWEL HILL
WZGÓRZE WAWELSKIE

📍 M5 🏛 Wawel Hill 🚌 114, 124, 169, 173, 504 🚊 1, 2, 6, 8, 10, 13, 18 🕐 Hours vary, check website 🌐 wawel.krakow.pl

Once the seat of Polish royalty, Wawel Hill is today a symbol of the country's national, cultural and spiritual identity. Sitting atop the hill is an impressive fortified complex, which includes the Wawel Royal Castle and the Wawel Cathedral, alongside many other sights.

Fortifications and Towers
Mury Obronne

The Vistulanians (p52) were the first to build a citadel on this limestone outcrop, with successive dynasties developing and extending the site. As a result, the fortifications surrounding Wawel Hill date from many different periods.

Three massive towers – Złodziejska (the Thief's Tower), Sandomierska and Lubranka (Senator's Tower) are some of the most dominant features of the architectural silhouette of the Wawel. They date from the second half of the 15th and early 16th centuries, when the royal residence was rebuilt by the Jagiellonians (p53).

New fortifications designed by Jan Pleitner and mainly constructed from earth, were erected under Władysław IV between 1644 and 1646 on the castle's northern terrace. The southeast bastion and redan (fortification of two parapets) were constructed in the early 18th century for King August II. Later in the century, star-shaped fortifications were built on the side of the Vistula River. The Austrians expanded the system between 1849 and 1852. Two round towers, forming part of the Austrian additions, have survived. As a result of this ongoing development, Wawel Hill was transformed into an imposing fortified citadel surrounded by a complex defence system.

Located on the eastern edge of Wawel Hill's fortifications are a series of pretty gardens, including a fruit orchard and a Renaissance-style garden. You can explore both the gardens, the ramparts and more on the "Wawel Architecture and Gardens" tour (book at the visitor centre).

② Archaeological Site

Archeologiczny teren

The archaeological site located on Wawel Hill is an open area where the foundations of medieval buildings can be seen. The buildings here were numerous and once formed a small town. A vicarage in the Renaissance style was among them. All of the buildings were demolished by the Austrians in 1803–04 and replaced by a drill ground. The lower parts of the walls of St Nicholas, a small Romanesque church which was rebuilt in the Gothic style during the reign of Kazimierz the Great *(p53)*, are of particular note. This church was an interesting example of a single nave church, supported on one central column. The plan of the small church of St George is also easy to discern.

③ Statue of Tadeusz Kościuszko

Pomnik Tadeusza Kościuszki

The statue of Tadeusz Kościuszko *(p55)*, a general and the main leader of the 1794 Uprising in Poland, as well as a participant in the American Revolution, was erected in 1921. Kościuszko is buried in the national pantheon which is found within the royal crypt of Wawel Cathedral *(p102)*.

The bronze statue, which depicts Kościuszko on horseback, was designed by the Polish architect Leonard Marconi. It was destroyed by the Nazis in 1940, while they were occupying Wawel Hill. The present reconstruction was given to the city of Kraków by the citizens of Dresden in Germany in 1960.

When approaching the Władysław bastion, where the statue stands, you can see a number of plaques mounted in the brick wall. These plaques commemorate the donors who contributed to the restoration works carried out within the castle during the interwar years. Found nearby and also of interest is the Coat of Arms Gate by Polish architect Adolf Szyszko-Bohusz.

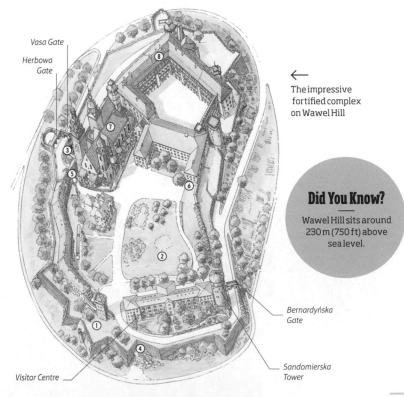

← The impressive fortified complex on Wawel Hill

Vasa Gate
Herbowa Gate
Bernardyńska Gate
Sandomierska Tower
Visitor Centre

Did You Know?

Wawel Hill sits around 230 m (750 ft) above sea level.

99

④
Dragon's Lair
Smocza Jama

🕐 Sep & Oct: 10am-5pm; May & Jun: 10am-6pm; Jul & Aug: 10am-7pm

Within Wawel Hill there are a number of rock caves. According to legend, one of the caves was home to a ferocious cattle-eating dragon who terrorized the inhabitants of ancient Kraków. It is said that the beast was eventually slain by King Krakus (or in some accounts a humble yet brave shoemaker, named Skuba) who tricked the monster into eating a sheep stuffed with sulphur. The dragon swallowed the bait. When the sulphur heated its gut, the dragon drank so much water from the Vistula that its body burst. In the second version of the story, King Krakus rewards the shoemaker by giving him the hand of his daughter in marriage.

Today it's possibly to visit the "lair" of the dragon, found at the foot of the Thieves' Tower on the western slope

↑ The metal dragon statue found in front of the Dragon's Lair

of the hill. Some 135 spiral steps lead down into these atmospheric caves, which in the 17th and 18th centuries housed a subterranean pub. There are 200 m (660 ft) of tunnels in total, of which 80 m (265 ft) can be explored by visitors. The lair is open only during the summer months. A bronze statue of the dragon, designed by the renowned Polish sculptor Bronisław Chromy, stands at the exit.

Made in 1972, this metal monster belches fire and is seen as a major attraction by younger visitors.

---

⑤
Cathedral Museum
Muzeum Katedralne

🕐 9am-5pm Mon-Sat (Nov-Mar: to 4pm) 🌐 katedra-wawelska.pl

The Cathedral Museum was established in September 1978 by the then Archbishop of Kraków Karol Wojtyła, who was later to become Pope John Paul II. The display inside the museum consists of objects from the cathedral's Crown Treasury. Among the exhibits are a sword, which was purposely broken in two places at the funeral of the last Jagiellonian king, Zygmunt August; the coronation robe of Stanisław August Poniatowski; the replica of the royal insignia found inside the royal coffins buried beneath the cathedral; and the stirrup of the Grand Vizier Kara Mustafa which was presented to the cathedral by

→ The imposing fortified complex sitting atop Wawel Hill

King Jan III Sobieski following his victory at the Battle of Vienna (1683). The outstanding collection of reliquaries, church vessels and vestments includes objects found in the tomb of Bishop Maur, as well as memorabilia of John Paul II.

---

 ⑥ ⊘

"Lost Wawel" Exhibition
Wawel Zaginiony

🕐 Apr-Oct: 9:30am-1pm Mon, 9:30am-5pm Tue-Fri, 10am-5pm Sat & Sun; Nov-Mar: 9:30am-4pm Tue-Fri, 10am-4pm Sat & Sun (last adm 1 hour before closing) 🚫 Public hols 🌐 wawel. krakow.pl

Arranged in the basement of the former royal kitchen (now occupied by the administration office), this special exhibition will appeal to those interested in the medieval history of Wawel Hill. The exhibition is centred on the remains of the Rotunda of the Virgin Mary (Sts Felix and Adauctus), just one of possibly ten churches that previously existed on Wawel Hill. The church, which was unearthed in 1917, is thought to be the oldest in Kraków, as well as one of Poland's most well-preserved Romanesque churches. It is believed that the circular rotunda formed part of the first palatium (the seat of the first ruler of Wawel), and was built sometime in the late 10th or early 11th century. Its plan resembles a quatrefoil, with strong evidence of Czech influences in the design of the structure. The rotunda was almost completely destroyed in the 19th century.

The exhibition also includes a virtual computer model of the architecture of the Wawel Hill complex, which enables visitors to explore the history of the hill in the middle ages. The computer reconstruction of selected medieval buildings, based on archaeological, architectural, photographic and conservational evidence, shows the state of current research into the early history of Wawel. There are also several scale models of buildings on Wawel Hill, including one of the Rotunda of the Virgin Mary, which help to give a clear picture of the overall layout of the hill.

The exhibition also includes a room filled with an extensive collection of Renaissance tiles and a number of lapidariums featuring early stonework.

DRINK

Słodki Wawel
Charmingly located within the grounds of the Wawel, this excellent café and chocolaterie makes for the perfect spot to enjoy a hot chocolate after exploring the hill's many sights. It also has a pleasant terrace overlooking the river.

📍 M5 🏛 Zamek Wawel 9 🌐 wawel.com.pl

WAWEL CATHEDRAL

KATEDRA NA WAWELU

EXPERIENCE Wawel Hill and Around

🏛 Wawel Hill 3 🕐 Hours vary, check website for details 🌐 katedra-wawelska.pl

An arresting mish-mash of architectural styles, Wawel Cathedral was once the coronation and burial site of the Polish monarchy. Today, it is seen by many as a symbol of the nation.

Two earlier churches stood on this site before the present cathedral, also known as the Cathedral of Saints Stanisław and Wacław, was erected in the 14th century. It was built by Władysław the Short, the first king to be crowned on Wawel Hill, to house the relics of St Stanisław (p53). Added to over the years, the cathedral is today an eclectic mix of architectural styles. Inside are a series of chapels, including the spectacular Zygmunt Chapel – surmounted by a gilt dome, it is a Renaissance masterpiece. A number of impressive tombs are located in the cathedral, including that of St Stanisław himself and of Jadwiga, Poland's first female monarch. Beneath the cathedral lie the royal crypts, both the final resting place of Polish kings and queens, and a national pantheon for distinguished Poles, including cultural heroes.

Zygmunt Bell (1520) is the largest bell in Poland; its diameter is over 2 m (6 ft).

The top of the 14th-century clock tower is decorated with statues of saints and a fine Baroque dome, added in 1715.

Main entrance

↑ The impressive interior of the cathedral

Timeline

1521
▽ The huge Zygmunt Bell is hung.

1895-1910
The cathedral is renovated.

1020
△ Laying of the foundation stone of the cathedral

c 1890
△ Crypt becomes a national pantheon.

The church's gilded high altar

↑ The eclectic exterior of Wawel Cathedral

In front of the grand high altar are Baroque oak stalls, made around 1620.

A silver coffin holding relics of St Stanisław, the bishop of Kraków, was cast in 1669–71 by Pieter van der Rennen, a goldsmith from Gdańsk.

Zygmunt Chapel is a mausoleum of the rulers of the Jagiellonian dynasty.

Baroque sarcophagi in the Royal Tombs were made for members of the royal Vasa dynasty.

↑ An illustration of the spectacular Wawel Cathedral

Did You Know?

Above the cathedral's entrance hang the bones of an "ancient creature", reputedly Kraków's dragon.

⑧ 🛠 🎵 💻 🏛

WAWEL
ROYAL CASTLE
ZAMEK KRÓLEWSKI NA WAWELU

🅰 Wawel Hill 🕐 Hours vary, check website for details 🅦 wawel.krakow.pl

This impressive castle is one of the most magnificent Renaissance residences in Central Europe. Its sumptuous rooms, for centuries home to Poland's kings and queens, are filled with a cornucopia of priceless artworks and glittering treasures.

The Wawel Royal Castle was commissioned for Zygmunt I, the penultimate ruler of the Jagiellonian dynasty. Built in 1502–36, the four-winged palace was designed and constructed by the Italian architects Francisco Fiorentino and Bartolomeo Berrecci, and incorporates the 14th-century walls of a Gothic building that once stood on the site. After the royal court was transferred to Warsaw in 1609, the palace fell into neglect, deteriorating further under the Swedish occupation of the early 18th century, and during the era of the Partitions. At the beginning of the 20th century, the castle was returned to the city by the occupying Austrian army, and an extensive programme of restoration began. After World War II, the castle was decreed a national museum; today its Italian-inspired interiors have been returned to their former glory and house a vast collection of royal treasures.

State Rooms

A sumptuous array of art and furnishings can be seen in the State Rooms (Komnaty Królewskie), the chambers where much of Poland's state ceremony took place until the capital was transferred to Warsaw. Spread throughout the rooms is Sigismund Augustus's famed collection of Renaissance Flemish tapestries, which depict Bible scenes, mythological themes or fanciful landscapes prowled by wild beasts. Highlights include the Tournament Room, named for the frieze of jousting knights that runs around the walls, and the Envoy's Room, whose ceiling is

decorated with 30 exquisitely sculpted heads; this room was where sittings of the lower house of the Sejm (parliament) were held.

Private Royal Apartments

Learn about the lifestyle of Poland's royalty in the Private Royal Apartments (Prywatne Apartamenty Królewskie). Don't miss the rooms once inhabited by King Sigismund the Old, containing a rich collection of Renaissance furnishings, or the opulent royal guest room, with its Flemish tapestries and painted ceiling beams.

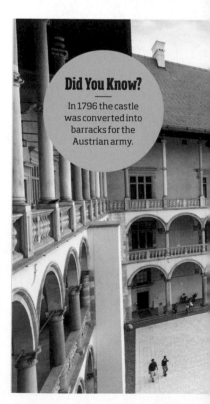

Did You Know?

In 1796 the castle was converted into barracks for the Austrian army.

TICKET GUIDE

Visiting the courtyard is free of charge, but separate tickets must be bought for each individual section of the castle and its museums. Tickets to the state rooms and royal apartments have a designated time slot - it's wise to come early in the day to avoid waiting, or to visit the museums while awaiting your slot.

← An ornate silver eagle, among the acollections of the Crown Treasury

↑ The beautifully decorated Envoy's Room, one of Wawel Royal Castle's State Rooms

Crown Treasury and Armoury

The Crown Treasury and Armoury *(Skarbiec koronny i Zbrojownia)* is two displays in one, presenting the crown jewels of Poland as well as pre-modern military hardware. The treasury contains a fascinating display of the crowns, sceptres and orbs used as symbols of authority by Poland's rulers, as well as gold-and-silver platters and chalices. The armoury collection includes a formidable array of helmets, maces and horse armour used by military commanders during the days of the Polish-Lithuanian Commonwealth. There are also countless rows of muskets and crossbows, and a forest of halberds.

Oriental Art Collection

When King Jan Sobieski defeated the Ottomans in 1683 he amassed a huge amount of booty, including guns, horse saddles and the exquisite textiles of the Ottoman commanders' tents. All of this is on display in the Oriental Art Collection *(Sztuka Wschodu)*, alongside Central Asian carpets, and Chinese and Japanese ceramics.

← The castle's Italianate arcaded inner courtyard

②

CHURCH OF SAINTS PETER AND PAUL

KOŚCIÓŁ ŚW. PIOTRA I PAWŁA

◉N4 ⌂Ulica Grodzka 54 ▦1, 6, 8, 10, 13, 18, 20 ◷Apr-Oct: 9am-5pm Mon-Sat, 1:30-5:30pm Sun; Nov-Mar: 11am-3pm Tue-Sat, 1:30-5:30pm Sun ▣apostolowie.pl

Guarded by statues of the 12 Apostles, this was the first Baroque church to be built in Kraków. Inside, you'll find the longest Foucault's Pendulum in Poland, as well as a national pantheon dedicated to illustrious Poles.

The Church of Saints Peter and Paul was built in 1596–1619. It is modelled on the Jesuit Church of Il Gesù in Rome and is widely considered to be one of the most magnificent Early-Baroque churches in Central Europe. It is home to a 46.5-m-(153-ft-) long Foucault's Pendulum, whose slowly circling swing is evidence of the Earth's rotation; visit at 10am, 11am or noon every Thursday to see this incredible device in action. In 2012, the crypt of the church was designated the site of a national pantheon where cultural figures will be buried.

> 💬 INSIDER TIP
> **Music to Your Ears!**
>
> The church hosts classical music concerts every day at 8pm, with a variety of well-known classical pieces performed by the Kraków Chamber Orchestra of St Maurice.

↑ The sumptuous Baroque interior of the church

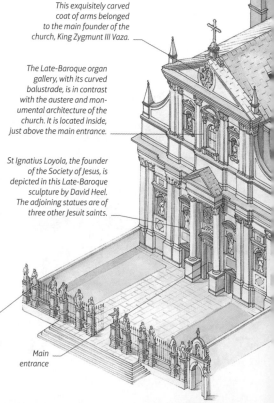

This exquisitely carved coat of arms belonged to the main founder of the church, King Zygmunt III Vaza.

The Late-Baroque organ gallery, with its curved balustrade, is in contrast with the austere and monumental architecture of the church. It is located inside, just above the main entrance.

St Ignatius Loyola, the founder of the Society of Jesus, is depicted in this Late-Baroque sculpture by David Heel. The adjoining statues are of three other Jesuit saints.

The railing in front of the church is decorated with statues of the 12 Apostles. They are copies of statues originally carved between 1715 and 1722.

Main entrance

→ The impressive exterior of the Church of Saints Peter and Paul

→ Statues of the 12 Apostles standing in front of the church

Created in 1622–39, the stuccowork above the high altar includes scenes from the lives of Saints Peter and Paul, patrons of the church.

Made in 1726–28, the high altar was conceived to convey a call for unity between the Roman Catholic and Orthodox Churches.

The monumental decoration of the tomb of Bishop Andrzej Trzebicki, created in 1695–96, commemorates the bishop with true Baroque ostentation.

Entrance to the Skarga Crypt

Statue of Piotr Skarga, the author of the political treatise Parliamentary Sermons. A Jesuit priest, he died in 1612 and was buried in the crypt beneath the high altar.

↑ Cut-away illustration of the Baroque Church of Saints Peter and Paul

Did You Know?

Foucault's Pendulum rotates clockwise in the northern hemisphere and counterclockwise in the southern.

↑ The striking interior of the Franciscan Church, decorated with murals

3

FRANCISCAN CHURCH
KOŚCIÓŁ FRANCISZKANÓW

📍M4 🚇 Wszystkich Świętych Sq 🚊1, 6, 8, 13, 18, 20
🕐10am–4pm Mon–Sat, 1:15–4pm Sun, public holidays
and during services 🌐franciszkanska.pl

One of Kraków's most colourful places of worship, the Franciscan Church is best known for its magnificent Art Nouveau stained-glass windows.

The church was built in 1255 on the orders of Duke Bolesław the Chaste. Badly damaged during the great fire of Kraków in 1850, it was rebuilt in a mix of Neo-Gothic and Neo-Romanesque styles. Its rather plain exterior belies a kaleidoscopic interior, including walls decorated with polychrome murals. The undisputed highlight, however, is a series of expressive Art Nouveau stained-glass windows by renowned Polish artist Stanisław Wyspiański (p49).

↑ The simple red-brick exterior of the Franciscan Church

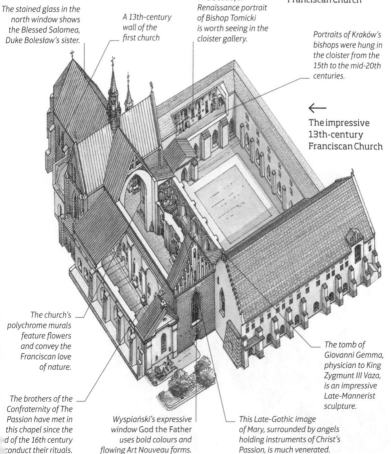

The stained glass in the north window shows the Blessed Salomea, Duke Bolesław's sister.

A 13th-century wall of the first church

This beautiful Renaissance portrait of Bishop Tomicki is worth seeing in the cloister gallery.

Portraits of Kraków's bishops were hung in the cloister from the 15th to the mid-20th centuries.

← The impressive 13th-century Franciscan Church

The church's polychrome murals feature flowers and convey the Franciscan love of nature.

The tomb of Giovanni Gemma, physician to King Zygmunt III Vaza, is an impressive Late-Mannerist sculpture.

The brothers of the Confraternity of The Passion have met in this chapel since the end of the 16th century conduct their rituals.

Wyspiański's expressive window God the Father uses bold colours and flowing Art Nouveau forms.

This Late-Gothic image of Mary, surrounded by angels holding instruments of Christ's Passion, is much venerated.

EXPERIENCE MORE

4

Grodzka Street
Ulica Grodzka

📍 N4 🚋 1, 6, 8, 10, 13, 18, 20

This picturesque street is one of the oldest in all of Kraków – it was built even before the city received its charter in 1257. In the past this charming cobbled stretch formed part of the important Salt Route from Hungary to Greater Poland. It was also part of the Royal Route and as such bore witness to the coronations and funeral processions of Polish kings.

Grodzka Street was once lined with many regal palaces and quite a few churches. Many of the palaces were later rebuilt and converted into town houses.

Today, Grodzka remains one of the loveliest streets in the city, one that is full of character, owing to its irregular plan and diverse architecture.

5

Church of St Martin
Kościół św. Marcina

📍 N5 🏠 Ulica Grodzka 58a 🚋 6, 8, 10, 13, 18 ⏰ 10am–1pm Mon-Sat 🌐 krakow.luteranie.pl

The first church on this site was probably built in the 12th century. In 1612 the Discalced Carmelite Nuns were brought here. The old church was demolished and in 1637–40 the nuns commissioned a new, rather small church in the Early-Baroque style. After the convent was closed down, the church was taken over by the Protestant community. Following this, the interior was converted according to the needs of the Lutheran liturgy.

The high altar features a 14th-century crucifix and *Christ Calming the Storm* by Henryk Siemiradzki, a famed painter of Academic art.

6

Church of St Andrew
Kościół św. Andrzeja

📍 N4 🏠 Ulica Grodzka 56 📞 12 422 16 12 🚋 1, 6, 8, 10, 13, 18, 20 ⏰ 7am-5pm daily

The Church of St Andrew in Okół is regarded as one of the finest examples of Romanesque architecture in Poland. It was built between 1079 and 1098 on the orders of Sieciech, a nobleman who was also the powerful Palatine to Duke Władysław Herman. It was rebuilt around 1200, with the towers and aisles extended and a transept added. It is said that this was the only church in Kraków to resist the Tatar invasion of 1241.

Around 1702 it was remodelled in the Baroque style to the designs of the Italian stuccoist and architect Baldassare Fontana, who also covered the internal walls and vaulting with stuccowork.

↑ The ornate interior of the Church of St Giles, showing the cross of Katyn

Statue of Piotr Skarga
Posąg Piotra Skargi

📍N4 🏛 Plac Marii Magdaleny 🚊1, 6, 8, 10, 13, 18, 20

Dominating the small piazza that connects Kanonicza Street with Grodzka Street is a modern statue of the leading Polish Jesuit Piotr Skarga (1536–1612). Skarga was a powerful orator and preacher, something captured admirably in this animated sculpture by Czesław Dźwigaj.

Mural paintings complete the church's interior decoration. Furnishings worth noting are the pulpit, in the form of a boat, and the high altar with an ebony tabernacle.

The treasury in the convent adjoining the church houses a mosaic depicting the Virgin Mary, which dates from the end of the 12th century, 14th-century marionettes and medieval reliquaries.

Royal Arsenal
Arsenał Królewski

📍N5 🏛 Ulica Grodzka 64 🚊6, 8, 10, 13, 18 🕐To the public

During the first half of the 16th century Zygmunt the Old built an arsenal and a cannon foundry next to the city wall. They formed part of Kraków's fortifications.

The arsenal was remodelled in 1927 by architect Stanisław Filipkiewicz, who juxtaposed the Baroque structure of the building with a rather austere extension.

←

Charming, cobbled Grodzka Street, illuminated at dusk

The building now houses the Centre of Polish Language and Culture in the World, part of the Jagiellonian University.

Church of St Giles
Kościół Św. Idziego

📍N4 🏛 Ulica Św Idziego 1 🚊6, 8, 10, 13, 18 🕐10am–1pm & 3–5pm Tue–Fri, 10am–1pm Sat 🌐krakow. dominikanie.pl/w-krako wie/kosciol-sw-idziego

According to historical evidence, this charming church was constructed at the end of the 11th century by Duke Władysław Herman, after his wife Judith bore a son through the intervention of St Giles. The story has been immortalized in song by Ewa Demarczyk of the famous Piwnica pod Baranami Cabaret (p39). The church as it is seen today was built in the early 14th century. In 1595 the Dominicans took over and soon remodelled it.

Among the furnishings, the stone stalls are particular highlights. They were made in 1629 by reusing fragments of the fine Renaissance tomb of St Jacek (also known as St Hyacinth) from the city's magnificent Dominican Church (p80).

SHOP

Kobalt Pottery
Unique hand-painted ceramics from Poland's leading studios. Expect mugs, plates and jugs decorated in everything from traditional floral designs to bold modern patterns.

📍N5 🏛 Grodzka 62 🌐kobalt.com.pl

Bajo Wooden Toys
This well-known Polish brand creates quality hand-made wooden toys. From baby rattles to rocking horses to building blocks, there's something for everyone's early years.

📍N5 🏛 Grodzka 60 🌐bajo.eu

Ciuciu Cukier Artist
Calling itself the "world's smallest sweet factory", Ciuciu sells old-school lollies and sticks of candy using traditional flavours. The sweets are made right before your eyes.

📍N4 🏛 Grodzka 38 🌐ciuciukrakow.pl

10

Kanonicza Street
Ulica Kanonicza

 N4 🚊 **1, 6, 8, 10, 13, 18, 20**

Kanonicza Street formed the last stretch of the Royal Route leading towards Wawel Hill (p98). From the 14th century onwards it was lined with the houses of Kraków's canons. They were the priests who managed Wawel Cathedral (p102) and had an elite status within the church. The canons were given the use of these houses for life when they took up office in the Chapter of Kraków. Each successive inhabitant would usually modernize their house. As a result, Gothic buildings acquired arcaded Renaissance courtyards, Baroque doorways or Neo-Classical façades. The great

---

Did You Know?

Up until 1390 the building at number 25 Kanonicza Street served as the royal bathhouse.

 Colourful, pastel-hued houses lining picturesque, cobbled Kanonicza Street

diversity of architectural styles which can be found within this gently curving street gives it a truly picturesque character.

Originally located in the Gothic house at number 5 was the Cricot 2 Theatre, founded in 1955 by the theatre director Tadeusz Kantor (p139).

11

Deanery
Dom Dziekański

N5 ⬛ **Ulica Kanonicza 21** 🚊 **1, 6, 8, 10, 13, 18, 20**

The Deanery is considered to be the most beautiful of all the canons' houses in Kraków. The medieval house was completely rebuilt in the 1580s, probably by the architect and sculptor Santi Gucci. The arcaded courtyard with its magnificent decoration, carved in stone, the impressive portal with an inscription reading *Procul este profani* ("keep away, you profane ones"), and the *sgraffiti* on the façade all

date from this period. The statue of St Stanisław in the courtyard was added in the 18th century. Interestingly, in the 1960s this house was the home of the future Pope John Paul II, then the Suffragan Bishop of Kraków, Karol Wojtyła.

12

Archdiocesan Museum
Muzeum Archidiecezjalne

N5 ⬛ **Ulica Kanonicza 19** 🚊 **1, 6, 8, 10, 13, 18, 20** ⏰ **10am–5pm Tue–Sun** 🌐 **archimuzeum.pl**

This house is traditionally associated with the residence of St Stanisław while he was a canon in Kraków, hence the name, St Stanisław's House. It was built in the 14th century but entirely remodelled in the late 18th century.

Today, the building is home to the fascinating Archdiocesan Museum. It runs a programme of temporary exhibitions of sacred art based on loans from church treasuries in the Kraków Archdiocese. A number of highly interesting goldwork displays have taken place here.

Part of the museum is given over to a reconstruction of one of the rooms found in the Deanery nearby. It has been faithfully recreated to look just as it did when Karol Wojtyła, who became Pope John Paul II, lived in the Deanery.

Bishop Erazm Ciołek Palace
Pałac biskupa Erazma Ciołka

📍 N4 🏠 Ulica Kanonicza 17
🚊 1, 6, 8, 10, 13, 18, 20
🕐 10am–4pm Tue–Sun
🌐 mnk.pl

This museum was once home to the great diplomat and patron of the arts Bishop Erazm Ciołek (1474–1522). A magnificently distinguished residence built in a mix of Gothic and Renaissance styles, it has been extensively renovated and now houses the National Museum's *(p158)* large and notable collection of Polish Art. This expansive collection ranges from the 12th to the 18th centuries. The latter includes stunning exhibits such as Late-Gothic altarpieces, Gothic statuary and a room dedicated to the highly ceremonial funerary culture of 17th-century Poland. Fixed to the ceilings of the galleries are beautifully restored examples of ceiling painting taken from ancient wooden churches. In the building's restored cellars are 800 fragments of valuable sculptures collected from all over Poland.

A separate section on the opposite side of the courtyard houses one of the oldest and most valuable collections of Orthodox religious icons in all of Central Europe. The icons featured here are mostly from the eastern parts of Poland where large communities of both Orthodox and Uniate Christians still live.

> **Fixed to the ceilings of the galleries are beautifully restored examples of ceiling painting taken from ancient wooden churches.**

EAT

Pod Nosem
A locally sourced and seasonally changing menu of modern Polish cuisine.

📍 N5 🏠 Ulica Kanonicza 22 🌐 podnosem.com

ⓩⓩⓩ

Art Restauracja
Offers an innovative take on traditional Polish cuisine, with five- or seven-course tasting menus.

📍 N4 🏠 Ulica Kanonicza 15 🌐 artresauracja.com

ⓩⓩⓩ

Copernicus
Classic Polish cuisine in an intimate restaurant.

📍 N5 🏠 Ulica Kanonicza 16 🌐 copernicus.hotel.com.pl

ⓩⓩⓩ

Polish art on display at the Palace of Bishop Erazm Ciołek ↑

14

Bernardine Church

Kościół Bernardynów

⊙N6 **△**Ulica Bernardyńska 2 **⊞**6, 8, 10, 13, 18 **⊙**During services only **W**bernardyni.com.pl

Giovanni da Capistrano, the reformer of the Franciscan Order, arrived in Kraków in 1453 to preach repentance and the renouncement of wealth. Some Cracovians influenced by this, took up the habit of the Reformed Franciscans, known as the Bernardines in Poland. Cardinal Zbigniew Oleśnicki built a small timber church for this new monastic community, and later a large brick church at the foot of Wawel Hill *(p98)*.

In 1655, while preparing to defend Kraków against the Swedes, Polish general Stefan Czarniecki gave orders to set fire to the church so that the invaders could not use it for their own protection. The statue of the *Virgin and Child with St Anne*, from Veit Stoss's workshop, and remnants of Mannerist tombs are the only surviving features.

The new Bernardine Church was built in the Baroque style between 1659 and 1680. The marble shrine of Blessed Simon of Lipnica was erected in 1662 and the high altar between 1758 and 1766. Don't miss *The Dance of Death*, a macabre painting depicting people dancing with skeletons.

15

Archaeological Museum

Muzeum Archeologiczne

⊙M4 **△**Ulica Poselska 3 **⊟**504 **⊞**1, 6, 8, 10, 13, 18, 20 **⊙**9am-3pm Mon, Wed & Fri; 9am-6pm Tue & Thu; 11am-4pm Sun (Jul & Aug: 10am-5pm Mon-Fri, 10am-3pm Sun) **W**ma.krakow.pl

Begun in 1850 and known then as the Museum of Antiquities, the Archaeological Museum is housed in the former Friary of the Discalced Carmelites, founded in 1606. Its collection includes artifacts that tell the earliest history of the Lesser Poland region. The statue of the idol Światowid, salvaged from the Zbrucz River, jewellery found in the tomb of a Scythian princess in Ryżanówka, gold objects from the tomb of a Hun from Jakuszowice and iron objects used as a form of payment are some are the highlights. There are also Egyptian mummies.

The basement of the museum (accessed via a doorway in the garden) was once the site of St Michael's Prison, one of Kraków's most notorious jails. The cells here were used by the Austrian, Nazi, and post-war Communist authorities to incarcerate Polish political prisoners. In 1945, a group of imprisoned soldiers was rescued following heroic action by the Home Army (AK). The cells here were also used to hold Nazi war criminals, including Rudolf Höss, commandant of Auschwitz, and Amon Göth, head of the Płaszów Concentration Camp *(p140)*.

 A tram running though pretty All Saints' Square

16
All Saints' Square
Plac Wszystkich Świętych

N4 🚊1, 6, 8, 10, 13, 18, 20
🌐infokrakow.pl

Intersecting with the northern section of Ulica Grodzka, bustling All Saints' Square is constantly busy with pedestrians and trams. Marking its southern side is the eye-catching **Wyspiański Pavilion** (Pawilon Wyspiańskiego), a modern building opened in 2007 to house a branch of the tourist office. The pavilion also contains a trio of stained glass windows made to original designs by Art Nouveau-era artist Stanisław Wyspiański. Executed in swirling colours, each of the windows portrays a key figure from Polish history: Saint Stanisław, King Kazimierz the Great and Henry the Pious – the Polish prince who was valiantly defeated by the Mongols at the Battle of Legnica in 1241.

Just to the east of the pavilion is the Wielopolski Palace (Pałac Wielopolskich), a former aristocratic seat that now houses the city council. The progressive 19th-century

Spectacular interior of the Bernardine Church at the foot of Wawel Hill

mayor Józef Dietl (1804-78) is honoured with a statue outside the palace, sculpted by Xavery Dunikowski in 1936.

Wyspiański Pavilion
🚪Plac Wszystkich Świętych 2
🕐9am-5pm daily
🌐infokrakow.pl

17
Church of St Joseph and the Convent of the Bernardine Nuns
Kościół św. Józefa i klasztor Bernardynów

N4 🚪Ulica Poselska 21
🚊1, 6, 8, 10, 13, 18, 20
🕐9am-6:30pm daily
🌐bernardynki.com

A small convent was established in Poselska Street in 1646. The Church of St Joseph was later built here between 1694 and 1703 for the nuns. Though small and modest, the church's interior displays splendid furnishings which include altars and a pulpit. The miraculous image of St Joseph and Child in the high altar was a gift from Jakub Zadzik, Bishop of Kraków, who possibly received it from Pope Urban VIII.

A 17th-century statue of the child Jesus in the side altar is much venerated. It originally came from the Church of the Nuns of St Colette in Stradom.

STAY

Mundo Hostel
Nicely placed between the Old Town and Kazimierz, Mundo offers cute double rooms, each with décor themed around a particular country.

P4 🚪Ulica Józefa Szarego 10
🌐mundohostel.eu

🅩🅩🅩

Hotel Royal
A 19th-century hotel that has been kept in good order, set among the lawns and flowerbeds of Planty Park. Rooms are neat and unfussy, many with original parquet floors.

🚩N5 🚪Ulica sw. Gertrudy 26-29
🌐amwhotele.pl

🅩🅩🅩

Hotel Copernicus
A historic town house with Gothic and Renaissance features, the Copernicus has antique furniture, swish bathrooms and faultless service.

🚩N4 🚪Ulica Kanonicza 16 🌐copernicus.hotel.com.pl

🅩🅩🅩

Hotel Senacki
A charming hotel with smart rooms located in an 18th-century tenement house. Some rooms have wonderful views of Ulica Grodzka.

🚩N4 🚪Ulica Grodzka 51
🌐hotelsenacki.com

🅩🅩🅩

A SHORT WALK
OKÓŁ

Distance 800 m (875 yds) **Nearest tram stop** Filharmonia **Time** 10 minutes

South of Kraków's medieval centre is the historic Okół district, a picturesque area with curving streets lined with incredible architecture. Fortunately, the great fire of Kraków in 1850 (p80) did not damage the buildings in Okół, and much of the original architecture can still be seen here, including the spectacular Church of Saints Peter and Paul and striking Bishop Erazm Ciołek Palace. Stroll along the historic streets of Kanonicza and Grodzka to follow in the footsteps of royalty – both streets were part of the Royal Route, the coronation path trod by Poland's monarchy.

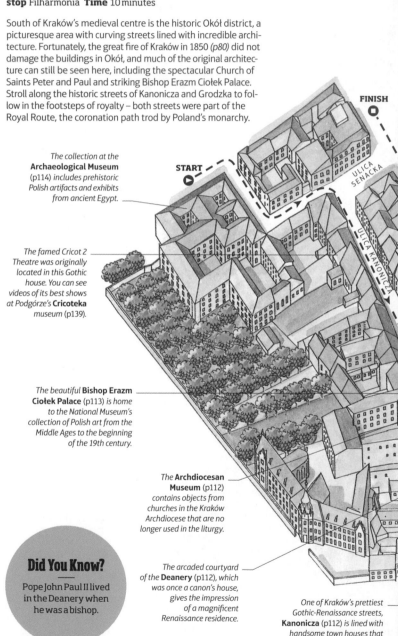

FINISH

START

ULICA SENACKA

ULICA KANONICZA

The collection at the **Archaeological Museum** (p114) includes prehistoric Polish artifacts and exhibits from ancient Egypt.

The famed Cricot 2 Theatre was originally located in this Gothic house. You can see videos of its best shows at Podgórze's **Cricoteka** museum (p139).

The beautiful **Bishop Erazm Ciołek Palace** (p113) is home to the National Museum's collection of Polish art from the Middle Ages to the beginning of the 19th century.

The **Archdiocesan Museum** (p112) contains objects from churches in the Kraków Archdiocese that are no longer used in the liturgy.

Did You Know?

Pope John Paul II lived in the Deanery when he was a bishop.

The arcaded courtyard of the **Deanery** (p112), which was once a canon's house, gives the impression of a magnificent Renaissance residence.

One of Kraków's prettiest Gothic-Renaissance streets, **Kanonicza** (p112) is lined with handsome town houses that once belonged to the city's clergy.

↑ Picturesque Grodzka Street, beautifully illuminated at night

Locator Map
For more detail see p94

| 0 metres | 50 | N |
| 0 yards | 50 | |

The Early-Baroque **Church of Saints Peter and Paul** *(p106) is a masterpiece of 17th-century Polish architecture. The façade, with its rich sculptural decoration, is remarkable.*

The town houses situated along **Grodzka Street** *(p110), one of the oldest streets in Kraków, were once palaces.*

The **Church of St Andrew** *(p110) is the best preserved example of Romanesque architecture in Kraków.*

The small Early-Baroque **Church of St Martin** *(p110) was taken over by the Protestant community in the early 19th century.*

ULICA GRODZKA

The rather modest Gothic **Church of St Giles** *(p111) dates from the 14th century.*

The entrance to the **Royal Arsenal** *(p111) is a beautiful 17th-century doorway.*

↑ The Romanesque façade of the Church of St Andrew

BĄBELSTE

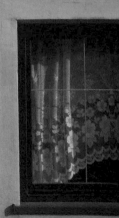

KAZIMIERZ

Founded by Kazimierz the Great in 1335, this area, south of Wawel Hill, began life as a royal town separate from Kraków, complete with its own churches, market place and town hall. Following a fire in the Old Town in 1495, Polish King Jan Olbracht settled Kraków's Jewish population in the eastern part of Kazimierz, which subsequently emerged as a thriving centre of Jewish life and culture. A wall dividing the Jewish and Christian parts of Kazimierz was torn down in 1822, and the area became a bustling multicultural suburb of the growing city of Kraków. Kazimierz was all but destroyed during World War II, its Jewish inhabitants forcibly moved first to the ghetto in nearby Podgórze and then to concentration camps such as Auschwitz–Birkenau. The area was seriously neglected under the country's Communist regime and fell into disrepair. It was only during the 1990s – following the fall of the Communist government and the release of Steven Spielberg's award-winning film *Schindler's List*, which portrayed the history of the area during World War II – that Kazimierz began to rejuvenate. Since then it has undergone a revival and is now one of the most vibrant places in Kraków, known as much for its old-world bars and quirky cafés as it is for its historic synagogues and cemeteries, the latter serving as evidence of the area's Jewish heritage.

St Adalbert's Church

Planty

Dominican Church

FRANCISZKAŃSKA

DOMINIKAŃSKA

ŚW. GERTRUDY

WIELOPOLE

STAROWIŚLNA

Franciscan Church

Planty

POSELSKA

OKÓŁ

Archaeological Museum

GRODZKA

Church of Saints Peter and Paul

JÓZEFA SAREGO

ZWIERZYNIECKA

F. STRASZEWSKIEGO

PLAC NA GROBLACH

POWIŚLE

PODZAMCZE

ŚW. SEBASTIANA

Natural History Museum

STRADOM

JÓZEFA DIETLA

ŚW. SEBASTIAN

BRZOZOWA

STRADOMSKA

Wawel Hill

Vistula

BERNARDYŃSKA

WAWEL HILL AND AROUND
p94

Tempel Synagogue ③

Kupa Synagogue ⑦

MIODOWA

⑤ Isa
Synago

⑥

Częstochowa Seminary

SMOCZA

New Square ⑬

MARII KONOPNICKIEJ

JÓZEFA DIETLA

BOŻEGO CIAŁA

KRAKOWSKA

AUGUSTIAŃSKA

PAULIŃSKA

NOWA

JÓZEFA

ESTERY

Corpus Christi Church ⑩

Most Grunwaldzki

ŚW. STANISŁAWA

Church of St Catherine ⑪

SKAŁECZNA

The Ethnographic Museum in Kraków ⑫

PLAC WOLNICA

ŚW. WAWRZYŃC

② BOCHEŃSKA

Paulite Church "On the Rock" ⑮

PIEKARSKA

KRAKOWSKA

MOSTOWA

BARSKA

MARII KONOPNICKIEJ

BULWAR MIKOŁAJA ZYBLIKIEWICZA

SKAWIŃSKA

H. WIETORA

TRYNITARSKA

Church of
Order of St
John of Goo

PODGÓRSK

WIERZBOWA

BARSKA

RYBAKI

Most
J. Piłsudskiego

LEGIONÓW

Vistula

0 metres   300

0 yards   300

N
↑

PODGÓRZE
p132

JANA DŁUGOSZA

WILGA

KAZIMIERZ

Must See

1 Old Synagogue

Experience More

2 Isaak's Synagogue
3 Tempel Synagogue
4 High Synagogue
5 Galicia Jewish Museum
6 Remuh Synagogue and Cemetery
7 Kupa Synagogue
8 New Jewish Cemetery
9 Museum of Municipal Engineering
10 Corpus Christi Church
11 Church of St Catherine
12 The Ethnographic Museum in Kraków
13 New Square
14 Father Bernatek Bridge
15 Paulite Church "On the Rock"

Eat

① Lody na Starowiślnej
② Good Lood
③ 2 Okna Café

Drink

④ Singer
⑤ Alchemia
⑥ Les Couleurs

1 🏛️ 🏛️

OLD SYNAGOGUE
STARA SYNAGOGA

📍 G8 🏠 Ulica Szeroka 24 🚌 3, 18, 22, 19, 24, 52 🕐 Apr-Oct: 10am-2pm Mon, 9am-5pm Tue-Sun; Nov-Mar: 10am- 2pm Mon, 9am-4pm Tue-Sun 🚪 First Sat & Sun of each month; Nov-Mar: Wed 🌐 muzeumkrakowa.pl

This synagogue is the oldest surviving example of Jewish religious architecture in Poland. Found within its airy interior is a museum that provides a compelling insight into Jewish life in Poland.

The Old Synagogue was used in the past as a temple and was also a seat of the local Kahal (governing body) and other offices of the Jewish community. As a result, the religious and social life of the surrounding area was concentrated here.

The brick building dates back to the mid-15th or beginning of the 16th century. Inside, the hall used for prayer is almost bare, in accordance with the rule of the Jewish religion. The elegant *bimah*, an elevated platform with a wrought-iron balustrade used for readings from the Torah, is the only piece of furnishing.

No longer a working synagogue, it is now part of the Historical Museum of the City of Kraków with exhibits dedicated to the history and culture of Kraków's Jews. The women's prayer room also hosts temporary exhibits.

↑ The simple red-brick exterior of the Old Synagogue

Did You Know?

The synagogue was known as the "Fortress Synagogue" due to the defensive buttresses built into it.

THE SYNAGOGUE DURING WORLD WAR II

This chapter of the Old Synagogue's history was incredibly tumultuous. After the Nazis took control of Kraków, they ransacked the synagogue, badly damaging it and stealing its Jewish relics and beautiful artworks. For the rest of the Nazi occupation, the synagogue was used as a magazine to store large quantities of ammunition. In 1943 30 Polish hostages were executed against the wall of the synagogue. A simple memorial dedicated to these Poles can be found outside the building.

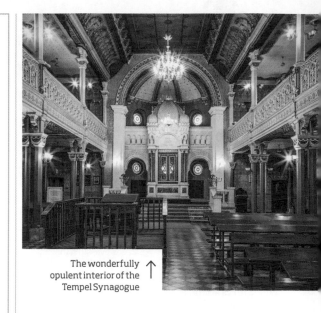

The wonderfully opulent interior of the Tempel Synagogue ↑

EXPERIENCE MORE

↑ The unadorned interior of the synagogue, illuminated by chandeliers

Isaak's Synagogue

Bożnica Izaaka

G7 ⬛ Ulica Kupa 18 ☎ 12 430 22 22 🚋 3, 18, 19, 22, 24, 52 🚌 504 ⏰ 8am-6pm Sun-Thu, 8:30am-4:30pm Fri

This synagogue (1638–1644) was built on the orders of Izaak Jakubowicz, a wealthy Jewish elder. Its large nave's barrel-vaulted ceiling is decorated with stuccowork and the walls are covered with remnants of Jewish sculptures. It is currently undergoing renovation but remains open to the public.

Tempel Synagogue

Synagoga Tempel

F7 ⬛ Ulica Miodowa 24 ☎ 12 430 54 11 🚋 3, 18, 19, 22, 24, 52 🚌 184, 484 ⏰ 10am-4pm Sun-Thu, 10am-dusk Fri

The newest of the synagogues found in the Kazimierz quarter,

HISTORY OF THE JEWS IN POLAND

Before the Holocaust, Poland had one of the most vibrant Jewish communities in the world. Polish rulers allowed them to settle and protected them from persecution. Anti-Semitic unrest in 1495 saw the removal of Jews from central Kraków and their settlement in Kazimierz. By the outbreak of World War II there were over 3.5 million Jews in Poland. Less than 10% of them survived the war.

the Tempel was built in the Neo-Renaissance style between 1860 and 1862. During World War II, it was used as a warehouse and a stable for horses. Today it is used by non-Orthodox Jews. Inside note the stained glass and period decoration. Concerts are occasionally held here.

↑ Ornate decor on
the walls of the
High Synagogue

④ 🔀 High Synagogue
Bożnica Wysoka

📍 G8 🏠 Ulica Józefa 38
📞 12 430 68 69 🚋 19, 24
🕐 10am–7pm daily

This synagogue dates from
1556 to 1563. A picturesque
structure supported by buttresses, its name derives from
the prayer hall being on the
upper floor. One highlight is
the synagogue's Renaissance
portal. Only a few furnishings
have survived, including a
money box and the remains
of an altar. There is a good
bookshop on the ground floor.

⑤ 🔀 Galicia Jewish Museum
Żydowskie Muzeum Galicja

📍 G8 🏠 Ulica Dajwór
18 🚋 3, 19, 24 🕐 10am–
6pm daily (Jun–Aug:
to 7pm) 🌐 galicia
jewishmuseum.org

Housed in a restored
prewar factory, this
museum was founded in
2004 by photographer Chris
Schwartz to commemorate
the once-thriving Jewish
culture of southeastern Poland.
Schwartz's evocative
photographs of synagogues
and graveyards fill the
exhibition halls. There are
also changing exhibitions
on Jewish historical themes.

---

⑥ 🔀 Remuh Synagogue and Cemetery
Bożnica i Cmentarz Remuh

📍 G7 🏠 Ulica Szeroka 40
📞 12 429 57 35 🚋 3, 18, 19,
22, 24, 52 🕐 9am–4pm
Sun–Fri (May–Sep: to 6pm)

This synagogue is one of two
in Kraków that are still in use.
It was built around 1557 by

RABBI MOSES BEN ISSERLES
Founder of the Remuh
Synagogue, Rabbi
Moses Isserles (1530–
1570) was one of the
leading Talmudic
scholars of his age,
helping Kazimierz gain
its reputation as a major
centre of Jewish learn-
ing. He is celebrated for
his additions to the
Shulkhan Arukh, or
code for everyday life,
which became the most
widely accepted book
of Jewish law. His grave-
stone in the Remuh
Cemetery remains a
focus of pilgrimage.

Izrael ben Józef for his son
Mojżesz Isserles, a great author
and philosopher known as
Remuh. Inside, the *bimah*
(reading platform) and an
ornamental *aron hakodesh*
(Torah ark) are worth noting.
Behind the synagogue is one
of Europe's most important
Jewish cemeteries. Established
in 1533, it contains many gravestones and sarcophagi decorated with rich floral and animal
motifs. This style is unusual
for a Jewish cemetery as it is

Tombstones in Remuh
Cemetery, some dating
↓ from the 16th century

↑ The beautiful interior of the renovated 17th-century Kupa Synagogue

normally not headstones, stone slabs which are positioned horizontally over a grave. Despite the damage caused by World War II, many of the cemetery's tombstones have survived, including the tomb of Remuh, which still attracts pilgrims from all over the world. Fragments of the shattered tombstones have also been built into the cemetery wall (known as the Wailing Wall) abutting Ulica Szeroka.

7

Kupa Synagogue
Synagoga Kupa

🅠 F7 **🅐 Ulica Miodowa 27**
📞 124295735 **🚃 3, 19, 24**
**🕐 10am-5pm Sun-Thu
(to 2pm Fri)**

Dating from the 16th century, the plain exterior of the Kupa

Did You Know?

Kupa Synagogue is attached to a small section of Kazimierz's old defensive walls.

synagogue hides a vibrant interior, which is covered with wall paintings executed in the 1920s and only recently restored. Depicting zodiac symbols and views of holy cities, they are best viewed in the women's section of the synagogue (open to both women and men), reached by ascending an outdoor staircase.

8

New Jewish Cemetery
Nowy Cmentarz Żydowski

🅠 G7 **🅐 Ulica Miodowa 55**
🚃 3, 19, 24 **🕐 9am-4pm
Sun-Fri**

Established in the early 19th century, this huge cemetery is the burial place of the most renowned members of the city's Jewish community who lived during the 19th and 20th centuries. All Kazimierz's rabbis and many of Kraków's great benefactors rest here. They include Józef Oettinger and Józef Rosenblatt (both professors of the Jagiellonian University), Józef Sare (the city's President) and Maurycy Gotlieb (one of the foremost Polish artists of the 19th century). This cemetery is fully functioning to this day.

9

Museum of Municipal Engineering
Muzeum Inżynierii Miejskiej

🅠 G8 **🅐 Ulica Świętego
Wawrzyńca 15** **🚃 3, 19, 24**
**🕐 Jun-Sep: 10am-6pm Tue,
Thu & Sun, 10am-4pm Wed,
Fri & Sat; Oct-May: 10am-
4pm Tue-Sun** **🆆 mim.
krakow.pl**

This museum is set in a late-19th-century former tram depot. The collection consists of motor cars through the ages, including Polish-made vehicles that are no longer manufactured. For kids, there are hands-on displays and lots of trams in the tram shed.

2 Okna, one of the many cafés that have helped to revitalize Kazimierz

Corpus Christi Church

Kościół Bożego Ciała

9 F8 **⌂** Ulica Bożego Ciała 26 **🚌** 504 **🚊** 3, 6, 10, 13 **🕐** 9am-6pm daily **✕** Closed during holy masses

According to legend, this church was built on marshland where a monstrance (religious container) with the Eucharist stolen from the Collegiate Church of All Saints had been found; a mysterious light indicated where it had been left. Founded by King Kazimierz the Great, the church's construction was started in 1340. It was bestowed with lavish furnishings by local burghers, most of which have survived.

From 1634 to 1637 the high altar was decorated with a painting of *The Nativity* by Tommaso Dolabella, court artist to Zygmunt III Vaza. The stalls for monks were made in 1632. A 17th-century gilded altarpiece with the relics of the priest Stanisław Kazimierczyk is located in the north aisle.

The magnificent gilded interior of the Corpus Christi Basilica and *(inset)* its simple façade ↑

Church of St Catherine

Kościół św. Katarzyny

9 F8 **⌂** Ulica Augustiańska 7 **🚌** 504 **🚊** 6, 8, 10, 13 **🕐** 4 May-31 Oct: 10am-4pm Mon-Fri, 11am-2pm Sat; Nov-Apr: 10am-4pm daily **🌐** parafia-kazimierz. augustianie.pl

According to the chronicler Jan Długosz, the Church of St Catherine was built by Kazimierz the Great as a penance for murdering Father Marcin Baryczka in 1349. However, other sources suggest that the construction of the church actually began in 1343 and continued until the early 16th century. Regarded as one of the most beautiful Gothic churches in Kraków, its furnishings were lost in the 19th century when it was briefly used as a warehouse. The Baroque high altar, decorated with the *Mystical Marriage of St Catherine*, has survived. Worth visiting is the Gothic cloister which features Late-Gothic murals and large 17th-century paintings. Two chapels adjoin the cloister: one houses the miraculous *Madonna of Consolation* and the other, the relics of Blessed Isaiah Boner.

The Ethnographic Museum in Kraków

Muzeum Etnograficzn w Krakowie

9 F8 **⌂** Plac Wolnica 1 **🚌** 504 **🚊** 6, 8, 10, 13 **🕐** 10am-7pm Tue-Sun **✕** Public hols **🌐** etnomuzeum.eu

Kazimierz's Renaissance Town Hall is now home to the Ethnographic Museum. It displays a rich collection of costumes from all over

> Two chapels adjoin the cloister: one houses the miraculous Madonna of Consolation and the other the relics of Blessed Isaiah Boner.

Poland, as well as traditional Kraków Christmas cribs, folk art and musical instruments. There is also a section on seasonal folk festivals and a fantastic display of recreated house interiors. Temporary exhibitions are housed in a separate 16th-century palace known as the **House of Esther**.

House of Esther

⌂ Ulica Krakowska 46
🕐 10am-7pm Tue-Sun

13

New Square
Plac Nowy

📍 F7 🚊 6, 8, 10, 13

Today the centre of Kazimierz's vibrant nightlife, New Square was the main market square in the 19th century. The red-brick rotunda in the centre was once a kosher slaughterhouse, but is now home to fast-food outlets selling late-night snacks. The square hosts daily markets, including one for antiques on a Saturday.

14

Father Bernatek Bridge
Kładka Ojca Bernatka

📍 G9 ⌂ Ulica Mostowa to Ulica Nadwiślańska
🚊 3, 6, 8, 10, 13, 19, 24

This graceful cycle- and footbridge, connecting the popular Kazimierz quarter with the less visited south bank, opened in 2010. It is

> 🔍 HIDDEN GEM
> ### Jan Karski Monument
> A short walk from New Square is a statue of Jan Karski, the Polish underground hero who infiltrated the ghetto in Warsaw to collect evidence of the Holocaust and inform the Allies.

named after Father Laetus Bernatek (1847–1927), who campaigned to build the first modern hospital in Kazimierz.

15

Paulite Church "On the Rock"
Kościół Paulinów Na Skałce

📍 E8 ⌂ Ulica Skałeczna 15 🚌 504 🚊 6, 8, 10, 13
🕐 Church: 9am-5pm Mon-Sat, 1-5pm Sun; Crypt: Apr-Oct: 9am-5pm daily; Nov-Mar: on request 🌐 skalka.paulini.pl

A church of St Michael "On the Rock" was recorded back in the 11th century. This was the site where Bishop Stanisław of Szczepanów, later canonized, was murdered. In the 14th century this Romanesque church was replaced by a Gothic one. It was rebuilt in Late-Baroque style, from 1733. A small font in the church is decorated with a statue of St Stanisław. The tormentors of the saint threw his cut-off finger into the font; the water is said to have had healing properties ever since.

In 1870, the church's crypt was turned into a national pantheon for key contributors to Polish culture. Tombs include those of poet Adam Asnyk, writer Lujan Siemieński and artist Stanisław Wyspiański.

EAT

Lody na Starowiślnej
There's always a queue outside this legendary hole-in-the-wall ice cream shop.

📍 G7 ⌂ Starowislna 83

💰💰💰

Good Lood
Belonging to a new generation of craft ice-cream makers, Good Lood offers additive-free ices and sorbets in a staggering range of flavours.

📍 F8 ⌂ Plac Wolnica 11 🌐 goodlood.com

💰💰💰

---

2 Okna Café
This cute café offers excellent coffee, a great range of snacks and a hidden garden.

📍 G8 ⌂ Ulica Józefa 40

💰💰💰

↑ The simple exterior of the sacred sanctuary of Paulite Church "On the Rock"

A SHORT WALK
SZEROKA STREET AREA

Distance 800 m (875 yds) **Nearest tram stop** Stradom **Time** 10 minutes

The Jewish quarter was initially located in the eastern part of Kazimierz and concentrated first around Szeroka Street, then Libusza Square (later known as New Square). As well as the Jews relocated here in the late 15th century from Kraków, Czech and German refugees also came to live in Kazimierz. The area became an active centre of Judaic culture and learning, and many synagogues, baths, schools and cemeteries were established. During the Nazi occupation of Kraków, however, the Jewish community was forcibly displaced from the area and move into the ghetto in Podgórze; as a result Kazimierz quickly declined. Yet, since the 1990s the area has been rejuvenated, with many of its spectacular synagogues and cemeteries restored, allowing visitors to explore both its poignant past and rich Jewish heritage.

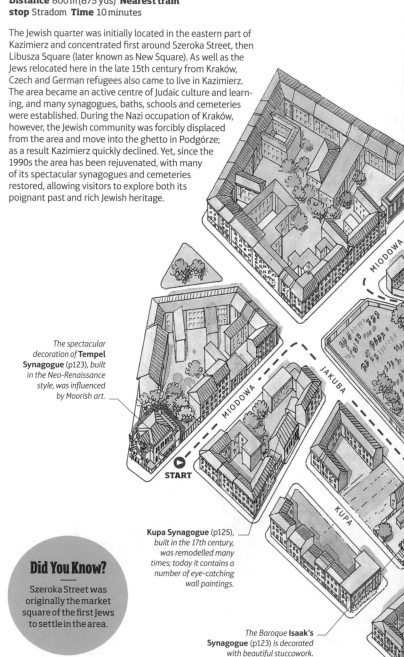

The spectacular decoration of **Tempel Synagogue** (p123), built in the Neo-Renaissance style, was influenced by Moorish art.

START

Kupa Synagogue (p125), built in the 17th century, was remodelled many times; today it contains a number of eye-catching wall paintings.

Did You Know?

Szeroka Street was originally the market square of the first Jews to settle in the area.

The Baroque **Isaak's Synagogue** (p123) is decorated with beautiful stuccowork.

Locator Map
For more detail see p120

↑ Some of the beautifully carved gravestones
found in the atmospheric Remuh Cemetery

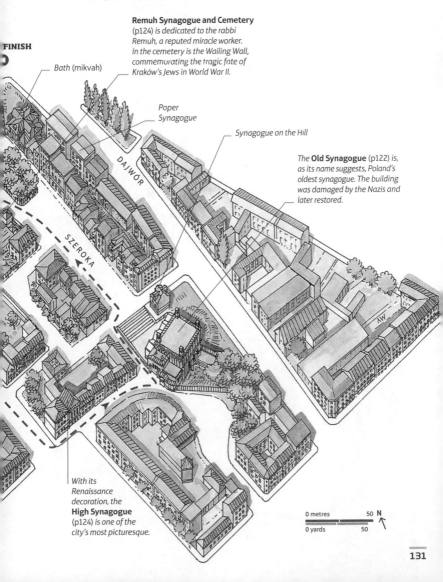

Remuh Synagogue and Cemetery
(p124) *is dedicated to the rabbi
Remuh, a reputed miracle worker.
In the cemetery is the Wailing Wall,
commemorating the tragic fate of
Kraków's Jews in World War II.*

FINISH

Bath (mikvah)

*Poper
Synagogue*

Synagogue on the Hill

The **Old Synagogue** (p122) *is,
as its name suggests, Poland's
oldest synagogue. The building
was damaged by the Nazis and
later restored.*

*With its
Renaissance
decoration, the*
High Synagogue
(p124) *is one of the
city's most picturesque.*

0 metres   50   N
0 yards   50

PODGÓRZE

Located on the south bank of the Vistula river and joined to Kazimierz by several bridges, Podgórze has been inhabited for at least 2,000 years. The area's impressive Krakus Mound – an artificial hill believed to be the resting place of Kraków's legendary founder, King Krakus – was erected sometime around the 1st century AD. For centuries the area was covered by a loose collection of villages, but over years the settlement closest to the river (what is today the centre of Podgórze) grew into a bustling town. In 1784, Podgórze was declared a free city by the Habsburg Emperor Joseph II; it remained so for over 130 years, before being incorporated into the city of Kraków in 1915. In the late-19th and early-20th centuries, Podgórze became ever more industrialized and a large number of factories were built. These drew economic migrants from the surrounding countryside, turning the district into a proudly working-class area quite different from the more historic parts of Kraków.

In March 1941 Podgórze was chosen by Kraków's Nazi occupiers as the site of a Jewish ghetto, separated from the rest of the city by a wall. Many Jews were deported from the ghetto to camps over the next two years, including to the Plaszów camp, located in heathland just south of Podgórze. In March 1943, the ghetto was cleared: the remaining inhabitants were either sent to camps or were murdered in the ghetto. The area saw little development following World War II and has only recently undergone a revivial, thanks in part to the opening of Schindler's Factory in 2010. Both this museum and other sights, such as the Eagle Pharmacy, have made Podgórze into a major centre of remembrance.

D   E   F   G

PLAC
NOWY

JÓZEFA DIETLA

BOŻEGO CIAŁA

JAKUBA

Old
Synagogu

JÓZEFA

KAZIMIERZ

AUGUSTIAŃSKA

Corpus Christi
Church

ŚW. WAWRZYŃCA

Museum of
Municipal
Engineering

SKAŁECZNA

PLAC
WOLNICA

KRAKOWSKA

KAZIMIERZ
p118

SKAWIŃSKA

H. WIETORA

9

WIERZBOWA

Most
J. Piłsudskiego

Vistula

LEGIONÓW

K. BRODZIŃSKIEGO

CELNA

Podgorski
Market **3**

RYNE
PODGÓ

BARSKA

KOMANDOSÓW

MARII

PRZY MOŚCIE

JANA DŁUGOSZA

T. REJTANA

PLAC
NIEPODLEGŁOŚCI

Church o
St Josep

KONOPNICKIEJ

Wilga

ORAWSKA

J. KRASICKIEGO

STROMA

JANA ZAMOJSKIEGO

SMOLKI

Park W.
Bednarskieg

10

LUDWINÓW

KALWARYJSKA

PTO RYSTÓW

REDEM

KRZEMIONKI

PODSKALE

JANA ZAMOJSKIEGO

CZYŻÓWKA

TV Kraków

H. KAMIEŃSKIEGO

H. KAMIEŃSKIEG

11

PODGÓRZE

Must See

1 Schindler's Factory and MOCAK

Experience More

2 Eagle Pharmacy
3 Podgorski Market
4 Ghetto Heroes Square
5 Ghetto Wall
6 Galeria Starmach
7 Cricoteka
8 Płaszów Concentration
   Camp
9 Podgórze Museum
10 Old Podgórze Cemetery
11 Church of St Benedict
12 St Benedict Fort
13 Krakus Mound

12

ŁAGIEWNICKA

KSIĘDZA JÓZEFA TISCHNERA

F   G

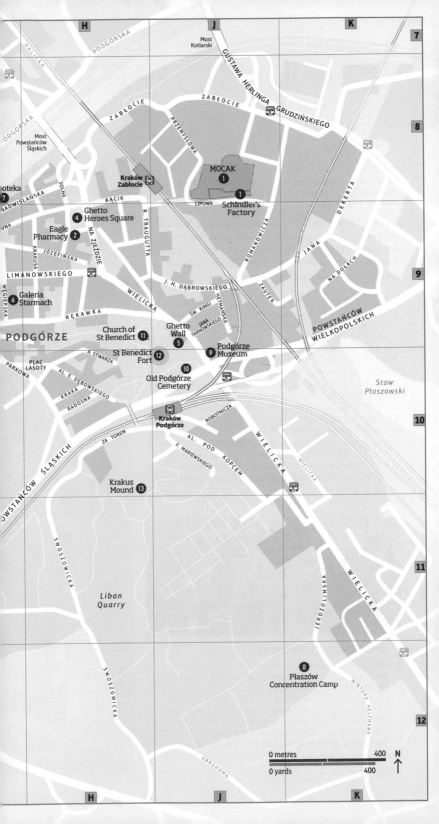

① ✍ ⓜ ◻ 🛍

SCHINDLER'S FACTORY AND MOCAK

FABRYKA SCHINDLERA MOCAK

📍 J8 🏠 Ulica Lipowa 4 🚌 3, 18, 24 🕐 Schindler's Factory: Hours vary, check website for details; MOCAK: 11am–7pm Tues–Sun 🌐 Schindler's Factory: muzeumkrakowa.pl; MOCAK: mocak.pl

A powerful symbol of humanitarian courage, Schindler's Factory tells the story of life in Kraków during the Nazi occupation. Attached to the building is the eye-catching MOCAK (Museum of Contemporary Art in Kraków), an energetic and constantly evolving art gallery.

Did You Know?

After his death in 1974, Schindler was buried in the cemetery on Mount Zion in Jerusalem.

In 1943, Oskar Schindler, the factory's German owner, saved over 1,000 Jews from deportation to the death camps by employing them and claiming that they were essential to the running of his business. Now part of the Historical Museum of Kraków, the factory hosts an exhibition entitled "Kraków Under Nazi Occupation 1939–45". Daily life for Kraków's Jewish and Polish inhabitants – from the last pre-war summer of 1939 through the Nazi occupation to the arrival of the Red Army in January 1945 – is illustrated using original documents, radio and film recordings, photographs and multimedia installations. The fate of the Jewish population is a major theme, though the lives of other citizens are also covered in detail. Poignant exhibits include Schindler's desk and photographs of some of those that Schindler saved.

Next door, MOCAK's main exhibition halls display the cream of Polish contemporary art in striking minimalist surroundings. Adjacent spaces host an engaging array of changing exhibitions by international artists.

SPIELBERG'S SCHINDLER'S LIST

Based on Thomas Keneally's novel *Schindler's Ark*, Steven Spielberg's 1993 film *Schindler's List* brought the story of factory-owner Schindler to a global audience. Most of the filming took place in Kraków, using real-life locations in Kazimierz and Podgórze as much as possible. Scenes set in Płaszów concentration camp were shot in a nearby quarry, because the Płaszów skyline had changed too much. Much of the film's extraordinary power is due to Oscar-winning Polish cinematographer Janusz Kamiński.

← MOCAK Museum
of Contemporary
Art in Kraków

→ MOCAK collection, with
works by Krištof Kintera
and Rafat Bujnowski

↑ Exploring the
exhibition at
Schindler's Factory

Poignant mementos of the ghetto found in the Eagle Pharmacy ↑

EXPERIENCE MORE

❷ Eagle Pharmacy
Apteka pod Orłem

H9 🏛 **Plac Bohaterów Getta 18** 🚊 3, 18, 19, 24, 52 🕐 10am–2pm Mon, 9am–5pm Tues–Sun 🌐 muzeumkrakowa.pl

Located on the southern side of the Vistula river, the suburb of Podgórze was chosen by the Nazis to be the site of a Jewish ghetto in 1941, with the area's non-Jewish residents required to relocate to other areas of the city. Declining to be moved from Podgórze, Dr Tadeusz Pankiewicz, a Polish pharmacist, continued to run his pharmacy; it was the only one left operating in the ghetto. As well as providing medication, often for free, the Eagle Pharmacy became a social hub for the Jewish population. Dr Pankiewicz documented his experiences in a moving book entitled *The Kraków Ghetto Pharmacy*. In this moving memoir, Pankiewicz describes how he and his staff risked their lives to undertake numerous clandestine operations: smuggling food and information, and offering shelter on the premises for those Jews facing deportation to the camps.

Now a small but fascinating museum, the pharmacy (which is a branch of the Historical Museum of the City of Kraków) has been recreated to look as it did during the war. Multimedia displays, as well as photographs and personal effects hidden in drawers, tell the devastating stories of those who lived in the ghetto during the Nazi occupation.

Did You Know?

Dr Pankiewicz is recognized as one of the Righteous Among the Nations for his brave deeds.

❸ Podgorski Market
Rynek Podgorski

G9 🚊 3, 19, 24

Formerly the main market square of Podgórze, this plaza

INSIDER TIP

Bednarski Park

Hidden away behind Podgorski Market is Bednarski Park, one of Kraków's most attractive green spaces. With stretches of woodland and a kids' playground, it's a great place for a stroll and a picnic.

is overlooked by the soaring spires of St Joseph's Church, a magnificent Neo-Gothic building consecrated just before World War I. On the eastern side of the square stands a splendid 19th-century town hall.

❹ Ghetto Heroes Square
Plac Bohaterów Getta

H9 🚊 3, 18, 19, 24, 52

This former market square was where Kraków's Jewish community unloaded their belongings and waited to be allocated accommodation in the Podgórze ghetto. Two years later, they assembled here again, prior to their deportation to the work camps and death camps. The remaining residents of the ghetto were murdered in March 1943.

This history of traumatic arrivals and departures is marked in Piotr Lewicki and Kazimierz Łatak's installation of oversized iron chairs scattered across the square. The chairs serve as a reminder that when the ghetto was cleared in 1943, bits of abandoned furniture were all that was left of Kraków's Jewish community.

5

Ghetto Wall

Mury getta

J9 Ulica Lwowska 25-29 69, 669 3, 19, 24

The largest surviving fragment of the wall which once surrounded Podgórze's Jewish ghetto is this 12-m (40-ft) stretch on the southwestern side of Ulica Lwowska. A plaque in Polish and Hebrew bears the words: "Here people lived, suffered and died at the hands of Hitler's henchmen. And from here they were taken on their final journey to the extermination camps."

6

Galeria Starmach

G9 Ulica Wegierska 5 3, 9, 24 11am-6pm Mon-Fri starmach.eu

One of Poland's leading private art galleries, Starmach has a reputation for promoting contemporary artists and the exhibitions held here are well worth catching. The gallery occupies the restored red-brick building of the Zucker Synagogue, opened in 1881 and abandoned in World War II.

7

Cricoteka

G8 Ulica Nadwiślańska 2-4 11am-7pm Tue-Sun 3, 18, 19, 24, 52 cricoteka.pl

The Centre for Documentation of the Art of Tadeusz Kantor Cricoteka – often referred to simply as Cricoteka – is dedicated to the work of Tadeusz Kantor, the artist and theatre director who founded the famed Cricot 2 theatre in 1955.

Stage props, costumes and a video archive of classic Cricot 2 performances are some of the undoubted highlights of the museum. There's also an ever-changing array of events and workshops on offer. Plus, the building – a striking structure made from rusted metal and mirrors that hovers on stilts above a 19th-century electricity plant – is an attraction in itself.

TADEUSZ KANTOR

Much of Kraków's reputation as a city of the avant-garde comes from Tadeusz Kantor (1915–1990). Through Cricot 2, his experimental theatre company, he created drama that was subversive, socially profound and hysterically funny. His performances often took place in semi-official spaces such as art galleries, which only added to their legendary nature. Kantor's tours abroad turned contemporary Polish theatre into an international brand. He also reawakened interest in Witkacy, the Polish cultural maverick of the interwar years whose dramas enjoy cult status today.

→ The striking mirrored exterior of the Cricoteka

8

Płaszów Concentration Camp
Płaszów obóz koncentracyjny

⊠ K12 ⬛ Jerozolimska
🚋 3, 6, 11, 13, 23, 24
🌐 muzeumkrakowa.pl

Two kilometres (1.25 miles) southeast of Ghetto Heroes Square (p138), an area of untended open parkland marks the spot of this concentration camp, today part of the Historical Museum of the City of Kraków.

Many of Kraków's Jews were subjected to forced labour here in 1942–4; it also became the site of mass executions. Unlike other Holocaust sites, there are few memorials or markings for visitors. However, it is a deeply evocative site suited to quiet contemplation.

> 🔍 HIDDEN GEM
> **Liban Quarry**
>
> The abandoned Liban Quarry on the south side of Lasota hill stood in for Płaszów Concentration Camp in the film *Schindler's List*. Parts of the set are still visible in wild undergrowth beside cliffs.

↑ A memorial sculpture found at Płaszów Concentration Camp

→ One of the fascinating exhibits found in the Podgórze Museum

9

Podgórze Museum
Muzeum Podgórze

⊠ J10 ⬛ Powstanców Wielkopolskich 1 🚌 107, 127, 143, 158, 243, 643
🚋 24 🕐 9.30am-5pm Tue-Sun 🚫 Mon & every second Wed of the month
🌐 muzeumkrakowa.pl

This compelling museum chronologically traces the history of the Podgórze area over the centuries, with a particular emphasis on social history.

Podgórze was little more than a village at the start of the 19th century, and its growth into a bustling industrial town (and subsequently a suburb of Kraków) was sudden and rapid. Swift urbanization provided Podgórze with a neighbourly working-class identity that made it markedly different from the rest of Kraków.

Exhibits in the museum include objects sourced from the local community, alongside compelling photographs and documents. There's an interesting interactive section and play area for children in the building's basement. There are also temporary themed exhibitions focusing on specific aspects of Podgórze life.

10

Old Podgórze Cemetery
Stary Cmentarz Podgórski

⊠ J10 ⬛ Ulica Limanowskiego 🚋 24
🕐 April-Sep: 7am-8pm daily; Oct-Mar: 7am-6pm daily

Despite being much reduced in size due to 20th-century construction projects, this cemetery is a beautiful example of a 19th-century graveyard, with dignified monuments set among trees and shrubs. Many of the graves display sculptural details such as angels, Christ figures and urns. The grave of independence campaigner Edward Dembowski (1822-1846), shot by the Austrians while leading a protest march, is a popular focus of remembrance.

11

Church of St Benedict
Kościół św. Benedykta

⊠ H9 ⬛ Ulica Porucznika Antoniego Stawarza, Lasota Hill 🚋 3, 9, 24
🕐 Jul-Sept: 10am-1pm Sat

Located on a hilltop meadow, this church was probably founded by Benedictines from Tyniec in the 11th century. One of the smallest, oldest

> **Did You Know?**
>
> A scene from *Schindler's List* was filmed on Lasota Hill, site of the Church of St Benedict.

churches in Kraków, it has a steep shingle-clad roof and sloping buttressed walls, with a rustic appearance totally unlike any other church in the city. The high ground around Lasota Hill was associated with pagan worshipping rites (rites preserved in the springtime Rękawka Festival to this day), and it is thought that the church was possibly built here in order to ward any remaining pagans off.

 St Benedict Fort
Fort św. Benedykta

H10 **Ulica Porucznika Antoniego Stawarza, Lasota Hill** 69, 669 3, 9, 24 To the public

Standing on a ridge above the Krzemionka cliffs on the south side of Lasota Hill, this fort is a 16-sided red-brick tower that was built by the Austrians in 1856. It was just one part of a huge system of defences ringing the city, built in the hope that Kraków would look so impregnable that no invader would ever dare attack it. It is one of the finest surviving examples of the so-called "Maximilian" towers (named after defence chief Archduke Josef Maximilian d'Este), which were built across the Habsburg Empire during the mid-19th century. The fort is currently derelict, but makes for a hauntingly impressive sight.

 Krakus Mound
Kopiec Krakusa

H10 **Franciszka Maryewskiego** 3, 6, 11, 13, 23, 24

The southern limits of Podgórze area are marked by the grassy, man-made hill known as Krakus Mound.

Archaeologists believe it was raised in the 2nd–1st century BC for religious purposes, although popular folklore maintains that it is the burial mound of Kraków's legendary founder, King Krakus – no bones have been found in the mound, however.

Visitors can enjoy an excellent view over central Kraków from the summit. It is not a difficult climb, and a footpath leads to the top.

↑ Walking along the footpath that winds around Krakus Mound

WESOŁA, KLEPARZ AND BISKUPIE

Stretching north and east around the Old Town, Wesoła, Kleparz and Biskupie started out as separate villages in the early Middle Ages and gradually grew into larger towns. As there were no specific boundaries between them (and land ownership often changed), the settlements north and east of the city walls developed to constitute a complex urban mosaic. First mentioned in 1184, Kleparz (originally called Florencja after its Church of St Florian) was centred on a huge market; Wesoła and Biskupie, meanwhile, developed as privately owned towns. Due to their position outside the city walls, all three settlements were repeatedly burned and pillaged by invading armies, which is why little pre-18th-century architecture survives today. In 1791, in order to force merchants and craftmen living here to pay taxes, the City Council decided to incorporate these quarters into the city of Kraków. A construction boom during the 19th century covered all three areas with apartment blocks and offices. In 1847, a grand railway station was opened at the place where Wesoła and Kleparz bordered each other; as a result, many grand hotels were later built there.

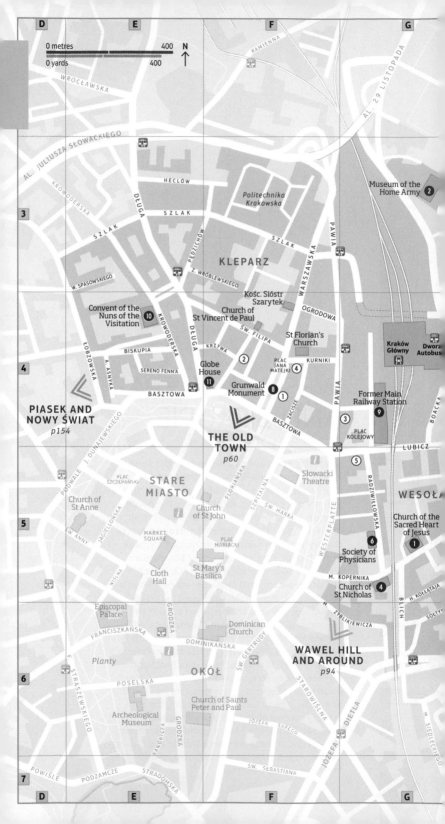

D **E** **F** **G**

0 metres 400
0 yards 400

N ↑

WROCŁAWSKA

AL. JULIUSZA SŁOWACKIEGO

1

KROWODERSKA

SZLAK

DŁUGA

HECŁÓW

SZLAK

Politechnika
Krakowska

KAMIENNA

AL. 29 LISTOPADA

Museum of the
Home Army **②**

2

SZLAK

W. SPASOWSKIEGO

PĘDZICHÓW

Z. WRÓBLEWSKIEGO

KLEPARZ

SZLAK

WARSZAWSKA

PAWIA

OGRODOWA

3

ŁOBZOWSKA

BISKUPIA

A. ASNYKA

KROWODERSKA

DŁUGA

KRZYWA

Convent of the
Nuns of the
Visitation **⑩**

Kośc. Sióstr
Szarytek

Church of
St Vincent de Paul

ŚW. FILIPA

St Florian's
Church

Kraków
Główny

Dwor
Autobus

4

SERENO FENN'A

BASZTOWA

Globe
House **⑪**

②

Grunwald
Monument **⑧ ①**

PLAC
JANA
MATEJKI **④**

KURNIKI

TARGIELE

BASZTOWA

PLAC
KOLEJOWY

PAWIA

Former Main
Railway Station **⑨**

LUBICZ

BOACKA

**PIASEK AND
NOWY ŚWIAT**
p154

**THE OLD
TOWN**
p60

5

PODWALE J. DUNAJEWSKIEGO

PLAC
SZCZEPAŃSKI

ŚW. ANNY

JAGIELLOŃSKA

Church of
St Anne

**STARE
MIASTO**

FLORIAŃSKA

SZPITALNA

ŚW. MARKA

Church
of St John

WISLNA

MARKET
SQUARE

PLAC
MARIACKI

Cloth
Hall

St Mary's
Basilica

Słowacki
Theatre

WESTERPLATTE

RADZIWIŁŁOWSKA

⑤

Society of
Physicians **⑥**

M. KOPERNIKA

Church of
St Nicholas **④**

WESOŁA

Church of the
Sacred Heart
of Jesus **①**

6

F. STRASZEWSKIEGO

Planty

Episcopal
Palace

FRANCISZKAŃSKA

GRODZKA

Dominican
Church

DOMINIKAŃSKA

ŚW. GERTRUDY

M. ŻYBLIKIEWICZA

BLICH

H. KOŁŁĄTAJA

SOŁTY

**WAWEL HILL
AND AROUND**
p94

7

POWIŚLE

PODZAMCZE

PODZAMCZE

POSELSKA

Archeological
Museum

KANONICZA

GRODZKA

Church of Saints
Peter and Paul

JÓZEFA

SAREGO

STAROWIŚLNA

ŚW. SEBASTIANA

JÓZEFA

DIETLA

H. SIEDLECKIEGO

STRADOMSKA

D **E** **F** **G**

WESOŁA, KLEPARZ AND BISKUPIE

Must Sees

1. Church of the Sacred Heart of Jesus
2. Museum of the Home Army

Experience More

3. Jagiellonian University Botanical Gardens
4. Church of St Nicholas
5. Monastery of the Discalced Carmelite Nuns
6. Society of Physicians
7. Church of the Immaculate Conception of the Virgin Mary
8. Grunwald Monument
9. Former Main Railway Station
10. Convent of the Nuns of the Visitation
11. Globe House

Eat

1. Glonojad
2. Stary Kleparz

Stay

3. Vienna House Andel's Cracow
4. Red Brick Apartments
5. Hotel Europejski

Rakowicki Cemetery

ARSZAWSKIE

Akademia Ekonomiczna

RONDO MOGILSKIE

Monastery of the Discalced Carmelite Nuns 5

Astronomical Observatory

Church of the Immaculate Conception of the Virgin Mary 7

Jagiellonian University Botanical Gardens 3

GRZEGÓRZECKA

AZIMIERZ p118

WESOŁA, KLEPARZ AND BISKUPIE

❶ CHURCH OF THE SACRED HEART OF JESUS

KOŚCIÓŁ NAJŚWIĘTSZEGO SERCA PANA JEZUSA

**📍 G5 🏛 Ulica Kopernika 26 🚋 3, 10, 20, 24, 52
📞 12 629 33 00 🕐 9:30am–noon daily**

A beguiling blend of styles, from Romanesque to Modernist, the Church of the Sacred Heart of Jesus is an architectural gem. Its striking interior is decorated with magnificent wall paintings.

This monumental church, one of the largest in Kraków, was built in 1909–21 to designs by the architect Franciszek Mączyński. He applied a number of historic architectural styles, modifying and combining them in new ways to create one of Poland's most interesting ecclesiastical buildings. Highlights include the soaring 68-m- (223-ft-) high tower and the exquisite interior. The latter was decorated by leading artists, including the sculptor Xawery Dunikowski, who designed the imposing south portal facing Kopernika Street, and the painter Jan Bukowski, who adorned the walls of the church with murals of striking beauty. Don't miss the mosaic above the high altar, by the artist Piotr Stachiewicz – this evocative work of art depicts Polish saints as well as Władysław II Jagiełło and Jadwiga, the first king and queen of the longstanding Jagiellonian dynasty.

The main entrance to the church is through the monumental south portal. Note the exquisite ornaments and figures which are all regarded as outstanding examples of Polish sculpture of the early 20th century.

Entrance

Illustration of the ↑ Church of the Sacred Heart of Jesus

FRANCISZEK MĄCZYŃSKI

Born in Wadowice in 1874, famed Polish architect Franciszak Mączyński studied in Kraków, Paris and Vienna. He became known for working in the Polish Art Nouveau style and during the course of his career left a profound mark on the architecture of Kraków. Examples of his works are dotted across the city, including the Globe House *(p153)*, Palace of Art *(p84)* and Piłsudski Mound *(p176)*.

← The exterior of the church showing the south portal and impressive tower

↑ The colourful interior of the Church of the Sacred Heart of Jesus

The murals decorating the nave vaulting contribute to the rich and monumental character of the interior.

The confessionals were designed by Jan Bukowski in the style of the Baroque Revival and are freely decorated with ornaments.

1900

Franciszak Mączyński won an international architecture competition in this year.

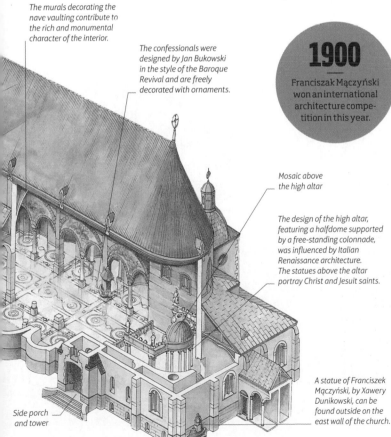

Mosaic above the high altar

The design of the high altar, featuring a halfdome supported by a free-standing colonnade, was influenced by Italian Renaissance architecture. The statues above the altar portray Christ and Jesuit saints.

Side porch and tower

A statue of Franciszek Mączyński, by Xawery Dunikowski, can be found outside on the east wall of the church.

❷

MUSEUM OF THE HOME ARMY
MUZEUM ARMII KRAJOWEJ

📍 G3 🏠 Ulica Wita Stwosza 12 🚌 105, 129, 179, 405, 501 🚊 3, 5, 17, 47
🕐 10am–5pm Mon–Fri, 11am–6pm Sun 🌐 muzeum-ak.pl

Housed within an imposing 19th-century red-brick command post, this compelling museum is devoted to the Home Army, Poland's underground resistance movement during World War II.

Opened in 2012, this multimedia museum chronicles the complex and fascinating story of the Home Army all the way from 1939 to 1945. The history of this often overlooked movement (which was actually one of the biggest resistence organizations in Europe) is movingly told with the aid of photos, weaponry and personal recollections. The museum also looks at what life was like for civilians and resistence fighters alike under both Nazi and Soviet occupation, with a particular emphasis on the beliefs and motivations of the Home Army soldiers.

Alongside the main exhibition, the museum hosts temporary exhibitions which focus on different aspects of World War II, such as the lives of those soliders who fought alongside Allied troops. Excellent guided tours are also available and the museum is free on Sundays.

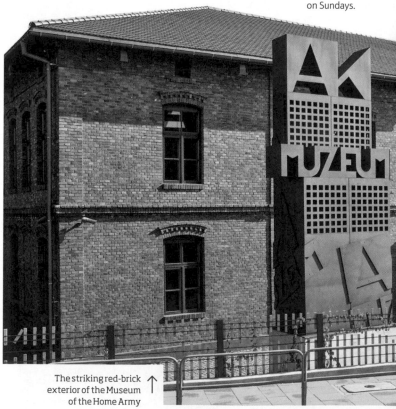

↑ The striking red-brick exterior of the Museum of the Home Army

1 An array of glass cabinets filled with different types of guns used during World War II

2 The spectacular glass roof of the atrium of the Museum of the Home Army, located within the centre of the museum.

3 A massive V2 rocket, one of the many exhibitions of World War II weaponry that is on show in the museum.

THE MUSEUM'S V2 ROCKET

One of the most striking things on display in the Museum of the Home Army is the crumpled remains of a V2 rocket, once tested by the Germans on Polish territory. These powerful weapons, developed by the Nazis, were the first long-range guided ballistic missiles ever built. The Germans began testing the rocket near Mielec in southeastern Poland in 1943. Polish intelligence observed the tests, and passed the information to the British, who were able to launch bombing raids on V2 production sites. The rocket was later recovered by Polish underground agents.

EXPERIENCE MORE

Did You Know?

The gardens of the Jagiellonian University are the oldest botanical gardens in Poland.

3

Jagiellonian University Botanical Gardens

Ogród botaniczny UJ

📍J5 🚪Ulica Kopernika 27a
🚍124, 125, 152, 182, 184, 192, 352, 424, 482, 501, 502
🚊2, 4, 5, 7, 9, 10, 14, 19, 20, 50, 52 ⏰Gardens: 9am-7pm daily; greenhouses: 10am-6pm Sat-Thu; Museum of Botanical Gardens: 10am-2pm Thu & Fri, 11am-3pm Sun ⏱Mid-Oct-mid-Apr
🌐ogrod.uj.edu.pl

The Botanical Gardens of the Jagiellonian University are located on the former grounds and lodge of the Czartoryskis, an important Polish noble family during the 18th century.

Established in 1780 by Jan Jaśkiewicz, a professor of natural history at the Jagiellonian University, the gardens were designed by the skillful Viennese gardener Franz Kaiser.

An impressive 500-year-old oak tree in the depths of the garden, as well as exotic and native plants, are particularly worth seeing. Also of interest are Late-Gothic pillars, originally from the Collegium Maius (p74), used here as plinths supporting plant pots.

Two of the gardens' palm houses are very interesting examples of 19th-century architectural structures. They are complemented by a third, 20th-century palm house which was built in 1964 to mark the sixth centenary of the Jagiellonian University. Busts of celebrated botanists decorate the gardens.

4

Church of St Nicholas

Kościół św. Mikołaja

📍G5 🚪Ulica Kopernika 9
🚊3, 10, 20, 24, 52
⏰During services only
🌐parafiamikolaj-krakow.pl

Recorded in the first half of the 13th century, this is one of the oldest churches in Kraków. Initally constructed in the Romanesque style, it was rebuilt in the Gothic style after it was burned down during the Swedish occupation in 1665. The present building is the result of a Baroque remodelling in 1677–82. It is still possible to see remnants of both the Romanesque and Gothic architecture inside the church, especially in the chancel. Furnishings were commissioned by the Academy of Kraków, whose patronage over this collegiate foundation goes back to 1465. A coat of arms of the academy decorates the backs of the stalls. The high altar, featuring an effigy of St Nicholas, was likely designed by the Italian architect Francesco Placidi.

One of the greenhouse at the Jagiellonian University Botanical Gardens ↑

The church also houses a Late-Gothic triptych, depicting the Coronation of the Virgin, and a Renaissance Madonna and Child with Saints Adalbert and Stanisław. A bronze font, from 1536, is another highlight.

In front of the church is a "lantern of the dead" (small towers indicating the position of a cemetery) which previously stood by a church in Kleparz.

↑ One of the stained glass windows found in the Society of Physicians building

Monastery of the Discalced Carmelite Nuns

Kościół Karmelitanek Bosych

📍H5 🏛Ulica Kopernika 44 🚌124, 152, 502 🚊2, 4, 7, 10, 14, 20, 52 🕐During services only 🌐karmelitankibose. krakow.pl

This large convent was built between 1720 and 1732. The church found inside the complex is small and has a Greek cross groundplan. The sumptuous façade is decorated in the Late-Baroque style. The interior, with its many columns, is impressive, as is the painting on the high altar is of Saint Theresa of Avila, to whom the church is dedicated.

Due to the strict rule of the order, the church is only open to the public during services.

Society of Physicians

Gmach Towarzystwa Lekarskiego

📍G5 🏛Ulica Radziwiłłowska 4 📞12 422 75 47 🚊3, 10, 20, 24, 52 🕐Oct-Jun: 4–8pm Wed

This building was constructed in 1904 for the Kraków Medical Society. The building's rather modest Neo-Classical exterior contrasts with its sumptuous interior, which was designed by the famous artist Stanisław Wyspiański (p49) in the Art Nouveau style. Many of the rooms within the building are decorated with naturalistic motifs, including flowers such as roses and geraniums. Wyspiański also designed the metal balusters and furniture, as well as the exquisite stained-glass windows that overlook the staircase. Entitled *Apollo, The Solar System*, the windows are a colourful representation of the solar system formulated by Copernicus (p75).

Church of the Immaculate Conception of the Virgin Mary

Kościół Niepokalanego Poczęcia

📍G5 🏛Ulica Kopernika 19 🚊2, 4, 7, 10, 14, 20, 52 🕐8am–4pm daily 🌐parafia-azory.pl

This church, also known as the Church of St Lazarus, was once used by novices of the order of the Discalced Carmelites. Built between 1634 and 1680, the rigidity of its Baroque architecture reflects the strict building regulations of the Carmelite order. Large and complex, the high altar dominates the small interior. Modelled on the high altar in the Carmelite Church of Santa Maria della Scala in Rome, it was made in 1681 of black marble sourced from the Dębnik quarry.

→

Grunwald Monument, standing in the middle of Jan Matejko Square

8

Grunwald Monument
Pomnik Grunwaldzki

 F4 Plac Jana Matejki
154, 192, 304 2, 4, 7, 13, 15, 20, 24, 52

This monument, featuring King Władysław Jagiełło on horseback, was raised to mark the 500th anniversary of the joint Polish and Lithuanian victory in 1410 at Grunwald (Tannenberg in German) over the Teutonic Knights. The statue was commissioned by the renowned statesman, composer and pianist, Ignacy Jan Paderewski.

The monument was inspired by the grandiose German monuments of the second half of the 19th century. It was generally quite well received but some critics mocked the theatrical treatment of the figures. Some even suggested that the only life-like figure was that of the dead Grand Master Ulrich von Jungingen. The monument was destroyed by the Nazis in 1939 during World War II, and was not reconstructed until 1975 by the sculptor Marian Konieczny.

Did You Know?

King Władysław Jagiełło was the founder of Poland's royal Jagiellonian dynasty.

9

Former Main Railway Station
Budynek dawnego dworca głównego

 G4 Plac Jana Nowaka Jeziorańskiego 3 2, 4, 7, 10, 14, 20, 24, 52

Between 1844 and 1847 a new station was built north of the city. It was soon considered to be one of the most elegant railway stations in Europe. Over the years it was remodelled several times. In 1898 Teodor Talowski, known for his eclectic architectural style, constructed a viaduct next to the station, in the Romanesque Revival style. Following the construction of Kraków Główny, the city's main transport hub, the building was no longer used as a station. Today it hosts a wide variety of large-scale events, including art installations. It is also home to **HistoryLand**, a quirky attraction that brings Kraków's history to life using lots of LEGO® figures and multimedia displays.

HistoryLand
 10am–6pm daily
historyland.pl

INSIDER TIP
Local Delicacies

The streets around the Former Main Railway Station are full of vendors selling popular snacks, including *obwarzanki* (hoop-shaped pretzels) and *oscypek* (smoked sheep's cheese from the Tatras).

 10

Convent of the Nuns of the Visitation
Kościół Wizytek

 E4 🏠 Ulica Krowoderska 16 🚊 2, 4, 7, 14, 24, 52 🕐 During services only 🌐 wizytki.pl

The convent was founded by Bishop Jan Małachowski as a votive offering after he was miraculously saved from drowning in the Vistula river.

Built from 1686 to 1695, the church found within the convent is an interesting example of Kraków's Baroque ecclesiastical architecture. Its graceful façade is richly decorated with a number of sculptures and ornaments. Some lavish decoration is also found within the interior which, although small, is very elegant.

The unusual high altar found inside the church was made in 1695 by the sculptor Jerzy Golonka. The 18th-century murals that can be seen decorating the vault have been much altered since their origination.

11

Globe House
Dom pod Globusem

 F4 🏠 Ulica Długa 1 🚌 124, 152, 304 🚊 2, 4, 7, 14, 24, 52 🕐 To the public

This house was built in 1904 to 1906 for the Chamber of Commerce and Industry. It was designed by the architects Franciszek Mączyński and Tadeusz Stryjeński. The building – an asymmetrical structure with a pyramidal tower topped by a globe – is considered to be one of the best examples of the Art Nouveau style in Polish architecture. The interior decoration, including murals in the great hall, is mainly the work of the famed artist Józef Mehoffer. Stained-glass windows above the stairs depict allegorical subjects such as the progress of mankind through industry and commerce, thus reflecting the function of the building. Today, the building houses publishers Wydawnictwo Literackie.

The striking Globe House, one of the city's best Art Nouveau buildings ↓

PIASEK AND NOWY ŚWIAT

West of the Old Town, Piasek ("Sand") and Nowy Świat ("New World") grew out of a complicated medieval patchwork of farming hamlets and royal hunting grounds. Their development was hindered over the years by frequent invasions and a lack of fortifications to prevent them.

Named after the sandy terrain surrounding the Carmelite Church, Piasek was originally known as Garbary ("Tanners") after the leather-workers that congregated here in the late Middle Ages. Nowy Świat, meanwhile, was named after the fact that it was seen as a new area of expansion for the growing city in the early 19th century. The demolition of Kraków's city walls in the 1830s opened up Piasek and Nowy Świat to a wave of urban development, leading to the construction of both aristocratic palaces and handsome apartment blocks. During the 1930s, the south west of Piasek became the focus of several prestige building projects, with the Jagiellonian Library, the National Museum, and the Academy of Mining and Metallurgy providing this part of the city with a bold modern face. Several more university departments were added after World War II and the whole area remains a bustling student hub.

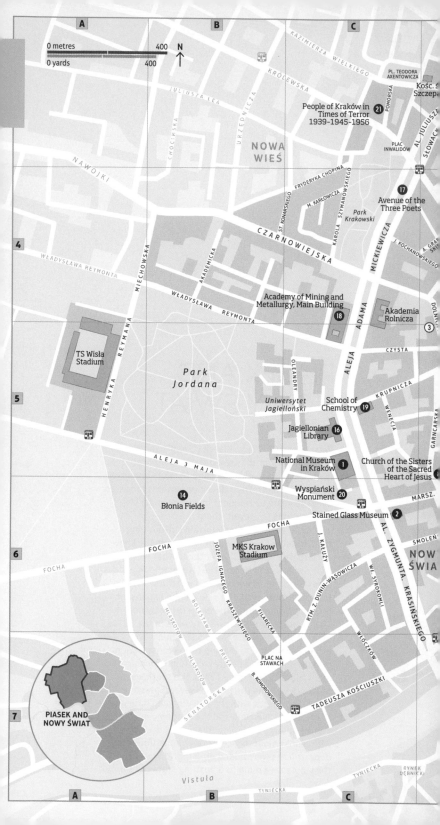

PIASEK AND NOWY ŚWIAT

PIASEK AND NOWY ŚWIAT

Must See
① National Museum in Kraków

Experience More
② Stained Glass Museum
③ Former Museum of Industry and Technology
④ Church of the Felician Nuns
⑤ Church of the Merciful God
⑥ Philharmonic Hall
⑦ Małopolska Garden of Arts
⑧ Church of the Sisters of the Sacred Heart of Jesus
⑨ Emeryk Hutten-Czapski Museum
⑩ Retoryka Street
⑪ Europeum
⑫ Capuchin Church
⑬ Józef Mehoffer House
⑭ Błonia Fields
⑮ The Józef Czapski Pavilion
⑯ Jagiellonian Library
⑰ Avenue of the Three Poets
⑱ Academy of Mining and Metallurgy, Main Building
⑲ School of Chemistry
⑳ Wyspiański Monument
㉑ People of Kraków in Times of Terror 1939-1945-1956
㉒ Spider House
㉓ Museum of Illusions
㉔ Carmelite Church

Eat
① Tektura
② Dynia Resto Bar

Drink
③ Tytano
④ Café Szafe

Shop
⑤ Massolit

Did You Know?

In World War II the museum building was used by the German military as a casino.

The colourful ↑
Ukrzesłowienie I by
Andrzej Wróblewski

NATIONAL MUSEUM IN KRAKÓW

MUZEUM NARODOWE W KRAKOWIE

📍C5 🏠 Aleja 3 Maja 1 🚌109, 144, 152, 164, 169, 173, 179, 194, 249, 292, 249, 304, 424, 502, 503 🚊20 🕐9am–5pm Tue–Fri, 10am–6pm Sat, 10am–4pm Sun 🌐mnk.pl

This monumental museum is the main building of the National Museum in Kraków. A vast treasure trove of incredible art and historic artifacts, it's best-known for its impressive collection of 20th- and 21st-century Polish art.

Housed in a vast modern building that took over 50 years to build, this museum is home to three permanent galleries. In the XX + XXI Gallery of Art, you'll find a spectacular collection of Polish works which date from the late 19th to the early 21st centuries. The gallery underwent an extensive three-year renovation between 2017 and 2020, and was expanded to include, amongst other items, a collection of applied arts. Highlights of the exhibition include works by the artists of the Młoda Polska ("Young Poland") movement (p49), including paintings by Józef Mehoffer (p166) and Stanisław Wyspiański (p49).

The museum also houses the Gallery of Decorative Arts, the largest collection of its kind in the country. Spanning the Middle Ages to the Art Nouveau period, items exhibited include ceramics, clothing and glassware; keep an eye out for the display of silk *kontusz* sashes dating from Poland's Sarmatian period. The Gallery Arms and Armour in Poland, meanwhile, explores the country's military history through 2,000 pieces of militaria. Alongside displays of armour and weaponry are items belonging to famous Polish commanders, including Józef Piłsudski (p56). The museum also hosts a number of excellent temporary exhibitions.

THE SARMATIAN PERIOD

Many of the historic costumes displayed in the National Museum date from the 17th century Sarmatist period, when Polish noblemen adopted Iranian-inspired styles of dress. Sarmatism was based on the idea that the Polish aristocracy was descended from the Sarmatians, an Iranian group who swept across Europe in the 1st century AD. Influenced by the idea that their ancestors came from the East, Polish noblemen adopted such things as scimitars, *kontusz* (long robes) and silk *kontusz* sashes, as well as hairstyles associated with their Near-Eastern neighbours.

→ Dressing up in armour at the Gallery of Arms and Armour in Poland, one of the museum's main exhibitions

↑ The striking exterior of the main building of the National Museum in Kraków

↑ Beautiful works on display in the Stained Glass Museum

EXPERIENCE MORE

Stained Glass Museum
Muzeum Witrażu

📍C6 📍Aleja Zygmunta Krasinskiego 🚌109,124, 144,164,169,179,194,304, 409,424,503 🚋20 🕐Only via guided tour: on the hour noon–5pm Tue–Sat 🌐muzeumwitrazu.pl

This fascinating museum is housed in the historic studio of Stanisław Gabriel Żeleński, one of Poland's most famous stained-glass artists. Opened in 1902, the studio was a meeting place for the foremost artists of the Młoda Polska ("Young Poland") movement (p49), including Stanisław Wyspiański (p49). Since its establishment, the studio has made countless stained-glass windows, over 200 of which decorate buildings across the city, including the Franciscan Church (p108).

Today, this still-working studio is also a museum dedicated to preserving this part of Kraków's cultural heritage. A one-hour tour of the building will teach you all about the processes involved in creating stained-glass. Along the way you'll see displays of stained-glass and examples of glass from throughout the ages. The tour also allows you to observe craftspeople at work.

Former Museum of Industry and Technology
Gmach dawnego Muzeum Techniczno - Przemysłowego

📍D6 📍Ulica Smoleńsk 9 🚋2, 8,13,18,20 🕐To the public

This museum was established in 1868 by Andrzej Baraniecki, who presented the city with both his library and large collection of decorative arts. The museum ran courses in fine art, as well as a school of painting for women. It also played an important role in the development of Polish applied art.

The building housing the museum was constructed in 1908–14. Famed Polish artist Józef Czajkowski designed the elegant façade, which is rich in geometrical forms. The structure of the building, which uses reinforced concrete, was considered novel at the time. It is a leading example of Modernist architecture in Poland.

The Museum of Industry and Technology was closed down in 1952 and today the Faculty of Industrial Design of the Academy of Fine Arts is housed here.

Church of the Felician Nuns
Kościół Felicjanek

📍D6 📍Ulica Smoleńsk 6 🚋2, 8,13,18,20 🕐8:30am–6pm daily 🌐felicjanki.pl

The church of the Felician Nuns is one of the largest churches built in Kraków in

---

💬 INSIDER TIP
Get Creative

Design your own colourful masterpiece at the Stained Glass Museum. Choose from creative two-hour classes to comprehensive two-day courses where you can learn about the whole process.

DRINK

Tytano
Hip eating and drinking venue. Its courtyard is packed with bars serving craft beers.

📍D5 📍Ulica Dolnych Młynów 10 🌐tytano.org

Café Szafe
Characterful café with retro furnishings, live music and stand-up comedy.

📍D6 📍Ulica Felicjanek 10 🌐cafeszafe.com

---

the 19th century. This basilica in the Romanesque Revival style was built between 1882 and 1884 to designs by Polish architect Feliks Księżarski, but was later modified by Sebastian Jaworzyński. The monumental and austere forms are striking, but softened inside through lavish decoration of the altars.

The church houses relics of Blessed Maria Angela Truszkowska, the foundress of the Order, who died in 1899.

5
Church of the Merciful God
Kościół Miłosierdzia Bożego

📍 D6 🏛 Ulica Bożego Miłosierdzia 1 ☎ 12 423 12 06 🚋 2, 8, 13, 18, 20 🕐 During services only

In 1555 Jan Żukowski established in Nowy Świat a home for the destitute and a small church. The church was consecrated in 1665. Located outside the city wall, both buildings were badly

damaged during a number of invasions, but the church has survived. On the outside wall facing Smoleńsk Street, remnants of a Gothic sepulchre, with a kneeling figure of a knight, can be seen.

Among the rather modest Baroque furnishings found inside the church, the one of most interest is the image of the *Misericordia Domini* (The Suffering Christ and Sorrowful Mary), found in the chancel.

Adjacent to the church is a presbytery, constructed in the Eclectic style in 1905–6 by Jan Zubrzycki, a Polish architect.

6
Philharmonic Hall
Filharmonia

📍 D6 🏛 Ulica Zwierzyniecka 1 🚋 1, 2, 6, 8, 13, 18, 20 🕐 For performances only 🌐 filharmonia.krakow.pl

Established in 1945, the Kraków Philharmoic was the

first philharmonic orchestra to be established in Poland following World War II.

Today one of the most respected and renowned musical institutions in the whole country, the orchestra and choir are beautifully complemented by the famed chamber orchestra, Capella Cracoviensis.

The Kraków Philharmonic is housed in what was once the home of the Catholic Cultural Institution. This building was erected in 1928–30 in the Neo-Classical style that was popular with many Polish architects at the time. Its design was inspired by the striking Maison du Peuple in Brussels.

The impressive façade ↑ of Kraków's renowned Philharmonic Hall

↑ The Małopolska Garden of Arts, housed in a strikingly contemporary building

❼
Małopolska Garden of Arts

Małopolski Ogród Sztuki

📍 D5 🏛 Ulica Rajska 12
🚌 114, 139, 152, 159, 164, 169, 192, 352 🚊 4, 8, 13, 14, 18, 24 🕐 9am–7pm daily
🌐 mos.art.pl

This multifunctional arts complex, known locally as MOS, features several exhibition spaces, a concert hall, a small cinema and an excellent café, all wrapped up in a contemporary building that consists of a slatted clay façade, glass frame, industrial beams and a garden courtyard.

Opened in 2012, MOS was built on and around buildings belonging to the Juliusz Słowacki Theatre. The semi-enclosed spaces at the front and side of the building are peaceful areas in which to sit and relax. There are always events or exhibitions taking place at MOS, and many of Kraków's biggest cultural festivals use the centre as their main venue.

❽
Church of the Sisters of the Sacred Heart of Jesus

Kościół Sercanek

📍 D5 🏛 Ulica Garncarska 24
🚊 15, 18 🕐 During services only 🌐 sercanki.org.pl/nabo-e-stwa.html

The Convent of the Sisters of the Sacred Heart of Jesus was built between 1895 and 1900. The architects designed the building along Garncarska Street so as to close one side of a square located here. They adjusted the façade of the church and the adjoining buildings of the convent to fit the slight bend in the street.

The church is eclectic in style. The exterior walls show bare brickwork, ornamented in the Romanesque Revival style, as well as pseudo-Renaissance *sgraffiti* and Neo-Classical sculptures. The furnishings display Neo-Romanesque forms.

❾
Emeryk Hutten-Czapski Museum

Muzeum im Emeryka Hutten-Czapskiego

📍 D6 🏛 Ulica Piłsudskiego 12 🚌 124, 152, 424, 502
🚊 1, 2, 6, 8, 13, 18, 20,
🕐 10am–4pm Tue–Fri & Sun, 10am–6pm Sat 🌐 mnk.pl

This small palace in the Renaissance Revival style was built in 1884 for Hubert Krasiński, a Polish nobleman.

A few years later it was purchased by Emeryk Hutten-Czapski, a Polish count and keen scholar, who owned an exquisite collection of coins, prints and manuscripts. A pavilion, built to house this collection, was added in 1896. The inscription decorating the pavilion reads *Monumentis Patriae naufragio ereptis* ("To the national heritage salvaged from destruction"). In 1903 the Czapskis left the palace and collection to the city.

 10

Retoryka Street
Ulica Retoryka

📍 D6 🚋 1, 2, 6, 20

This street is named after the Retoryka *jurydyka* (a settlement owned by nobles), which was established in this area by the Ossolińskis, a Polish noble family, in the 18th century. In the late 19th century the

 HIDDEN GEM
Under the Singing Frog

Designed by Talowski, this house on Retoryka Street is famed for the chequerboard and swirl patterns on its façade. It is named after the noisy frogs who lived in a river that flowed near here.

construction of boulevards began along the Rudawa river, which ran here (in 1910 the river was enclosed in a tunnel beneath street level). The boulevards were lined with houses whose architecture was marked by imaginative forms and unusual decoration – many are interesting examples of Polish architecture at the dawn of the modern age. The houses designed by Teodor Talowski, whose eclectic style blended together everything from Art Nouveau to Historicism, are the most interesting. He used pseudo-antiquarian, intentionally damaged motifs such as mosaics and plaques bearing popular Latin inscriptions for the external decoration. The plaque on his own house reads *festina lente* ("hasten slowly") and that on the house named Under the Donkey, *faber est suae quisque fortunae* ("one makes one's own destiny").

---

 11 ✍️

Europeum

📍 D5 📍 Plac Sikorskiego 6
🚌 124, 152, 134, 144, 164, 169, 173, 179, 194, 292
🚋 2, 4, 8, 13, 14, 18, 20, 24
🕐 10am-4pm Tue-Fri & Sun, 10am-6pm Sat 🌐 mnk.pl

The Europeum is part of the National Museum in Kraków (*p158*). Housed in a renovated 17th-century granary, it covers

↑ Fragments from the city's historic buildings found in the Europeum

seven centuries of art and is home to the city's most important collection of non-Polish European works of art. Notable exhibits include works by renowned artists Lorenzo Lotto, Pieter Brueghel the Younger and Paolo Veneziano. Other highlights include a dramatic 16th-century *Suicide of Lucrecia* by an unknown Dutch master and *Dormition of the Virgin Mary* by an anonymous German painter known as "The Master of the Study of the Robes". Followers of Polish history will appreciate the portrait of Izabela Czartoryska by Alexander Roslin and the dramatic *Death of Chopin* by Felix-Joseph Barrias. There is also an excellent sculpture collection and an intriguing assortment of masonry fragments from the city's historic buildings.

> **The boulevards were lined with houses whose architecture was marked by imaginative forms and unusual decoration**

←
House Under the Singing Frog, a former music school, Retoryka Street

The striking Małopolska Garden of Arts

Capuchin Church
Kościół Kapucynów

D5 **Ulica Loretańska 11**
124w, 152, 192, 502
2, 4, 8, 13, 14, 15, 18
**9:30am-4:30pm &
5-7pm daily** **krakow.
kapucyni.pl**

The Capuchin friars arrived
in Kraków in 1695. They began
constructing this church and
friary a year later. The church's
simple interior reflects the
strict rule of the Order which
espouses extreme poverty.
The altars, however, feature
some excellent paintings. They
include *The Annunciation* by
Pietro Dandini; *St Erasmus and
St Cajetan*, two 18th-century
effigies by Łukasz Orłowski;
and *St Francis of Assisi* by
Szymon Czechowicz.

A wooden crucifix in front
of the church indicates the
tomb of the Confederates of
Bar who fell in a rebellion
against the Russians in 1768.
Between 1712 and 1719 an
external Loreto Chapel was
built to a design by the Polish
architect Kacper Bażanka;
this is linked to the church
through a cloister. It houses
a Neo-Classical altar with a
miraculous statue of the
Madonna of Loreto and
a beautiful tabernacle, also
designed by Bażanka.

An impressive Christmas crib is
erected here every year, featuring a variety of historic
Polish characters.

Józef Mehoffer House
Dom Józefa Mehoffera

D5 **Ulica Krupnicza 26**
4, 8, 13, 14, 24 **10am-
4pm Tue-Fri & Sun; 10am-
6pm Sat** **mnk.pl**

This small museum, part of
the National Museum in
Kraków *(p158)*, is located
in the house where Józef
Mehoffer, the leading Art
Nouveau stained-glass artist,
lived from 1932 until his
death. He was one of the
foremost Modernist artists
in Poland. The interiors have
been preserved in the tasteful
way that they were arranged
by the artist himself, including
original chandeliers, wall hang-
ings and clocks. The house
also contains furnishings
made by Mehoffer, as well
as some of his artistic works,
including paintings such as
the captivating *Portrait of the
Artist's Wife*, plus stained glass
and murals. Interestingly,
the house was also the birth-
place of the artist and writer
Stanisław Wyspiański *(p49)*.

Located behind the house
is the excellent Meho Café.

Set amid peaceful gardens,
it serves up tasty food and
good coffee.

Błonia Fields
Błonia

B6 **114, 124, 134,
152, 164, 173, 179, 192,
292** **15, 18, 20, 24**

This area once formed part
of the grounds owned by the
Convent of Premonstratensian
(Norbertine) Nuns who lived
in Zwierzyniec; the area was
originally used as pastures.
In 1366 the nuns made quite
a bad deal with the city's
authorities and exchanged
the Błonia Fields for a house in
Floriańska Street. The house
proved to be unprofitable and
was eventually destroyed by
fire. This gave rise to a joke
about the nuns who had
exchanged pastures for a
bonfire. For centuries the
nuns tried in vain to regain
the land but to this day the
Błonia Fields remain the
property of the City of Kraków.

↑ The simple interior of the
18th-century Capuchin Church

↑ Exploring Kraków's vast and verdant Błonia Fields

Błonia was used in the past as a venue for mass religious and national celebrations: the first football match in Kraków took place here in 1894 and Pope John Paul II said a Holy Mass here on four occasions. Today it is a wildlife sanctuary in the centre of Kraków and a popular place for recreation.

15

The Józef Czapski Pavilion
Pawilon Józefa Czapskiego

📍D6 🏠 Ulica Piłsudskiego 12 🚋1, 2, 6, 8, 13, 18, 20 🚌124, 152, 424, 502 🕐10am–4pm Tue–Fri & Sun, 10am–6pm Sat 🌐mnk.pl

Set in an elegant cube-shaped building in the garden behind the Emeryk Hutten-Czapski Museum (p162), the Józef Czapski Pavilion celebrates the life of Emeryk's grandson Józef (1896–1993). An accomplished painter as well as an outstanding writer and patriotic activist, Józef Czapski was instrumental in uncovering the truth about the Katyń massacres, where 20,000 Polish officers were murdered by the Soviet secret police during World War II. He went into exile after World War II and became an influential member of the émigré cultural community built around the Paris-based monthly Kultura, an acclaimed literary and political journal.

The exhibition in the small pavilion displays the artist's paintings, personal diaries, unseen documents and photos, and uses archival film and interview footage to tell the story of this remarkable man, including his time in captivity during the Nazi occupation. Visitors can see a reconstruction of the painter's room from the house of the Literary Institute in Maison-Laffitte, one of the suburbs of the city of Paris. This is where he wrote and painted for almost 40 years from when he was exiled until he died in 1993. The room also includes many fascinating furnishings, as well as mementoes of this remarkable man's life.

JÓZEF CZAPSKI

One of the most compelling figures in modern Polish history, Czapski was both a man of culture and a man of action. He interrupted his painting studies to join the Polish army in 1920, and then re-enlisted again as a 43-year-old after the Nazi-Soviet invasion of Poland in 1939. Captured by the Soviets, he avoided the Katyń massacres by chance, and spent the rest of his life publicizing the truth about the killings. His lifelong faith in humanity came through in his vibrant paintings.

 16

Jagiellonian Library
Biblioteka Jagiellońska

Q C5 **A** Ulica Oleandry 3 **15, 18** **144, 164, 169, 173, 179, 194, 292, 503** **8:15am–8:50pm Mon–Fri, 9am–4pm Sat** **W** bj.uj.edu.pl

For many centuries the library of the Jagiellonian University was housed in the Collegium Maius (p74). This new building was constructed between 1931 and 1939 to designs by Wacław Krzyżanowski, a Polish architect during the interwar period. It has impressive modern forms and a spacious and functional interior. It is not only the success of the design but also the high quality of craftsmanship and the use of luxurious materials that make this building an outstanding example of Kraków's architecture in the interwar years.

Another wing of the library, was completed in 2001, when the university celebrated the sixth centenary of its re-establishment. The additional wing matches the forms of the old

building and is one of the most interesting examples of architecture from the 1990s.

Themed exhibitions of books and manuscripts are held in the lobby. The reading rooms are for members only.

 17

Avenue of the Three Poets
Aleje Trzech Wieszczów

Q C4 **144, 164, 169, 173, 179, 194, 292, 503**

In the mid-19th century an earthen embankment was constructed along what is today a pretty avenue, and in 1887 to 1888 a railway line was laid for trains connecting Kraków to Płaszów. East of the embankment, new streets were laid out and new houses constructed in the Eclectic and Art Nouveau styles. When in 1910 the borders of Kraków were extended, the railway and the embankment were dismantled. They were replaced by a wide avenue comprising a dual carriageway with a belt of greenery in the middle.

Did You Know?

Founded by Casimir the Great in 1364, the Jagiellonian University is the oldest in Poland.

Kraków's answer to the Champs Elysées, parts of the avenue were named after Romantic poets: Krasiński, Mickiewicz and Słowacki.

 18

Academy of Mining and Metallurgy, Main Building
Akademia Górniczo-Hutnicza w Krakowie

Q C4 **A** Aleja Mickiewicza 30 **12 617 30 43** **144, 164, 169, 173, 179, 194, 292, 503** **20** **8am–3pm Mon–Fri**

The Academy of Mines was established in Kraków in 1919, with the Faculty of Metallurgy

← The impressive building of the Jagiellonian University Library

then added in 1922. After 1945 the academy was transformed into a large and well-equipped technological university. It has its own nuclear reactor and modern acoustic laboratory.

The enormous main building, with 110,000 sq m (1,183,600 sq ft) of floor space, was built between 1923 and 1935. It was designed in a Neo-Classical style that is particularly prominent in the façade and portico. The statues of miners and steel workers in front of the building are by Jan Raszka, a Polish sculptor and painter. They symbolize one of the city's key industries.

In German-occupied Poland the building became the seat of the Governor-General. A museum housed in Building C-1 is dedicated to the history of the academy. It houses a large collection of souvenirs related to St Barbara and St Florian, the patrons of metallurgists.

 19

School of Chemistry
Zespół Szkół Chemicznych

🗺 C5 🏛 Ulica Krupnicza 44 🚌 114, 164, 169, 173, 179 🚫 To the public 🌐 zschkrakow.pl

In 1834 the Institute of Technology was established in Kraków, funded by the bequest of Szczepan Humbert, a French architect who was granted Polish citizenship. It was later transformed into the State School of Industry.

This irregular, imposing red-brick structure is decorated with several Art Nouveau ornaments.

> Kraków's answer to the Champs Elysées, parts of the avenue were named after Romantic poets: Krasiński, Mickiewicz and Słowacki.

The building now houses the School of Chemistry and so is not open to visitors.

 20

Wyspiański Monument
Pomnik S. Wyspiańskiego

🗺 C6 🏛 Aleja 3 Maja 🚌 144, 164, 173, 179, 503 🚊 20

This striking monument, found in front of the National Museum in Kraków (p158), was unveiled in 1982 to mark the 75th anniversary of the death of Stanisław Wyspiański (p49). Wyspiański was a central figure in the Młoda Polska ("Young Poland") movement, a cultural movement tied to Art Nouveau. The monument shows Wyspiański wearing a cape, which was typical of the Młoda Polska era, and surrounded by the characters from two of his plays, The Wedding and November Night.

↑ Monument dedicated to the famous Polish artist Stanislaw Wyspiański

 A display inside the People of Kraków in Times of Terror 1939-1945-1956

People of Kraków in Times of Terror 1939-1945-1956

Krakowianie wobec teroru

Q C3 **A** Ulica Pomorska 2
🚌 64, 664 🚃 4, 8, 13, 14, 24
🕐 10am-5.30pm Tue-Sun
🚫 Mon 🌐 muzeum krakowa.pl

It was in an elegant Art Deco building known as the Silesian House *(Dom Śląski)* that the German Gestapo had their main headquarters during World War II. The building is now a museum, also known as the Gestapo Museum, which is part of the Historical Museum of the City of Kraków. Its gripping displays are devoted both to the terror of the Nazi occupation and to the tyranny of the Stalinist regime that followed it. Original photographs, audio recordings and documents reveal in harrowing detail how Polish citizens suffered at the hands of both regimes. The exhibition also highlights the often heartbreaking stories of individuals who lived through this incredibly distressing and harrowing period of Polish history.

The detention cells that the Gestapo used to imprison, torture and murder local people, have been preserved in their original condition.

Found in the building's cellars, the walls of the cells are covered with writing carved by those once imprisoned here – a shocking reminder of the horrors inflicted under both the Nazi and Soviet regimes.

Spider House

Dom pod Pająkiem

Q D4 **A** Ulica Karmelicka 35 🚃 4, 8, 13, 14, 24
🚫 To the public

Named after the spider that decorates the top of the building's façade, this house was built in 1889 by Teodor Talowski *(p163)*, one of the leading architects in Kraków in the late 19th century. His intention was to give this irregular structure "an ancient appearance" by adding a "Gothic" round corner tower and a high gable in the style of Netherlandish Mannerism. By using different architectural styles of the past Talowski wanted to pretend that the house had been rebuilt many times. He inserted, for example, a parapet modelled on the Renaissance Cloth Hall *(p70)* into the crenellated "Gothic" frieze. The decoration is rich in inventive detail.

Museum of Illusions

Museum Iluzji

Q E6 **A** Straszewskiego 15
🚌 504 🚃 2, 8, 13, 18, 20
🕐 10am-8pm daily
🌐 krakil.pl

A relatively new addition to Kraków's museum scene, the Museum of Illusions is packed with examples of how different combinations of light, pattern and colour can play havoc with our visual senses. As well as looking at holograms and visual tricks, visitors can enter upside-down rooms and experience all manner of disorienting but fun environments. There's also a hands-on selection of

QUEEN JADWIGA (HEDWIG)

The youngest daughter of King Louis of Hungary and Poland, Jadwiga was Poland's first independently crowned queen. Reigning from 1384 to 1399, she turned out to be a formidable ruler. Her marriage to the Grand Duke of Lithuania, Władysław II Jagiełło, cemented an alliance between Poland and Lithuania that lasted 400 years. Jadwiga took an active role in statecraft and diplomacy, and was a major donor to Kraków's university. Famously devout, she was canonized in 1997.

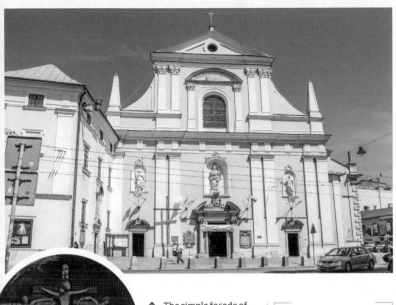

↑ The simple façade of the Carmelite Church and *(inset)* a calvary scene on its exterior

mind-bending puzzles, some of which can be purchased in the museum shop.

24

Carmelite Church
Kościół Karmelitów

Q D4 **A** Ulica Karmelicka 19 **🚌** 124, 169, 179 **🚋** 4, 8, 13, 14, 24 **🕐** 9:30am–4:30pm and 5–7pm daily **🌐** krakow.karmelici.pl

According to a legend, Duke Władysław Herman cured his skin disease by rubbing sand that he had taken from a site miraculously indicated by the Virgin Mary onto the infected areas. This site was therefore named *Piasek* (sand), and a votive church founded by the duke was built in 1087. Thus was born the legend of the Madonna of the Sand.

The church was actually founded by Queen Jadwiga in 1395. Legend tells that a mason who was employed in the construction of the church spoke to the queen about his poverty and inability to buy medicine for his wife. The queen is said to have removed a gold brooch from her shoe and given it to the man. A low cornerstone – which can be seen outside of the church – is said to bear her footprint.

The church built by Queen Jadwiga was almost entirely destroyed during the Swedish invasion in the 17th century and its remnants were incorporated into the new Baroque church which was consecrated in 1679. The magnificent high altar, made in 1698–99, is worth noting, as are the splendid stalls and the balcony with the organ. An icon of the Madonna of the Sand, painted directly on the wall, is much venerated.

In 1997, Pope John Paul II gave the church the title of a minor basilica.

EAT

Tektura
A specialist coffee shop that serves up aeropress and cold brews as well as espressos. Tektura also does delicious deli sandwiches and tortilla wraps. It's a great place for imaginative breakfasts.

Q D5 **A** Ulica Krupnicza 7

Dynia Resto Bar
This popular lunching and drinking spot offers a full range of café-bistro food, including soups, pasta dishes and outstanding cakes. It also has a relaxing walled garden.

Q D5 **A** Ulica Krupnicza 20 **📞** 12 430 0838

Experience

BEYOND THE CENTRE

A collection of scattered villages has long surrounded Kraków. Religious orders also founded abbeys here in the late Middle Ages, including the Benedictines at Tyniec and the Norbertine nuns in Zwierzyniec. These orders were major landowners and had access to the vast hunting grounds of the Wolski Forest, found to the west of the city. In the early 19th century, a memorial mound dedicated to national hero Tadeusz Kościuszko was erected in the forest; it was followed in the 1930s by another mound, this time in memory of independence leader Józef Piłsudski. After World War II, many of the area's villages were absobed into the large housing estates being built around the city, in part due to a rising population. Most famous of these was Nowa Huta, constructed in the 1950s as a planned Communist housing estate. This district was conceived as a working-class suburb whose population would be loyal to Communism, but it in fact became a centre of opposition to the regime.

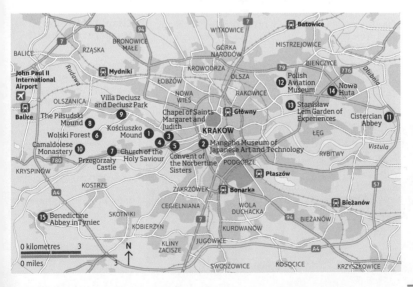

EXPERIENCE

1

Kościuszko Mound
Kopiec Kościuszki

📍 Aleja Waszyngtona 1
🚌 1, 2 🕐 Hours vary, check
website for details
🌐 kopieckosciuszki.pl

The Kościuszko Mound is
undoubtedly the most famous
of several memorial mounds
dotted across Kraków. It was
erected in 1820-23 in honour
of the leader of the 1794
insurrection against the
Tsarist Empire, Tadeusz
Kościuszko. He launched a
national uprising against the
Russians, and defeated them
with a makeshift army at the
Battle of Racławice in 1794.
Ultimately losing out to superior forces, Kościuszko tried to
interest Napoleon in the
Polish cause, before dying in
exile in Switzerland. At 34-m
(112-ft) high, the mound can
be climbed by a spiral pathway.
The views across Kraków from
the summit are breathtaking.

The red-brick fort at the
bottom of the mound was
built by the Austrians in the
1850s as part of the city walls.
The entrance fee includes entry
to the mound, fort and Chapel
of the Blessed Bronisława,
found at the base of the

 GREAT VIEW
Tea with a View

For epic views of Wawel
Castle looming over the
Vistula, head to the
Manggha Museum's
café. As well as the view,
you can enjoy an invi-
ting menu of leaf teas
and Japanese snacks.

mound – the church contains
an exhibit of objects related
to Kościuszko's life.

2

Manggha Museum of Japanese Art and Technology
Muzeum Sztuki i Techniki
Japońskiej Manggha

📍 Ulica Konopnickiej 26
🚌 124, 164, 169, 173, 179,
194, 304, 503 🚋 12, 18, 22,
52 🕐 10am-6pm Tue-Sun
🌐 manggha.pl

Occupying a contemporary
building, this museum was
opened in 1994 to exhibit
Japanese art and showcase
how it influenced Polish artists during the 19th century;
the museum also promotes

The Convent of the ↑
Norbertine Sisters
overlooking the Vistula

knowledge of Japanese culture.
It gets its name from Feliks
"Manggha" Jasieński, the
Kraków art critic and collector
who popularized Japanese
art in the city. His original
collection forms part of the
assortment of works on display,
which include paintings, drawings and watercolours.

3

Chapel of Saints Margaret and Judith
Kaplica św. Malgorzaty i św. Judyty

📍 Ulica Świętej Bronisławy
8 🚌 109, 409 🚋 1, 2 🕐 May-
Sept: 9am-1pm & 2-6pm
Thur-Sat; noon-5pm Sun

One of the most delightful
Baroque buildings in the city,
this wooden chapel is a single-
domed octagon emerging
from a grassy hillside. Inside is
a Late-Baroque altar brought
here from the nearby Church
of the Holy Saviour. Outside is

←

The famous Kościuszko
Mound, surrounded by a
red-brick fort

a monument to Pope John Paul II, who walked here frequently as a young priest.

❹
Church of the Holy Saviour

Kościół pw. Najświętszego Salwatora

📍 Ulica Świętej Bronisławy 9 🚋 1, 2 🚌 109, 409
🕐 During mass on Sun only
🌐 parafiasalwator.pl

Built on the site of a pagan temple, the Church of the Holy Saviour is one of the oldest in the city, and retains much of its Romanesque character. The presbytery of the church contains several fragments of 16th-century frescoes depicting Christ and the "Feeding of the 5,000".

Surrounding the church, there is a charming walled graveyard full of 19th-century tombstones as well as a 19th-century cottage that apparently belonged to the gravedigger. It is considered by many to be the most beautiful cemetery in the whole of the city.

❺
Convent of the Norbertine Sisters

Klasztor Sióstr Norbertanek

📍 Tadeusza Kościuszki 88
🚋 1, 2 🚌 109, 409
🕐 During services only
🌐 norbertanki.w.krakow.pl

Situated on a promontory overlooking the confluence of the Rudawa stream and the Vistula river, the Convent of the Norbertine Sisters was founded in the 12th century by Queen Agnieszka, wife of King Wladyslaw II. Destroyed by the Mongols in 1241 it was rebuilt and became a symbol of resistance to foreign invaders. Within the convent's high walls you'll find the Baroque Church of St Augustine and John the Baptist. It is entered through a Romanesque portal, which is the oldest surviving part of the building. The convent courtyard is the centre of the Emmaus festivities which take place every Easter Monday, with stalls selling sweets and wooden toys. The Lajkonik procession also starts here.

THE LAJKONIK

Every year, on the first Thursday after Corpus Christi, a parade led by the Lajkonik proceeds from the Convent of the Norbertine Sisters to the Main Market Square. The event commemorates a victory over the Tatars in 1287; after repelling the invaders, one of the Polish victors put on Tatar clothes and paraded around the city. Today, the Lajkonik taps spectators with his "mace" to bring good luck.

6

Wolski Forest
Las Wolski

Ulica Lesna 🚌134

Wolski Forest is a vast area of verdant woodland that stretches across the hills in Kraków's western suburbs. The forest is criss-crossed with paths – many of which are suited to mountain biking, hiking, horse riding and even cross-country skiing – making it the perfect destination for a day out.

Consisting primarily of oak, beech and birch, this expansive forest provides a habitat for deer, foxes and badgers, among other wildlife. Buses travelling from central Kraków stop at the zoo in the centre of the forest, from where trails lead off in all directions. A walk through the forest can easily be combined with a visit to other nearby attractions such as the Piłsudski Mound, Przegorzały Castle or Decius Park.

7

Przegorzały Castle
Zamek Przegorzały

Ulica Jodłowa 13
🚌109, 209, 229, 239, 249

Occupying a wooded hill at the southern end of Wolski Forest, this Neo-Gothic castle was built in the 1920s as a

JÓZEF PIŁSUDSKI

The founder of modern Poland, Józef Piłsudski started out as an underground opponent of Tsarist autocracy. Thrust into the role of defending Polish independence after World War I, he defeated the Red Army at the Battle of Warsaw (1920) and secured the nation's borders. Although he never held the office of president, Piłsudski was virtual ruler of Poland from 1926 to 1935. Despite authoritarian tendencies he provided stability at a time of international turbulence.

family home by Adolf Szyszko-Bohusz, then chief of the Wawel restoration team.

Taken over by the Nazis in World War II, the castle was renamed Schloss Wartenberg, and served as a recreation centre for Luftwaffe officers. Up until 2018 it belonged to the European Studies Department of Jagiellonian University, but it is now home to the U Ziyada restaurant.

8

The Piłsudski Mound
Kopiec Piłsudskiego

Aleja Do Kopca 🚌134

Located on the northern fringes of Wolski Forest, the Piłsudski Mound was built in 1934-37 to serve as an independence monument. It was subsequently named after the statesman who did most to restore Poland's freedom in 1918, Józef Piłsudski.

It has proved remarkably resilient over the years: the

Nazis tried to flatten it but gave up; the Communist authorities ignored it and planted trees to obscure the view; and the torrential rains of 1997 threatened to bring it down. Restored in 2002, this 35-m- (115-ft-) high mound has a viewpoint at the summit – it is the highest point in the Wolski Forest and offers truly excellent views over the surrounding landscape.

9

Villa Deciusz and Deciusz Park
Willa Deciusza i Park Deciusza

Ulica Krolowej Jadwigi
🚌102, 152, 292 🕐Park: 24 hours daily; Villa: closed to the public

Surrounded by a landscaped park, the Villa Decius was built by court secretary Jost Ludvik Dietz (or "Decius" in Latin) in 1535. Both park and villa were remodelled in the 19th century, when the villa

The Camaldolese Monastery and *(inset)* one of the paintings decorating its interior

HIDDEN GEM
Outdoor Gallery

Standing in the middle of Deciusz Park is the domed form of a former outdoor concert shell, now used as an unusual gallery dedicated to prolific local sculptor Bronisław Chromy (1925–2017).

was given its current Neo-Renaissance form. After serving as Nazi police headquarters during World War II and a boarding school in the years that followed, the villa was restored in 1996 and now houses a restaurant and a concert hall.

The park, which features colourful flowerbeds, expansive lawns and ancient hornbeam and lime trees, is the perfect place for a peaceful stroll. It's also home to a charming café.

← Looking over Wolski Forest from Piłsudski Mound

⑩

Camaldolese Monastery
Klasztor Kamedułów

⌂ Aleja Konarowa 1
🚌 109, 209, 229, 239
🕐 Hours vary, check website for details
🌐 kameduli.info

A walled compound on the southern edge of Wolski Forest, this monastery was founded by Crown Marshal Mikolaj Wolski in 1604. Members of the this strict order are only allowed a certain amount of human contact and conversation each day – hence the monastery's limited opening hours. The compound is home to a twin-towered, Late-Baroque church, and has an imposing façade featuring slabs of different coloured stone. Inside, lavishly decorated chapels feature delicate stuccowork. The church crypt contains cupboard-like niches in which the bones of deceased monks are kept. Note that the compound is usually open only to men, although women can visit on certain days throughout the year (see the website for more information).

EAT

U Ziyada
Serves delicious international cuisine with a focus on Kurdish and traditional Polish dishes. Amazing views from the terrace.

⌂ Ulica Jodłowa 13
🌐 uziyada.pl

ⓩ ⓩ ⓩ

⑪ Cistercian Abbey

📍 Ulica Klasztorna 11, Mogiła; 7 km (4 miles) E of Kraków 🚎 123, 153, 163 🚊 15 🕐 6am-7pm daily 🌐 mogila.cystersi.pl

The Cistercians were brought to Poland in 1222, or 1225, by Iwo Odrowąż, the Bishop of Kraków. The new monastery, around which a village grew up, was named *Clara Tumba* ("Bright Tomb" or "*Jasna Mogiła*" in Polish) because of its proximity to the reputed burial place of the legendary princess Wanda. According to the best-known version of the tale, Wanda was betrothed to a German prince, but refused to marry him. The offended prince attacked Polish lands in retalitation, but troops under Wanda's command repelled them. However, following the battle the princess threw herself into the Vistula as a sacrifice for the victory.

Found within the abbey, the Romanesque Cistercian Church followed the strict building regulations of the Cistercian order. The chancel ended with a flat perpendicular wall, and pairs of chapels with a square ground-plan were added to the transept. The church was destroyed by fire in 1447 and during its rebuilding Gothic forms were introduced. In the 16th century, the interior was decorated with Renaissance-style murals, which were later complemented by 18th-century furnishings. The Baroque façade was added as late as 1779–80.

The Gothic cloister built during the time of Kazimierz the Great is the most beautiful part of the abbey. It leads to the Chapter House, which features a series of 19th-century murals illustrating scenes from Wanda's life.

Not far from the abbey is the Church of St Bartholomew. Built in 1466, it is one of the oldest timber churches in all of Poland.

↑ A German plane from 1918 on display at the Polish Aviation Museum

⑫
Polish Aviation Museum
Muzeum Lotnictwa Polskiego

📍 Aleja Jana Pawła II 39 🚎 502 🚊 4, 5, 9, 10, 52 🕐 9am-5pm Tue-Sun 🌐 muzeumlotnictwa.pl

This museum is located on the historic Rakowice-Czyżyny airfield, one of the oldest military airfields in Europe (established in 1912) and the second largest in Poland prior to World War II. The museum features one of the best collections of early 20th-century aircraft. The collection consists of more than 200 aircraft, including pre-war Polish fighter planes, Spitfires, German Albatrosses and Soviet Kakaruzniks, plus 22 rare aeroplanes that were once part of the personal collection Hermann Göring, one of Nazi party's leaders. There are several displays in neighbouring hangars and a large open-air section.

Did You Know?

In 1978 Mirosław Hermaszewski became the first Pole in space.

⑬ Stanisław Lem Garden of Experiences
Ogród Doświadczeń im. Stanisława Łema

📍 Aleja Pokoju 68 🚎 64, 664 🚊 1, 4, 5, 9, 10, 14, 22, 52 🕐 Hours vary, check website for details 🌐 ogroddoswiadczen.pl

This park is filled with a wonderful wealth of hands-on installations that teach visitors all about the laws of science. Enormous prisms show how sunlight is refracted into different colours, wobbly shapes convey a sense of weight and balance, and musical chimes offer the chance to explore sound.

The garden is named after Stanisław Lem (1921-2006), the renowned Polish science-fiction writer famous for his novel *Solaris*.

⑭ Nowa Huta

📍 9 km (5.5 miles) W of Kraków 🚎 502 🚊 4, 10, 22 ℹ️ Osiedle Zgody 7; 12 354 27 14, 10am-7pm daily

Kraków was widely considered an anti-Communist town in the aftermath of World War II due to its patriotic, intellectual and clerical traditions. In order to change this, the Communist government undertook a programme of quick industrialization of the Kraków region to increase the working-class population. In 1948 a contract was signed between Poland and the Soviet Union for a steelworks. The construction of a new town for the workers of this steelworks, named Nowa Huta (New Steelworks), began in 1949. It was designed by Tadeusz Ptaszycki in the Socialist Realist style.

The housing estate, Centre, built between 1949 and 1955, is a bold exercise in urban planning. In this "model Communist town" there was no room for churches. However, after years of campaigning by the Nowa Huta people, the construction of churches finally began in the 1970s. Among these, the well-known Lord's Ark church is one of Poland's most outstanding examples of modern sacral architecture. The Maximilian Kolbe Church in Nowa Huta's Mistrzejowice district is another magnificent modern church.

During the period of Martial Law in Poland (1981–3), the workers residing in Nowa Huta clearly demonstrated that they were not the best allies of the Communists, and the town became famous for anti-regime protest.

💬 INSIDER TIP
Szkieletor

On the way to Nowa Huta you can't miss the tallest building in Kraków, the 102.5-m-(336-ft-) high Unity Tower. It was dubbed *"Szkieletor"* due to its skeletal appearance before it was finished.

Formerly known as the PRL Museum, the engaging **Nowa Huta Museum** is part of the Historical Museum of the City of Kraków. The museum is housed in the former Światowid cinema *(Kino Światowid)*, an impressive and imposing example of Socialist-Realist architecture constructed in 1957. The building can be found on a central alley known as the "Alley of Roses" *(Aleja Róż)* due to its many blooms. The museum hosts a number of themed exhibitions on the town's history, including fascinating exhibits about life for Nowa Huta's residents during the Communist period.

Nowa Huta Museum

 🄰 Osiedle Centrum E1
🕐 10am–5:30pm Tues–Sun
🌐 muzeumkrakowa.pl

15

Benedictine Abbey in Tyniec

🄰 Ulica Benedyktyńska 37; 10 km (6 miles) west of Kraków 🚌 112 🚃 12, 18, 22, 52 to Rondo Grunwaldzkie, then bus 🕐 9 May–Oct: 10am–6pm daily; Nov–Apr: 10am–4pm daily 🌐 tyniec. benedyktyni.pl

The picturesque Benedictine Abbey in Tyniec is situated on a rocky hill by the Vistula. The monks were brought to Kraków in 1044 and a Romanesque basilica was built here soon after. In the 12th and 13th centuries, when Poland was fragmented into principalities, the abbery was transformed into a fortress and played an important role during the struggles for the crown of the suzerain province of Kraków.

In the 15th century, the abbey's Romanesque church was replaced by a Gothic one; only a few architectural fragments of the original basilica have survived. Then at the end of the 16th century, due to the fact that the abbey was a strategic site that often came under attack, the fortifications were extended. The church was remodelled again in the 17th century in the Baroque style.

Tyniec's impressive Benedictine Abbey, overlooking the Vistula

A LONG WALK
ZWIERZYNIEC

Distance 2.5 km (1.6 miles) **Walking time** 40 minutes
Terrain Gently undulating, although with some rather
steep uphill sections, along paths and pavements
Nearest tram stop Salwator

This tranquil walk takes you through verdant Zwierzyniec, one
of Kraków's residential districts. In the 12th century, Zwierzyniec
was a small village, founded as the endowment to the Norbertine
nuns, whose convent was located by the Rudawa river, a tributary
of the Vistula. Over time, both royal gardens and the country
residences of the city's wealthy were established here. Despite
being incorporated into Kraków in the early 20th century,
Zwierzyniec has managed to retain its original village character.

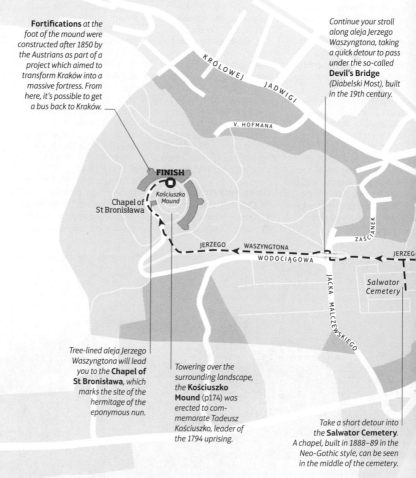

Fortifications *at the*
foot of the mound were
constructed after 1850 by
the Austrians as part of a
project which aimed to
transform Kraków into a
massive fortress. From
here, it's possible to get
a bus back to Kraków.

Continue your stroll
along aleja Jerzego
Waszyngtona, taking
a quick detour to pass
under the so-called
Devil's Bridge
(Diabelski Most), built
in the 19th century.

KRÓLOWEJ JADWIGI

V. HOFMANA

FINISH

Kościuszko
Mound

Chapel of
St Bronisława

ZAŚCIANEK

JERZEGO WASZYNGTONA JERZEG

WODOCIĄGOWA

JACKA MALCZEWSKIEGO

Salwator
Cemetery

Tree-lined aleja Jerzego
Waszyngtona will lead
you to the **Chapel of**
St Bronisława*, which*
marks the site of the
hermitage of the
eponymous nun.

Towering over the
surrounding landscape,
the **Kościuszko**
Mound *(p174) was*
erected to com-
memorate Tadeusz
Kościuszko, leader of
the 1794 uprising.

Take a short detour into
the **Salwator Cemetery***.*
A chapel, built in 1888–89 in the
Neo-Gothic style, can be seen
in the middle of the cemetery.

↑ The winding path leading upwards to the top of Kościuszko Mound

Locator Map
For more detail see p172

Zwierzyniec

BEYOND THE CENTRE

A **residential estate** *established in the early 20th century is located near the church. Its beautiful Art Nouveau architecture is definitely worth seeing.*

A little further uphill is the **Church of the Holy Saviour,** *surrounded by a charming walled graveyard.*

Begin your walk outside of the imposing **Convent of the Norbertine Sisters** *(p175). Pop into its church to admire the spectacular Neo-Classical decoration of the choir.*

| 0 metres | | 400 | N |
| 0 yards | | 400 | ↑ |

EMAUS

KRÓLOWEJ JADWIGI

ZYNGTONA

ŚW. BRONISŁAWY

Rudawa

Church of the Holy Saviour

START

SENATORSKA

Chapel of Saints Margaret and Judith

KSIĘCIA JÓZEFA

Vistula

Convent of the Norbertine Sisters

Leaving the church, go up the steep ulica Świętej Bronisławy. On your left is the Baroque **Chapel of Saints Margaret and Judith** *(p174), a delightful single-domed wooden chapel.*

→
The Baroque wooden Chapel of Saints Margaret and Judith

A LONG WALK
WOLSKI FOREST

Distance 8 km (5 miles) **Walking time** 2 hours
Terrain Undulating woodland paths that can get
muddy; in parts there are some steeper sections
Nearest bus stop Bielany Klasztor (nż)

Wolski Forest is the largest green area in Kraków. It has partly
retained its original character as a forest, while the remaining
ground is maintained as a park. Paths and lanes wind up and
down this hilly terrain, leading to many spots of outstanding
beauty, both natural and human-made. The lovely architecture
of the Camaldolese Monastery and Villa Deciusz and Deciusz
Park, both on the outskirts of the park, are worth exploring.
The walking route described below includes sights in both
the Wolski Forest and the surrounding neighbourhood.

*Follow aleja Do Kopca
(which translates as "Avenue
to the Mound") to reach the
Piłsudski Mound (p176).
Climb to the top to enjoy
epic views of the forest.*

↑ The leafy green and peaceful
   interior of Wolski Forest

*Leave the monastery by the same
route you arrived, turning right
once you get to aleja Wędrowników,
the main lane of Wolski Forest.*

*Turn right into
aleja Konarowa
and climb up the
Silver Mount.*

Piłsudski
Mound
AL. DO KOPCA

AL. DO KOPCA

Las Wolski

AL. WĘDROWNIKÓW

AL.
KONAROWA
Camaldolese
Monastery

AL. WĘDROWNIKÓW

KSIĘCIA

SKALNA

KRUCZA   JÓZEFA

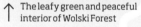 **START**

*Starting at the bus stop
found at the intersection of
aleja Wędrowników and ulica
Księcia Józefa, head down
aleja Wędrowników.*

*At the top of the hill
is the **Camaldolese
Monastery** (p177);
stop off to admire
its opulent chapels.*

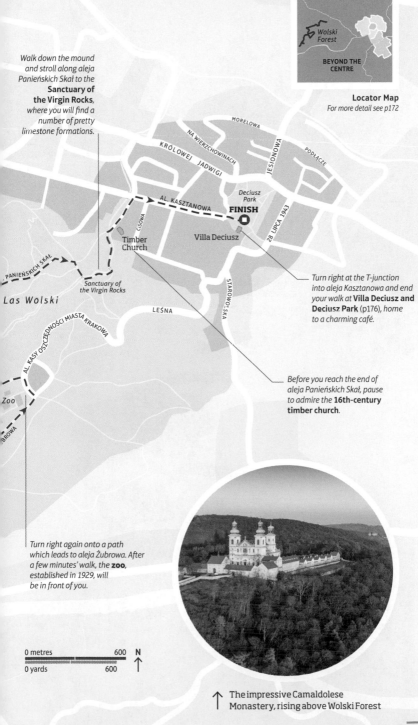

Walk down the mound and stroll along aleja Panieńskich Skał to the **Sanctuary of the Virgin Rocks**, where you will find a number of pretty limestone formations.

MORELOWA

NA WIERZCHOWINACH

KRÓLOWEJ JADWIGI

JESIONOWA

PODŁĄCZE

AL. KASZTANOWA

CISOWA

Deciusz Park

FINISH

28 LIPCA 1943

Timber Church

Villa Deciusz

PANIEŃSKICH SKAŁ

Sanctuary of the Virgin Rocks

Las Wolski

AL. KASY OSZCZĘDNOŚCI MIASTA KRAKOWA

LEŚNA

STAROWO-SKA

Zoo

ŻUBROWA

Turn right at the T-junction into aleja Kasztanowa and end your walk at **Villa Deciusz and Deciusz Park** (p176), home to a charming café.

Before you reach the end of aleja Panieńskich Skał, pause to admire the **16th-century timber church**.

Turn right again onto a path which leads to aleja Żubrowa. After a few minutes' walk, the **zoo**, established in 1929, will be in front of you.

| 0 metres | 600 | N |
| 0 yards | 600 | ↑ |

↑ The impressive Camaldolese Monastery, rising above Wolski Forest

DAYS OUT FROM KRAKÓW

Must Sees

1 Auschwitz-Birkenau Memorial and Museum

2 Wieliczka Salt Mine

3 Zakopane and Tatra National Park

Experience More

4 Ojców National Park

5 Niepołomice

6 Bochnia Salt Mine

7 Grodzisko

8 Kalwaria Zebrzydowska

9 Wadowice

10 Lanckorona

11 Pieskowa Skała Castle

The area around Kraków was the heartland of the Polish state from the 10th to the late 16th century, when the capital was moved to Warsaw. Not surprisingly, Kraków's environs are filled with the castles, palaces and churches built by noble families connected to the royal court. The area is also home to salt mines at Bochnia and Wieliczka – source of much of Kraków's medieval and Renaissance wealth – where cavernous chapels and galleries were laboriously carved by miners over centuries. The 19th century saw the development of the mountain villages of the Tatras, south of Kraków. Zakopane in particular was a source of artistic fascination for the Kraków intelligentsia. One site forever associated with Poland's fate during World War II is the Nazi concentration camp at Auschwitz–Birkenau; today it serves as a poignant and important reminder of the Holocaust.

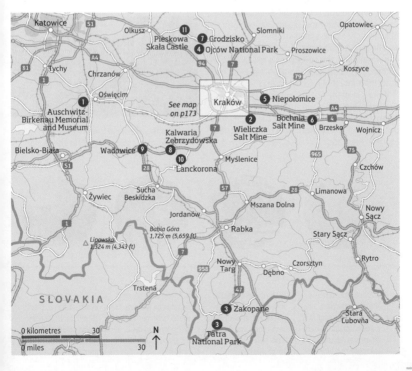

❶ ⊕ ⊛

AUSCHWITZ–BIRKENAU MEMORIAL AND MUSEUM

🏠 Oświęcim 🚌 From Kraków bus station 🕐 Hours vary, check website for details 🌐 auschwitz.org

Over a million people visit this site each year to pay their respects to the estimated 1.1 million people murdered here by the Nazis, most of whom were Jewish. The site consists of two camps: Auschwitz I, used to incarcerate Polish political prisoners, and Auschwitz II–Birkenau, the main site of Hitler's Final Solution – the extermination of European Jews. Today, the site is an important symbol of remembrance.

Auschwitz I

Auschwitz I opened in 1940 on the site of a former Polish army barracks. Originally built to incarcerate Polish political prisoners, its numbers were swelled by the arrival of Soviet prisoners of war, many of whom died of malnourishment, overwork or torture. Further buildings were added in the spring of 1941 as the number of prisoners continued to increase. From 1942 onwards, Auschwitz II–Birkenau (p188) was built to deal with the vast numbers of Jews brought to be murdered as part of the Nazis' Final Solution. While Birkenau was the main concentration and extermination camp, Auschwitz I was the administrative centre; it was here that the Nazis conducted sickening experiments on their prisoners and built the first gas chamber, using the pesticide Zyklon B as an instrument of mass murder.

When Germany's defeat seemed inevitable, the Nazis made hasty attempts to destroy the camps and thus the evidence of their activities, but much remains at both sites to bear witness to these most atrocious of crimes.

↑ A reconstruction of the wall near Block 11 used for summary executions

↑ A display showing the discarded shoes of people murdered at the camp

Timeline

1940
△ Oświęcim chosen as the site of the Nazis' new concentration camp; first mass transport of Polish citizens to Auschwitz takes place on June 14.

1942
△ The implementation of the Final Solution is agreed at the Wannsee Conference, and mass deportation to Auschwitz begins.

1944
△ As the Soviet Army closes in on the area, the SS begin destroying all evidence of the camp and its machinery of death.

1945
△ Most prisoners evacuated on a "Death March" on 18 January; Soviet soldiers liberate Auschwitz's remaining prisoners on 27 January.

VISITING THE CAMPS

The two camps are 3 km (2 miles) apart, on the western suburbs of the town of Oświęcim. Most of the displays telling the camp's history are at Auschwitz I; Birkenau is a large open site which involves a lot of walking. A free shuttle bus operates between the two. Crowds at Auschwitz are large and numbers are controlled; visitors are required to book a time-slot on the website before arrival.

"Work Sets You Free", the tragic message seen by prisoners entering the camp ↑

Auschwitz II-Birkenau

Birkenau was opened in March 1942 in the village of Brzezinka, where the residents were evicted to make way for it. The camp grew steadily to become the largest of all the camps in Nazi-occupied Europe, housing 90,000 prisoners by mid-1944.

While many other camps were built for slave labour, Birkenau was primarily a place for the extermination of Europe's Jewish population. It housed most of Auschwitz's machinery of mass murder, and the whole process was carried out systematically and on an enormous scale. In the six gas chambers in use at different stages of the camp's construction, over one million people were killed, 98 per cent of whom were Jewish. Victims included people from over 20 nations. The purpose of the remaining buildings on the site are now for remembrance.

> The camp grew steadily to become the largest of all the camps in Nazi-occupied Europe, housing 90,000 prisoners by mid-1944.

$\longrightarrow$
"Hell's Gate", the infamous entrance through which prisoners arrived by train

Memorial wall of photographs in the "sauna", where new arrivals were deloused and disinfected ↑

1 A pile of suitcases stolen from the prisoners comprises one of the museum's harrowing and moving exhibits.

2 The camp's primitive wooden barracks had lines of bunks inside, and were crammed with up to 600 prisoners at a time.

3 One of the ponds in the camp's surrounds, where tons of ash, the remains of so many victims, were dumped.

THE LIBERATION OF THE CAMPS

With the war all but lost, in mid-January 1945 the Nazi leaders gave the order for all the camps to be destroyed. So rapid was the collapse of the German army, however, that much of Birkenau remained intact. More than 56,000 inmates were evacuated by the Nazis and forced to march west; many died en route. When the Soviet army entered the camps on 27 January 1945, they found just 7,000 survivors.

WIELICZKA SALT MINE
KOPALNIA SOLI WIELICZKA

Ulica Daniłowicza 10, Wieliczka **Minibus from Kraków's Main Railway Station** **From Kraków's Main Railway Station and Kraków-Płaszów** **Apr–Oct: 7:30am–7:30pm daily; Nov–Mar: 8am–5pm daily** **1 Jan, Easter, 1 Nov, 24–25 & 31 Dec** **wieliczka-saltmine.com**

Hidden deep beneath the earth, the Wieliczka Salt Mine is a sparkling subterranean wonderland. This vast underground city, now a UNESCO World Heritage Site, was painstakingly sculpted by miners over centuries.

Located southeast of Kraków, the Wieliczka Salt Mine was active as early as the 11th century; for years its salt was regarded as a major natural asset of the Kingdom of Poland.

Inside the mine is a sprawling network of underground galleries, tunnels, chambers and pits that have been carved into the rock salt. Huge underground chapels and altars, in front of which the miners prayed for God's protection against accidents, were formed from salt blocks, as were striking statues.

Visitors can descend to depths of 65–135 m (210–440 ft) and explore sections of the mines. Highlights include the Chapel of St Kinga, with altarpieces, chandeliers and sculptures made of salt, and the Saltworks Museum, which has exhibits illustrating old mining methods and the tools that were used.

 INSIDER TIP
Underground Concerts

The Wieliczka Salt Mine is an amazing place to catch a concert, with regular classical and jazz events taking place in the atmospheric Chapel of St Kinga and other underground halls.

Did You Know?

The mine extends to a staggering 287 km (178 miles) of underground tunnels.

← The extraordinary Chapel of St Kinga, carved out of the rock salt

← Several of the exquisite rock salt statues found within the Wieliczka Salt Mine, carved by the miners

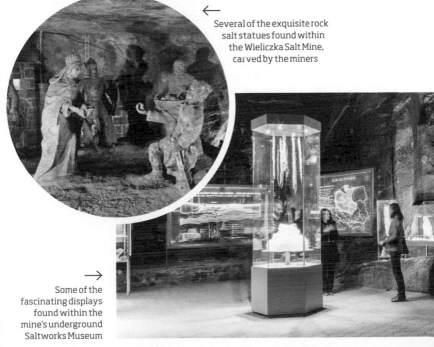

→ Some of the fascinating displays found within the mine's underground Saltworks Museum

 3

ZAKOPANE AND TATRA NATIONAL PARK

🏠 111 km (70 miles) S of Kraków 🚌🚂 ℹ️ Ulica Kościuszki 17; www.zakopane.pl

Lying on the boundary of Tatra National Park, Zakopane is one of Poland's most popular holiday destinations. This attractive town has long been regarded as the country's winter capital, on a par with alpine resorts as an upmarket winter sports and leisure centre. Its surrounding mountains are equally popular with summer visitors, lured by the network of hiking trails and the breathtaking scenery surrounding Mount Kasprowy Wierch and Morskie Oko lake.

① Gubalówka Funicular to Gubalówka Hill

Rising above Zakopane to the north, the green ridge of Gubalówka Hill is famous for its superb views of the Tatra peaks. A funicular railway runs up the hill from just behind Zakopane's central market, a ride that takes around three minutes. At the top of the hill there are plenty of marked trails offering easy walking, and a dry toboggan run that's popular with children.

② Willa Oksza Gallery of 20th-Century Art

🏠 Ulica Zamoyskiego 25
🕐 10am–6pm Tue–Sat, 11am–4pm Sun 🌐 muzeum tatrzanskie.pl

One of the most beautiful houses designed by artist and architect Stanisław Witkiewicz, creator of the "Zakopane Style" of architecture, is the Willa Oksza. Built in 1895, it now serves as a gallery devoted to 20th-century art. Zakopane was a popular resort among Polish artists, especially before World War I when the town was a ferment of creativity.

③ The Szymanowski Museum

🏠 Ulica Kaprusie 8
🕐 10am–5pm Tue–Sun
🌐 mnk.pl

From the 1930s until his death, Polish composer Karol Szymanowski (1882–1937)

Visitors strolling through the picturesque town centre of Zakopane

spent most of the year in the idyllic wooden house known as the Willa Atma. The house is now a museum devoted to Szymanowski's life and works, with period furnishings and personal effects mingling with touchscreen computers and multimedia displays. The exhibition devotes particular attention to *Harnasie* (1935), a ballet inspired by folk tales of Tatra mountain brigands.

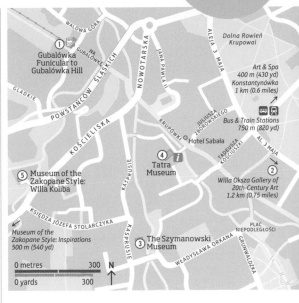

Gubalówka Funicular to Gubalówka Hill

Dolna Rowień Krupowai

Art & Spa 400 m (430 yd)
Konstantynówka 1 km (0.6 miles)

Bus & Train Stations 750 m (820 yd)

Hotel Sabała

④ Tatra Museum

⑤ Museum of the Zakopane Style: Willa Koliba

Willa Oksza Gallery of 20th-Century Art 1.2 km (0.75 miles)

Museum of the Zakopane Style: Inspirations 500 m (540 yd)

③ The Szymanowski Museum

PLAC NIEPODLEGŁOŚCI

| 0 metres | 300 |
| 0 yards | 300 |

N

④

Tatra Museum

🏠 Ulica Krupówki 10
🕐 10am–5pm Tue–Sat, 9am–3pm Sun 🌐 muzeum tatrzanskie.pl

The Tatra Museum (Muzeum Tatranskie) eloquently tells the story of how Zakopane came to occupy a central place in Polish culture. Photographs and mementos recall how the town was "discovered" by 19th-century Polish doctors, who concluded that the fresh mountain air would make it the perfect health resort. This, combined with Zakopane's rustic character (traditional music and dress could still be heard and seen on the streets) drew city folk in droves, and a host of pensions and sanatoria were opened to cater for them. The town became a major meeting-point for Polish society, with cultural figures spending weeks or months here every year. The museum's exhibits, including recreations of traditional interiors, paint a vivid picture of what this time was like.

↑ Learning about the fascinating history of Zakopane in the Tatra Museum

⑤

Museum of the Zakopane Style: Willa Koliba

🏠 Ulica Kościeliska 18
🕐 9am–5pm Wed–Sat, 9am–3pm Sun 🌐 muzeum tatrzanskie.pl

Before World War I, a group of Polish architects led by Stanisław Witkiewicz developed a house-building style based on the traditional timber dwellings found in the region. The Willa Koliba, designed by Witkiewicz in 1892, is a key example of this "Zakopane Style". Inside are models and sketches of other structures built in the style, and a display of portraits by Witkiewicz's son Stanisław Ignacy Witkiewicz.

The related **Museum of the Zakopane Style: Inspirations** displays folk crafts from the region and reveals how they influenced modern furniture and interior design.

Museum of the Zakopane Style: Inspirations
🏠 Droga do Rojów 6
🕐 9am–5pm Wed–Sat, 9am–3pm Sun 🌐 muzeum tatrzanskie.pl

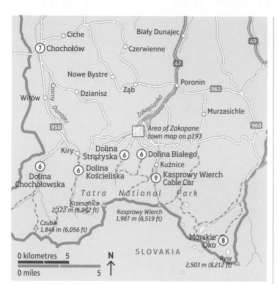

AROUND ZAKOPANE

⑥
The Mountain Valleys

The border of Tatra National Park lies on the southern outskirts of Zakopane. The massif is riven with scenic valleys (known as *doliny*), and it is here that some of the most popular hiking trails are to be found. Some of them are within walking distance of Zakopane; others are served by a regular minibus.

The closest valley to town is woody Dolina Białego; follow the trail along a stream. Running parallel to the west is the picturesque Dolina Strążyska, with a broad path passing the Siklawica Waterfall (Wodospad Siklawica). The path climbs up to the meadow of Hala Strążyska, which has superb views of the higher Tatra peaks. Combining this trail with the one through Dolina Białego makes for a good day-long circular walk.

Around 6 km (4 miles) west of Zakopane, Dolina Kościeliska is characterized by steep rocky sides pitted with caves. After about 4 km (3 miles) of gradual ascent, the path along the valley becomes steeper as it climbs towards the Hala Ornak mountain hut, which serves hot food and refreshments.

A further 2 km (1 mile) west of Dolina Kościeliska, Dolina

Chochołowska is arguably the most spectacular of the valleys, with steep sides darkened by dense pines. Nonetheless, the ascent is sufficiently gentle to ensure that it is a good family walking destination. The main target for hikers is the Polana Chochołowska mountain hut, which sits at 1,146 m (3,760 ft) and is just over 7 km (4 miles) from the valley entrance.

⑦
Chochołów

Along the main street of this 16th-century village stand traditional wooden cottages, the best examples of the region's highland architecture. The cottage at No 75 dates from 1889 and is open to the public. It houses the fascinating **Museum of the 1846 Chochołów Uprising**, which tells the story of this revolt against Austrian rule.

Chochołów has a local custom that involves cleaning the walls of the building once a year until they are white.

Museum of the 1846 Chochołów Uprising
Ⓢ ⌂ Chochołów 75
🕐 10am–2pm Wed–Sun
Ⓦ muzeumtatrzanskie.pl

→
Walking along paths atop Kasprowy Wierch, a mountain in Tatra National Park

> Surrounded by stark grey peaks, the high-altitude Morskie Oko ("Eye of the Sea") is the largest lake in Tatra National Park.

⑧ Morskie Oko

Surrounded by stark grey peaks, the high-altitude Morskie Oko ("Eye of the Sea") is the largest lake in Tatra National Park, and its most visited attraction for its spectacular beauty. It lies at the end of a 9-km (6-mile) paved trail from Polana Palenica, around 15 km (9 miles) east of Zakopane. Horse-drawn carts are available to take visitors up the scenic, forest-shrouded trail, although most people choose to walk. There is a hut serving refreshments beside the lake, and a choice of trails leading round the shore and up into the mountains.

Did You Know?

According to legend, an underground passage once connected Morskie Oko to the sea.

⑨ Kasprowy Wierch Cable Car

⏰ Hours vary, check website 🌐 pkl.pl

The settlement of Kuźnice, 3 km (2 miles) south of Zakopane, is the start of the cable-car ride to Kasprowy Wierch, the highest of the mountains in Zakopane's immediate vicinity at 1,987 m (6,519 ft). The ascent takes about 15 minutes and offers superb views – however, it's a very popular ride so it is advisable to buy tickets in advance from one of the automatic machines in central Zakopane. The summit boasts a stunning panorama of the ridges that make up the central part of the Tatra chain. From here you can walk back to Zakopane via the Hala Gąsienicowa meadow. Experienced walkers can use Kasprowy Wierch as the starting point for a number of high-altitude hikes, either westwards to Mount Giewont or east towards the challenging terrain of Orła Perć.

STAY

Art & Spa
Roomy doubles and apartments in an elegant mansion.

🏠 Ulica Kościuszki 18, Zakopane
🌐 artandspa.pl

Hotel Sabała
Comfortable rooms and a restaurant offering traditional Polish dishes, located in the heart of the town.

🏠 Ulica Krupówki 11, Zakopane
🌐 sabala.zakopane.pl

Konstantynówka
A lovely Zakopane-style building, offering spectacular hillside forest views.

🏠 Ulica Jagiellońska 18, Zakopane 📞 18 533 0363

Sunset over the majestic Tatra mountains

EXPERIENCE MORE

 4

Ojców National Park

📍 24 km (15 miles) NW of Kraków 🚌 From Kraków's main coach station 🌐 ojcow.pl

Poland's smallest national park, Ojców was established in 1956. The landscape here is characterized by a deep sandstone gorge eroded by the Prądnik river, steep cliffs overgrown with trees and stunning rock formations, including the 25-m- (82-ft-) high Hercules' Club.

A small village, also called Ojców, is the park's main entry point. It is home to the ruins of a castle built by Kazimierz the Great; its 14th-century tower has been renovated and now houses a small exhibition dedicated to the castle's history. In the **Museum of Ojcowskiego National Park** there are exhibits on the area's geology, flora and fauna.

Museum of Ojcowskiego National Park

📍 Ulica Ojcow 26 🕐 Mar–Nov: 9am–4:30pm; Dec–Apr: 8am–2:45pm 🌐 ojcowskipark narodowy.pl

 5

Niepołomice

📍 24 km (15 miles) SE of Kraków 🚌 Minibus from Ulica Worcella opposite Galeria Krakowska

The royal grounds in Niepołomice, situated on the outskirts of a vast woodland, were much favoured by Polish kings, who came here to rest and hunt. In the 14th century King Kazimierz the Great built a hunting lodge here. It was transformed by King Zygmunt August into the magnificent **Niepołomice Castle**, constructed between 1550 and 1571. Over the years a town grew up around it. The castle's regular plan and the central, square courtyard differ from other royal Renaissance houses in Poland. In 1637 massive stone arcades were added to the courtyard, helping to give it the nickname the second Wawel. Part of the castle is used to house the Niepołomice Museum, which showcases the history of this royal residence and also contains exhibits on painting and hunting. Another section of the castle houses the Hotel Zamek Królewski.

The town is also home to the **Church of Ten Thousand Martyrs**, also founded by King

---

 HIDDEN GEM
Łokietek Cave

One of the Ojców National Park's most impressive features is the 300-m- (984-ft-) long Łokietek Cave. It gets its name from Władysław the Short ("Łokietek"), who hid here from his enemies.

Taking in the ruins of the medieval Ojców Castle ↑

↑ Fascinating underground chapel in the Bochnia Salt Mine

Kazimierz the Great, between 1350 and 1358. Originally a Gothic building, it was later rebuilt in the Baroque style. Fragments of the rich stone decoration from the interior of the medieval church have survived and are displayed in the Old Sacristy.

The dense Niepołomicka Forest *(Puszcza Niepołomicka)* stretches right behind the town. Brown bears, bison, lynx, wildcat and deer are known to have inhabited it. Wild areas have been preserved, including part of the Poszyna forest which is now home to a bison sanctuary.

Just opposite Niepołomice Castle, the **Sound and Words Centre of Małopolska** contains a museum of record turntables and tape recorders throughout the ages. A row of listening booths allows visitors to play any of the museum's 2,000 vinyl records.

West of the castle is the Grunwald Mound, raised in 1910 to celebrate the 500th anniversary of the Battle of Grunwald, when Polish and Lithuanian armies secured victory against the Teutonic Order.

Niepołomice Castle
🏛 Close to the main car park 🕐 May–Sep: 10am–6pm; Oct–Apr: 10am–5pm 🌐 zamek krolewski.com.pl

Church of Ten Thousand Martyrs
🏛 Ulica Piękna 2 🕐 7am–6pm daily 🌐 parafianiepolomice.pl

Sound and Words Centre of Małopolska
 🏛 Ulica Zamkowa 4 🕐 10am–6pm daily 🌐 mcdis.pl

6

Bochnia Salt Mine
Kopalnia Soli Bochnia

🏛 43 km (27 miles) SE of Kraków 🚍🚆 Bochnia 🕐 For tours only, check website for details 🌐 bochnia-mine.eu

Located in the regional market town of Bochnia, the Bochnia Salt Mine was established in the 13th century and is the oldest salt mine in Poland. Visitors descend over 200 m (660 ft) and travel by underground train to explore the labyrinthine workings. It is sometimes referred to as an underground town. Particularly memorable is Blessed Kinga's Chapel, carved from bare rock, and the enormous Ważyn Chamber, part of which has been converted into a sanatorium due to the humid, mineral-rich air. One of the mine's chambers is flooded with water and visitors are ferried through it in rafts.

EAT

Pestka Restaurant
This stylish restaurant offers delicious Polish fare with a twist. Try the fried duck breast served with brussels sprouts, pickled ginger, and plum-and-cognac sauce.

🏛 Ulica Zatorska 17, Wadowice 🌐 pestkarestaurant.pl

ⓩⓩⓩ

Kawiarnia Niezapominajka
This cute-as-a-button café, found in the heart of Ojców National Park, offers a beguiling range of cakes and desserts.

🏛 Ojców 57a, Ojców National Park 🕐 10am–6pm Sat & Sun 📞 509 790 150

ⓩⓩⓩ

7

Grodzisko

🏛 28 km (17 miles) NW of Kraków 🚆 From Kraków main train station

The little village of Grodzisko is situated on the opposite bank of the Prądnik river from Ojców. It is most famous for being home to the **Church of the Blessed Salomea**, a tiny church dedicated to the first Mother Superior of a convent that was previously found in the village. It has several charming Baroque touches, like the elephant bearing an obelisk.

Church of the Blessed Salomea
🏛 Grodzisko nr 5 🕐 9–10am daily 🌐 ojcow-grodzisko.pl

 8

Kalwaria Zebrzydowska

🚗 30 km (19 miles) SW of Kraków 🚌 From Main Coach Station 🚆 From Kraków's main Railway Station, change at Kraków-Płaszów 🌐 kalwaria.eu

Poland's first calvary was built around 1600 near Kalwaria Zebrzydowska, a charming town nestled amid the foothills of the Carpathians. Calvaries, or Ways of the Cross, are an outdoor representation of the crucifixion of Jesus. They were introduced in the 16th century and were built throughout Europe to commemorate the Passion and Death of Christ.

The calvary at Kalwaria Zebrzydowska consists of 42 chapels, representing the Stations of the Cross, that were built atop Żary Hill on the orders of Mikołaj Zebrzydowski, an important administrator of the Kraków area. Both the impressive Franciscian monastery and the beautifully decorated Bernardine Church form part of the calvary. The whole complex has been named a UNESCO World Heritage Site.

"Mystery plays" (dramatized performances portraying scenes from the Bible) and religious feasts are staged in Kalwaria during Holy Week. The "funeral of the Virgin" takes place on the feast of the Assumption. During this event, crowds of pilgrims arrive to venerate the miraculous icon of the Mother of God, whose cult in the Bernardine Church goes back to the 17th century.

💬 **INSIDER TIP**
Cream Cakes

Wadowice is famous for its *kremówki* or cream cakes – delicious vanilla custard sandwiched between mille-feuille pastry. Local boy Karol Wojtyła (the future Pope John Paul II) was a big fan.

↑ Baroque interior of the Bernardine Church in Kalwaria Zebrzydowska

 9

Wadowice

🚗 40 km (25 miles) SW of Kraków 🚌 From Kraków's main coach station 🛈 Ulica Koscielna 4; www.it.wadowice.pl

Wadowice was first recorded in 1327, but the town came to international attention in 1978 when Karol Wojtyła, born here on 18 May 1920, was elected Pope. Almost immediately the town became a place of mass

→ Monument of Pope John Paul II, in Wadowice, the city where he was born

pilgrimage. The local sites associated with the Pope include the Baroque Church of the Presentation of the Virgin Mary, where he was baptized. The **Family House of John Paul II** now houses a museum dedicated to the pontiff. It contains an array of personal objects, including family photos.

Another site associated with John Paul II is the votive Church of St Peter the Arch-shepherd, which was built on the outskirts of Wadowice in thanksgiving for the Pope's survival of an assassination attempt on 13 May 1981. The walls of its nave seem to give way under the power of light, symbolizing the triumph of good over evil.

The town has had a chequered history, especially in the last century. While under German occupation during World War II, it was renamed Frauenstadt and the entire Jewish population was either executed on the spot or sent to nearby Auschwitz.

Family House of John Paul II

⌂ Ulica Kościelna 7 🕐 May-Sep: 9am-7pm daily; Nov-Mar: 9am-2:40pm daily; Apr & Oct: 9am-4:40pm daily 🅦 domjp2.pl

---

⑩

Lanckorona

⌂ 38 km (27 miles) SW of Kraków 🚉 Kalwarja Zebrzydowska 🚌 Lanckorona

Lanckorona, one of Poland's most attractive villages, is a short distance from the easternmost stations of Kalwaria Zebrzydowska's famous calvary trail. The picturesque market square is surrounded by traditional timber houses; many are painted in bright colours. Above the square, paths lead up to the ruins of a castle that was destroyed during the 17th-century Swedish invasion.

⑪

Pieskowa Skała Castle

⌂ 35 km (22 miles) NW of Kraków 🚌 From Kraków's main coach station 🕐 Hours vary, check website for details 🅦 pieskowaskala.eu

The Pieskowa Skała Castle was built by King Kazimierz the Great in the 14th century as part of the defence system on the Kraków-Częstochowa Uplands. It became private property in 1377. Between 1542 and 1544, enlargement of the castle was undertaken by Stanisław Szafraniec and his wife, Anna Dębińska.

The castle, which is a branch of the Wawel Royal Castle (p104), houses a fascinating museum. The main exhibition is dedicated to the history of Polish interiors from medieval times to the 19th century. Among the objects on display are pieces of furniture, tapestries and decorative objects, as well as a diverse array of art works.

The museum also contains an exhibit on the history of Pieskowa Skała and a gallery of English painting.

Pieskowa Skała Castle by the Pradnik river, Lesser Poland →

NEED TO KNOW

BEFORE YOU GO

Forward planning is essential for any successful trip. Be prepared for all eventualities by considering the following points before you travel.

AT A GLANCE

CURRENCY
Złoty (PLN)

AVERAGE DAILY SPEND

SAVE **260zł**

SPEND **550zł**

SPLURGE **800zł+**

BOTTLED WATER **3zł**

COFFEE **9zł**

BEER **12zł**

DINNER FOR TWO **150zł**

ESSENTIAL PHRASES

Hello	Cześć
Thank you	Dziękuję
Please	Proszę
Goodbye	Do widzenia
Do you speak English	Czy mówi pan angielsku?
I don't understand	Nie rozumiem

ELECTRICITY SUPPLY

Power sockets are type C and E, fitting two-pronged plugs. Standard voltage is 230 volts.

Passports and visas

Citizens of the EU, USA, Australia, Canada and New Zealand can enter Poland without a visa, on production of a valid passport. Poland is a member of the Schengen group of EU countries, which means that there are unlikely to be any border controls when entering Poland from another Schengen-zone country. Citizens of other countries should check the latest visa regulations on the website of Poland's **Ministry of Foreign Affairs** or with their local Polish embassy.
Ministry of Foreign Affairs
W gov.pl/diplomacy

Travel Safety Advice

The **UK Foreign and Commonwealth Office**, the **US State Department** and the **Australian Department of Foreign Affairs and Trade** provide up-to-date travel safety information.
Australia
W smartraveller.gov.au
UK
W gov.uk/foreign-travel-advice
US
W travel.state.gov

Customs Information

If you are travelling to Poland from another EU country there are few restrictions on what you can take in or out. Visitors from the UK should note that they are only allowed to take a maximum of 200 cigarettes home from Poland. Otherwise rules for EU citizens are as follows:
Tobacco Products 800 cigarettes, 400 cigarillos, 200 cigars or 1kg of smoking tobacco
Alcohol 10 litres of alcoholic beverages above 22% strength, 20 litres of alcoholic beverages below 22% strength, 90 litres of wine (80 litres of which can be sparkling) and 110 litres of beer.
Cash If you plan to enter or leave the EU with €10,000 or more in cash (or equivalent in other currencies), you must declare it to the customs authorities.
Visitors from outside the EU should check the customs regulations of their home country .

All visitors will need a licence to export any item more than 100 years old or any artwork more than 50 years old and exceeding 16,000zł in value. For more information on licences visit the Polish **Ministry of Finance** website.
Ministry of Finance
W finanse.mf.gov.pl

Insurance

It is wise to take out an insurance policy covering theft, loss of belongings, medical problems, cancellations and delays. Residents of the EU, the European Economic Area and Switzerland are entitled to free first-aid and emergency treatment in Poland on production of a European Health Insurance Card (EHIC). Additional medicines or non-essential treatment will have to be paid for. Visitors from outside those areas will need to have private health insurance or will be required to pay up-front for all treatment.
EHIC
W gov.uk/european-health-insurance-card

Vaccinations

No vaccinations are required for Poland.

Money

Major credit and debit cards are accepted in most shops, businesses and the main railway station. They can't always be used in smaller cafés, restaurants, snack bars, and the smaller B&Bs and hostels, so it is a good idea to carry some cash, too. Cash machines can be found at most banks, shopping malls and the city's railway station.

Booking Accommodation

Kraków offers an incredible variety of accommodation, from boutique hotels in historic buildings to spa resorts and backpacker hostels. It is worth booking well in advance in the summer months (from June to September), at Easter, and around the 1 May and 3 May public holidays, when lodgings tend to fill up fast and prices rise.

Travellers with Specific Needs

Most of Kraków's main sights and public buildings have wheelchair access. Hotels of four stars and above have wheelchair-friendly rooms, but these are often in short supply and ought to be booked in advance. Many trams and buses in the city are equipped with hydraulic ramps which allow for the boarding of wheelchairs. Electronic destination boards, found at many stops, especially those in the city centre, highlight wheelchair-accessible vehicles, together with the expected waiting time.

Accessible Poland Tours organize trips to Kraków for travellers with specific requirements, including those in wheelchairs, and the visually and hearing impaired.
Accessible Poland Tours
W accessibletour.pl

Language

The official language of Poland is Polish, a Slavic language related to Czech, Slovak and Russian. English is widely spoken in Kraków and throughout the tourist industry, but the same cannot be said for more rural areas surrounding the city.

Closures

Mondays Most tourist attractions are closed.
Sundays Most businesses, malls and shops are closed, except for small convenience stores. Visiting times in churches may be restricted due to Sunday masses.
Public holidays Post offices, banks, shops and most tourist attractions will be closed all day.

PUBLIC HOLIDAYS	
1 Jan	New Year's Day
6 Jan	Epiphany
Mar/Apr	Easter
1 May	Labour Day
3 May	Constitution Day
May/Jun	Pentecost Sunday/ Whit Sunday
May/Jun	Corpus Christi
15 Aug	Feast of the Assumption
1 Nov	All Saints' Day
11 Nov	Independence Day
25 Dec	Christmas Day
26 Dec	St Stephen's Day

GETTING
AROUND

Whether exploring Kraków by foot or public transport, here is all you'll need to know to navigate the city like a local.

PUBLIC TRANSPORT COSTS

SHORT TRIP

3.40zł

20 minutes

SINGLE JOURNEY

4.60zł

50 minutes

24-HOUR PASS

15zł

Central zone

72-HOUR PASS

42zł

All zones

TOP TIP

Tickets are valid on all trams and buses run by municipal transport authority MPK. Different tickets are required for trains and water taxis.

SPEED LIMIT

MOTORWAY

140 km/h

NATIONAL ROADS

100 km/h

REGIONAL ROAD

90 km/h

URBAN AREAS

50 km/h

Arriving by Air

More than 20 international airlines fly to Kraków's John Paul II International Airport, which is situated 15 km (9 miles) west of the city centre at Balice. The airport is connected to most European capital cities, as well as to Dubai and Chicago. The airport has a single passenger terminal and is well served with cafés, exchange facilities and car-hire desks.

Getting to and from Kraków airport is easy, with a choice of either train or bus for those without their own transport. Trains run from the airport to Kraków Główny, the city's main train station, every 30 minutes between 5am and 11pm. Tickets can be bought from a ticket machine in the terminal or from the conductor.

In addition bus No 208 runs from the airport to Kraków Główny (hourly from 4.30am to 9.30pm) and bus No 252 runs to Rondo Grunwaldzkie in the western part of the city (every 30min from 4.15am to 10.15pm). There is also a night bus, No 902, which runs to Kraków Główny (hourly between the hours of midnight and 4pm). Bus tickets can be bought from a machine in the terminal or from the bus driver if you have the correct change.

For information on journey times and ticket prices for transport between the airport and the city centre, see the table (opposite).

Several European budget airlines fly to Katowice airport, 110km (68 miles) northwest of Kraków in Pyrzowice. Most of the main car-rental firms have offices here. Minibus services (run by companies such as **Matuszek** and **Pyrzowice Ekspres**) connect the airport with Kraków city centre, although they should be booked well in advance to be sure of a seat.

Matuszek
w matuszek.com.pl
Pyrzowice Ekspres
w pyrzowiceekspres.pl

Train Travel

International Train Travel

The main train station, Kraków Główny, is served by direct trains from Prague, Vienna, Bratislava

GETTING TO AND FROM THE AIRPORT

Transport	Journey Time	Price
Train	20 min	9zł
Bus	35-45 min	4.60zł
Taxi	30 min	90zł

and Budapest, and is accessible from most other European capitals involving at least one change of train. Seat reservations are usually obligatory on international express trains and advance booking is advised.

You can buy tickets and passes for multiple international journeys from **Eurail** or **Interrail**, although you may still need to pay an additional supplement and reservation fee on the faster trains. Students and those who are under 26 can benefit from discounted rail travel. For more information on discounted rail travel to and within Poland, visit either the Interrail or Eurail websites.

Eurail
W eurail.com
Interrail
W interrail.eu

Domestic Train Travel

Local train lines can be very useful in reaching many of the destinations found outside of the city's boundaries (p184). Your most likely starting point is Kraków Główny, a busy train station whose ticket counters and pedestrian concourse are all located underground. Queues can build up at ticket counters and it can take time to find the right platform for your train, so always arrive with plenty of time to spare.

Trains in Poland are run by a variety of different companies, although tickets for all services can be bought from the main ticket counters at Kraków Główny. From here local train company **Koleje Małopolskie** runs services to Wieliczka and Bochnia, while **Przewozy Regionalne** operates trains to Oświęcim (for Auschwitz), Wadowice, Kalwaria Zebrzydowska and Zakopane. For onward travel within Poland, **PKP InterCity** runs fast trains to Warsaw, Gdańsk and other cities. Note that while all rail companies have timetables for their own services online, **Deutsche Bahn** has information for all train times in Poland.

Koleje Małopolskie
W malopolskiekoleje.pl
Przewozy Regionalne
W polregio.pl
PKP InterCity
W intercity.pl
Deutsche Bahn
W bahn.de

Domestic Bus Travel

There is a country-wide network of bus services run by a multitude of different companies. The city's main bus station (dworzec autobusowy) is the main point of departure for services to Oświęcim (Auschwitz), Kalwaria Zebrzydowska, Zakopane and other day-trip destinations. The bus station is immediately east of the railway station and is accessible via the pedestrian walkways that run underneath the railway platforms. It is equipped with easy-to-read departure boards, ticket counters and cafés, although it gets very busy at weekends and during holiday times, when there are long queues for tickets. During busy periods, many services may sell out well before departure time. It is not always possible to buy tickets online in advance, so it is advisable to book tickets in person at the bus station the day before travel.

Kraków Bus Station
W mda.malopolska.pl

Public Transport

Kraków's comprehensive network of tram and bus services are provided by the City Transport Company (Miejskie Przedsiębiorstwo Komunikacyjne or **MPK**). Both are easy to use, with well-marked stops and ticket machines, although all forms of transport are prone to overcrowding at peak times. It is worth noting that the city centre is relatively compact and many sights are within walking distance of each other.

Trams and Buses

Trams are the main form of transport in central Kraków, running round either side of the largely pedestrianized Old Town, and offer the best way of getting around central Kraków. They are the best means of travelling to and from the main bus and railway stations, and are also the quickest way of reaching outlying attractions such as Nowa Huta, Podgórze and Zwierzyniec. Trams run from around 5am to 11pm. There are three night-tram routes operating at hourly intervals between 11.30pm and 4am. Most tram routes operate every 10-15 minutes in the middle of the day, and every 20-25 minutes early in the morning and late in the evening.

Kraków's bus services cover all the out-of-centre suburbs with a dense network of lines. Bus routes are a good way of getting to suburban attractions such as Wolski Forest and Tyniec Abbey. Bus routes numbered from 100 to 194 operate within Kraków city, while buses numbered 201 to 297 continue to destinations just outside the city limits (these are included in Zone 2 of the public transport zoning system). Routes beginning with a 3 or a 5 are express services and only call at major stops along the way. Buses run at intervals of 10-20 minutes between 4.30am and 11.30pm. Bus routes beginning with 6 or 9 are night buses. These buses run about once an hour between 11:30pm and 4am, and cross the city in all directions. The fare is the same as for any other bus journey.

Tickets for both trams and buses can be bought from newspaper kiosks, from ticket machines placed at individual tram and bus stops, and from ticket machines inside the vehicles themselves. Most ticket machines take cash only (change is given) although some of the centrally located ones take cards. Tickets are validated by inserting them into one of the machines located inside the doors of the vehicle.

A number of different types of tickets are available. A 20-minute, single-journey ticket will suffice if you are travelling between central destinations such as the Old Town, Kazimierz and Podgórze. A 50-minute single-journey ticket will be required if you are travelling between the centre and the suburbs. If you think that you are going to be using a lot of public transport during your stay then significant savings can be made by purchasing a 24-hour, 48-hour, 72-hour or 7-day ticket. Periodic checks are carried out by ticket inspectors who will levy an on-the-spot fine if you are caught without a valid ticket.

There are two zones in Kraków: Zone 1 (Strefa 1) covers the city of Kraków, while Zone 2 (Strefa 2) covers the ring of settlements outside the city. Almost all the destinations you are likely to visit are in Zone 1, except Kraków airport. The 50-minute single-journey ticket is sufficient to reach most destinations in Zone Two. Otherwise purchasers of period passes should note that the 24-hour ticket and the 7-day ticket are available in two versions (Zone 1 and Zone 1+2). The 48-hour and 72-hour tickets are only valid for Zone 1 and extra tickets must be bought if you are travelling into Zone 2.

MPK
🆆 mpk.krakow.pl

Water Trams

The **Water Tram** (tramwaj wodny) is a boat service that operates on the Vistula River from May 1 to September 30. Services start on the riverbank in Kazimierz and run to the Convent of the Norbertine Sisters in Zwierzyniec, calling at Wawel Hill on the way. Services run every 65 minutes between 10.05am and 17.45pm. One daily service runs all the way to the Benedictine Abbey at Tyniec. Tickets on the Kazimierz-Zwierzyniec stretch cost 12zł each way; a ticket to Tyniec costs 30zł. Tickets are bought aboard the boat.

Water Tram
🆆 tramwajwodny.pl

Taxis

Taxi ranks can be found at the main points of arrival into the city: at the airport, at the bus station, and on the rooftop parking lot of the train station (take the elevator to the top level). There are also taxi ranks at the main entrances to the Old Town, such as ulica Sławkowska and plac Wszystkich Świętych. Flagging down taxis on the street is rarely possible and it is best to go to a rank or order a taxi by phone. **Wawel Taxi** and **Barbakan** are two reputable taxi companies. Most taxi journeys are metered, although you may be able to negotiate a fee if you are going a particularly short or long distance. Private taxis, which do not display a company name and phone number, should be avoided, and taxi touts at the airport or train station should be ignored, as their charges may be several times the official rate. **Uber** cars are available in Kraków for travellers who have the Uber app.

Wawel Taxi
📞 19666
Barbakan
📞 19661
Uber
🆆 uber.com

Driving

Driving to Kraków

Poland is increasingly integrated into the European motorway network. However routes from the west (through Germany) are faster than those from the south or east, where motorway construction is lagging behind. The principal motorway linking Western Europe to Kraków is the E40 (Dresden-Wrocław-Kraków). Travelling from Prague, Vienna, Bratislava or Budapest involves a combination of motorways and single carriageway roads.

In the event of a break down, **Emergency Road Services** can arrange a tow truck and advise on nearby garages.

Emergency Road Services

📞 9637

Driving in Kraków

Getting around by car in Kraków can be challenging and time consuming, with routes near the city centre particularly busy . There are also many confusing one-way systems. Note that Kraków's efficient and comprehensive public transport system is probably a much easier and less stressful way of getting around the city.

Outside of Kraków, the number of fast inter-city highways is increasing, and travel times between the major centres are getting shorter. Away from the main highways, however, progress can be slow, with columns of traffic building up on popular routes. Road surfaces in general are improving although rural routes may be bumpy. The area around Kraków is one of the most heavily touristed regions in the country, and traffic on all roads in and out of the city can be thick at weekends and holiday times. The road to Zakopane can be particularly busy, with long queues building up at peak holiday times.

Car Rental

All major international car rental companies operate in Kraków. It is best to book a particular make of car before arrival. Key conditions are a valid full driving licence and a minimum age of 21 or 25, depending on the hire company. Before signing the rental documents, it is also advisable to check the level of insurance cover provided. Travellers should themselves take out adequate insurance.

Parking

Finding an on-street parking space can be very difficult in Kraków; if you park elsewhere you risk getting fined or having your wheels clamped. Street parking in clearly signed areas costs 3zł for the first hour, 3.50zł for the second, 4.10zł for the third, and 3zł for each subsequent hour. Parking tickets can be bought from street-side ticket machines (although these do not give change, so it is a good idea to have smaller amounts of cash available) or from uniformed wardens. Charges for on-street parking apply between 10am and 8pm from Monday to Saturday (parking is free on Sundays). It is frequently more straightforward to find a parking garage or guarded parking lot *(parking strzeżony)*, of which there are several near the city centre, including **Parking Kraków Centrum** on ulica Karmelicka 26 and **Parking Wawel** on plac Na Groblach 24. These rarely cost more that 50-60zł per 24 hours. Hotels often have parking spaces for guests.

Parking Kraków Centrum

📞 690 666 284

Parking Wawel

🔲 parkingwawel.pl

Rules of the Road

The wearing of seat belts in Poland is compulsory. Children under the age of 12 are not allowed to travel in the front of the car, and small children must be strapped into special child seats. Headlights must be on, day and night, regardless of the weather conditions. Radar speed controls are frequent, and offenders will be given an on-the-spot fine. The use of mobile phones while driving is banned unless the phone is a hands-free model. The permitted alcohol content In blood is so low in Poland (two parts per thousand) that drinking and driving should be avoided altogether. It is obligatory for motorcyclists and their passengers to always wear helmets.

Cycling

Kraków is becoming more and more bike friendly, with an increasing number of cycling lanes and signed cycling routes. The city's green spaces – especially the Planty, a park surrounding the Old Town – are perfect for easy cycling. Cycling on the pavement is permissible in areas where bike lanes do not exist, which means that cyclists don't have to dodge traffic on the main roads. However, cyclists on pavements should always give way to pedestrians. Cycling under the influence of alcohol is strictly forbidden. Cycle theft is common and your bike should never be left unchained or unlocked.

The city-wide bicycle hire scheme operated by **Wawelo** allows you to pick up and drop off bikes at regular points throughout the city, once you have registered with a credit card. Offering a wider range of bikes (including mountain bikes, and bikes with child seats) are specialist bike rental outfits such as **KRK Bike Rental** and **Kraków Bike Tour**. Guided cycle tours are also available from agents such as Kraków Bike Tour and are a wonderfully invigorating way to see the city.

Wavelo

🔲 wavelo.pl

KRK Bike Rental

🔲 krkbikerental.pl

Kraków Bike Tour

🔲 krakowbiketour.com

PRACTICAL
INFORMATION

A little know-how gets you a long way in Kraków. Here you can find all the essential advice and information you will need during your stay.

AT A GLANCE

EMERGENCY NUMBERS

FIRE, POLICE AND AMBULANCE	MOUNTAIN RESCUE
112	**985**

TIME ZONE
CET/CEST. Central European Summer Time runs from the last Sunday in March to the last Sunday in October.

TAP WATER
Ordinary tap water in Poland is safe to drink. Outdoor taps not connected to the main supply will have a sign reading *woda niezdatna do picia* (not drinking water)

TIPPING

Waiter	10 per cent
Hotel Porter	10zł per trip
Housekeeping	10zł
Concierge	20zł
Taxi Driver	10 per cent

Personal Security

Kraków is a generally safe city in which to travel and visitors are unlikely to encounter difficulties providing they take the usual precautions against petty crime. Crowded bars, public transport, the train and bus stations, and busy markets are the places where petty thieves and pickpockets are most active. Pickpockets often work in gangs, and a sudden push or other distraction is rarely accidental. Car break-ins can occur and valuables should never be left unattended in the car. Use guarded car parks rather than on-street parking wherever possible. If you have anything stolen, report it to the police as soon as possible. Make sure you get a copy of the crime report in order to claim on your insurance. If you have your passport stolen, contact your embassy or consulate.

Tourists on the lookout for nightlife opportunities are particularly prone to being overcharged, so should avoid the tourist-trap bars and clubs. Late-night noisy behaviour in Kraków is a frequent annoyance, but outright public disorder is very rare.

LGBT+ Safety

Although homosexuality is not illegal in Poland, it remains a conservative country in which LGBTQ+ communities are not always met with across-the-board acceptance. An annual Equality Parade *(Parada Równości)* is held in Kraków every May, and there is a growing handful of hotels, bars and clubs that welcome members of the LGBTQ+ community. Outside the city centre, same-sex couples may elicit a negative response from locals and business-owners.

Health

Emergency treatment for citizens of the EU and Switzerland is free of charge. Popular remedies are available over-the-counter at local pharmacies, but for more specific drugs and medicines you will need a prescription authorized by a local doctor. Minor health problems can often be dealt with in a pharmacy, where trained staff

can provide advice on remedies. For more serious injury or illness, head for the emergency department of the nearest hospital.

Smoking, Alcohol and Drugs

Smoking is prohibited in all public places, restaurants, cafés and bars, with the exception of some bars which have an area specifically set aside for smokers.

The blood alcohol limit for drivers is 0.02 per cent, a very small amount which will be exceeded even if you only drink half a glass of wine – so it is best not to drink at all. Beware that riding a bicycle while under the influence of alcohol is also a punishable offence.

Custodial sentences are frequently applied to those in possession of illegal drugs, especially if you are buying or selling.

ID

Although checks on ID are rare in Poland, visitors are obliged to carry either their passport or identity card at all times.

Visiting Places of Worship

Poland is a devout Roman Catholic country and certain standards are expected when visiting churches. Visitors should refrain from making noise and use cameras discreetly. Strict dress codes apply: cover your torso and upper arms, and ensure shorts and skirts cover your knees. Shoes must be worn. Some of the synagogues in Kazimierz require male visitors to wear a black skullcap, available at the entrance.

Mobile Phones and Wi-Fi

Most hotels, cafés and bars offer free Wi-Fi to their customers. There are also free Wi-Fi hotspots in the main railway station and in the city centre, around the Main Market Square. Visitors travelling to Poland on EU tariffs are able to use their devices abroad without having to pay extra roaming charges on calls, SMS messages or data.

Post

Stamps can be bought from both post offices and newspaper kiosks. Allow around 6-9 days when sending post to Great Britain, and around 10-15 days when sending post to the United States or Australia.

Taxes and Refunds

The rate of VAT in Poland is 23 per cent. Non-EU residents are entitled to VAT tax refunds, providing you request a tax receipt and regular retail receipt when purchasing your goods. These must be presented to a tax refund office, together with your passport, when leaving the country.

Discount Cards

If you are a student and you have an **ISIC** (International Student Identity Card) you will qualify for discounts at tourist attractions and on public transport. All tourists are eligible for the **Kraków Tourist Card**, a visitors' pass which allows free access to public transport, free entrance to 40 of the city's museums, and discounts on car hire and on tours offered by local travel agents. The card is available in two-day or three-day versions (120zł and 140zł respectively). There is also a three-day "Museums and Attractions" card which does not include public transport (90zł). The cards are available online or from tourist offices.
ISIC
w isic.org
Kraków Tourist Card
w krakowcard.com

INDEX

PHRASE BOOK

SUMMARY OF PRONUNCIATION IN POLISH

ą *a nasal "awn" as in "sawn" or "an" as in the French "Anjou"*
  but barely sounded
c *"ts" as in "bats"*
ć, cz *"ch" as in "challenge"*
ch *"ch" as in Scottish "loch"*
dz *"j" as in "jeans" when followed by **i** or **e** but otherwise "dz"*
  as in "adze"
dź *"j" as in "jeans"*
dż *"d" as in "dog" followed by "s" as in "leisure"*
ę *similar to "en" in "end" only nasal and barely sounded, but if at*
  the end of the word pronounced "e" as in "bed"
h *"ch" as in Scottish "loch"*
i *"ee" as in "teeth"*
j *"y" as in yes*
ł *"w" as in "window"*
ń *similar to the "ni" in "companion"*
ó *"oo" as in "soot"*
rz *similar to the "s" in "leisure" or, when it follows **p**, **t** or **k**, "sh"*
  as in "shut"
ś, sz *"sh" as in "shut"*
w *"v" as in "vine"*
y *similar to the "i" in "bit"*
ź, ż *similar to the "s" in "leisure"*

EMERGENCIES

Help!	**pomocy!**	*pomotsi*
Call a doctor!	**zawołać doktora!**	*zawowach doctora*
Call an ambulance!	**zadzwonić po pogotowie!**	*zadzvoneech po pogotovee*
Police!	**policja!**	*poleetsya*
Call the fire brigade!	**zadzwonić po straż pożarną!**	*zadzvoneech po stras posarnAWN*
Where is the nearest phone?	**Gdzie jest najbliższa budka telefoniczna?**	*gjeh yest nIbleezhsha boodka telefoneechna*
Where is the hospital?	**Gdzie jest szpital?**	*gjeh yest shpeetal*
Where is the police station	**Gdzie jest posterunek policji?**	*gjeh yest posterunek politsyee*

COMMUNICATION ESSENTIALS

Yes	**Tak**	*tak*
No	**Nie**	*n-yeh*
Thank you	**Dziękuję**	*jENkoo-yeh*
No thank you	**Nie, dziękuję**	*n-yej jENkoo-yeh*
Please	**Proszę**	*prosheh*
I don't understand.	**Nie rozumiem.**	*n-yeh rozoom-yem*
Do you speak English? (to a man)	**Czy mówi pan po angielsku?**	*chi moovee pan po ang-yelskoo*
Do you speak English? (to a woman)	**Czy mówi pani po angielsku?**	*chi moovee panee po ang-yelskoo*
Please speak more slowly	**Proszę mówić wolniej.**	*proseh mooveech voln-yay*
Please write it down for me.	**Proszę mi to napisać.**	*prosheh mee to napeesach*
My name is...	**Nazywam się...**	*nazivam sheh*

USEFUL WORDS AND PHRASES

Pleased to meet you (to a man)	**Bardzo mi miło pana poznać**	*bardzo mee meewo pana poznach*
Pleased to meet you (to a woman)	**Bardzo mi miło panią poznać**	*bardzo mee meewo pan-yAWN poznach*
Good morning	**Dzień dobry**	*jen-yuh dobri*
Good afternoon	**Dzień dobry**	*jen-yuh dobri*
Good evening	**Dobry wieczór**	*dobri v-yechoor*
Good night	**Dobranoc**	*dobranots*
Goodbye	**Do widzenia**	*do veedzen-ya*
What time is it...?	**Która jest godzina?**	*ktoora yest gojeena*
Cheers!	**Na zdrowie!**	*na zdrov-yeh*
Excellent!	**Wspaniale**	*wspan-yaleh*

SHOPPING

Do you have...? (to a man)	**Czy ma pan...?**	*che ma pan*
Do you have...? (to a woman)	**Czy ma pani...?**	*che ma panee*
How much is this?	**Ile to kosztuje?**	*eeleh to koshtoo-yeh*
Where is the... department?	**Gdzie jest dział z...?**	*gjeh yest jawuh z*

Do you take credit cards? (to a man)	**Czy przyjmuje pan karty kredytowe?**	*chi pshi-yuhmoo-yeh pan karti kreditoveh*
Do you take credit cards? (to a woman)	**Czy przyjmuje pani karty kredytowe?**	*chi pshi-yuhmoo-yeh panee karti kreditoveh*
bakery	**piekarnia**	*p-yekarn-ya*
bookshop	**księgarnia**	*kshENgarn-ya*
chemist	**apteka**	*apteka*
department store	**dom towarowy**	*dom tovarovi*
exchange office	**kantor walutowy**	*kantor valootovi*
travel agent	**biuro podróży**	*b-yooro podroozhi*
post office	**poczta, urząd pocztowy**	*pochta, ooZHAWNd pochtovi*
postcard	**pocztówka**	*pochtoovka*
stamp	**znaczek**	*znachek*
How much is a postcard to...?	**Ile kosztuje pocztówka do...?**	*eeleh koshtoo-yeh pochtoovka do*
airmail	**poczta lotnicza**	*pochta lotneecha*

STAYING IN A HOTEL

Have you any vacancies? (to a man)	**Czy ma pan wolne pokoje?**	*chi ma pan volneh poko-yeh*
Have you any vacancies? (to a woman)	**Czy ma pani wolne pokoje?**	*chi ma panee volneh poko-yeh*
What is the charge per night?	**Ile kosztuje za dobę?**	*eeleh koshtoo-yeh za dobeh*
I'd like a single room.	**Poproszę pokój jednoosobowy.**	*poprosheh pokoo-yuh yedno-osobovi*
I'd like a double room.	**Poproszę pokój dwuosobowy.**	*poprosheh pokoo-yuh dvoo-osobovi*
I'd like a twin room.	**Poproszę pokój z dwoma łóżkami.**	*poprosheh pokoo-yuh z dvoma woozhkamee*
I'd like a room with a bathroom.	**Poproszę pokój z łazienką.**	*poprosheh pokoo-yuh z wazhenkAWN*
bathroom	**łazienka**	*wazhenka*
bed	**łóżko**	*woozhko*
bill	**rachunek**	*raHoonek*
breakfast	**śniadanie**	*shn-yadan-yeh*
dinner	**kolacja**	*kolats-ya*
double room	**pokój dwuosobowy**	*pokoo-yuh dvoo-osobovi*
full board	**pełne utrzymanie**	*pewuhneh ootzhiman-yeh*
guest house	**zajazd**	*za-yazd*
half board	**dwa posiłki dziennie**	*dva posheewuhkee jen-yeh*
key	**klucz**	*klooch*
restaurant	**restauracja**	*restawrats-ya*
shower	**prysznic**	*prishneets*
single room	**pokój jednoosobowy**	*pokoo-yuh yedno-osobovi*
toilet	**toaleta**	*to-aleta*

EATING OUT

A table for one, please.	**Stolik dla jednej osoby proszę.**	*stoleek dla yednay osobi prosheh*
A table for two, please.	**Stolik dla dwóch osób proszę.**	*stoleek dla dvooh osoob prosheh*
Can I see the menu?	**Mogę prosić jadłospis?**	*mogeh prosheech yadwospees*
Can I see the wine list?	**Mogę prosić kartę win?**	*mogeh prosheech karteh veen*
I'd like...	**Proszę**	*prosheh*
Can we have the bill, please?	**Proszę rachunek?**	*prosheh raHoonek*
Where is the toilet?	**Gdzie jest toaleta?**	*gjeh yest to-aleta*

MENU DECODER

baranina	*mutton, lamb*
barszcz czerwony	*beetroot soup*
bażant	*pheasant*
befsztyk	*beef steak*
bigos	*hunter's stew (sweet and sour cabbage with a variety of meats and seasonings)*
bukiet z jarzyn	*a variety of raw and pickled vegetables*
ciasto	*cake, pastry*
cielęcina	*veal*

cukier	sugar	
cukierek	sweet, confectionery	
dania mięsne	meat dishes	
dania rybne	fish dishes	
dania z drobiu	poultry dishes	
deser	dessert	
flaki	tripe	
grzybki marynowane	marinated mushrooms	
herbata	tea	
jarzyny	vegetables	
kabanos	dry, smoked pork sausage	
kaczka	duck	
kapusta	cabbage	
kartofle	potatoes	
kasza gryczana	buckwheat	
kaszanka	black pudding	
kawa	coffee	
kiełbasa	sausage	
klopsiki	minced meat balls	
lody	ice cream	
łosoś	salmon	
łosoś wędzony	smoked salmon	
makowiec	poppy seed cake	
naleśniki	pancakes	
piernik	spiced honeycake	
pierogi	ravioli-like dumplings	
piwo	beer	
prawdziwki	ceps (type of mushroom)	
przystawki	entrées	
pstrąg	trout	
rolmopsy	rollmop herrings	
sałatka	salad	
sałatka owocowa	fruit salad	
sok	juice	
sok jabłkowy	apple juice	
sok owocowy	fruit juice	
sól	salt	
śledź	herring	
tort	cake, gâteau	
wieprzowina	pork	
wino	wine	
woda	water	
ziemniaki	potatoes	
zupa	soup	

HEALTH

I do not feel well.	Źle się czuję.	zhleh sheh choo-yeh
I need a prescription for...	Potrzebuję receptę na...	potzheboo-yeh retsepteh na
cold	przeziębienie	pshef-yENb-yen-yeh
cough (noun)	kaszel	kashel
cut	skaleczenie	skalechen-yeh
flu	grypa	gripa
hayfever	katar sienny	katar shyienny
headache pills	proszki od bólu głowy	proshke od booloo gwovi
hospital	szpital	shpeetal
nausea	mdłości	mudwosh-che
sore throat	ból gardła	bool gardwa

TRAVEL AND TRANSPORT

When is the next train to...?	Kiedy jest następny pociąg do...?	k-yedi yest nastENpni pochAWNg do...
What is the fare to...?	Ile kosztuje bilet do...?	eeleh koshtoo-yeh beelet do
A single ticket to ... please	Proszę bilet w jedną stronę bilet do...	prosheh beelet v yednAWN stroneh beelet do
A return ticket to ... please	Proszę bilet w obie strony do...	prosheh beelet v obye strony do
Where is the bus station?	Gdzie jest dworzec autobusowy?	gjeh yest dvozhets awtoboosovi
Where is the bus stop?	Gdzie jest przystanek autobusowy?	gjeh yest pshistanek awtoboosovi
Where is the tram stop?	Gdzie jest przystanek tramwajowy?	gjeh yest pshistanek tramvl-yovi
booking office	kasa biletowa	kasa beeletova
station	stacja	stats-ya

timetable	rozkład jazdy	rozkwad yazdi
left luggage	przechowalnia bagażu	psheHovaln-ya bagazhoo
platform	peron	peron
first class	pierwsza klasa	p-yervsha klasa
second class	druga klasa	drooga klasa
single ticket	bilet w jedną stronę	beelet v yednAWN stroneh
return ticket	bilet powrotny	beelet povrotni
airline	linia lotnicza	leen-ya lotna-yeecha
airport	lotnisko	lotn-yeesko
arrival	przylot	pshilot
flight number	numer lotu	noomer lotoo
gate	przejście	pshaysh-cheh
coach (bus)	autokar	awtokar

NUMBERS

0	zero	zero
1	jeden	yeden
2	dwa	dva
3	trzy	tshi
4	cztery	chteri
5	pięć	p-yENch
6	sześć	shesh-ch
7	siedem	sh-yedem
8	osiem	oshem
9	dziewięć	jev-yENch
10	dziesięć	jeshENch
11	jedenaście	yedenash-cheh
12	dwanaście	dvanash-cheh
13	trzynaście	tshinash-cheh
14	czternaście	chternash-cheh
15	piętnaście	p-yEntnash-cheh
16	szesnaście	shesnash-cheh
17	siedemnaście	shedemnash-cheh
18	osiemnaście	oshemnash-cheh
19	dziewiętnaście	jev-yEntnash-cheh
20	dwadzieścia	dvajesh-cha
21	dwadzieścia jeden	dvajesh-cha yeden
22	dwadzieścia dwa	dvajesh-cha dva
30	trzydzieści	tshijesh-chee
40	czterdzieści	chterjesh-chee
50	pięćdziesiąt	p-yENchjeshAWNt
100	sto	sto
200	dwieście	dv-yesh-cheh
500	pięćset	p-yENchset
1,000	tysiąc	tishAWNts
1,000,000	milion	meel-yon

TIME

today	dzisiaj	jeeshl
yesterday	wczoraj	vchorl
tomorrow	jutro	yootro
tonight	dzisiejszej nocy	jeeshAYshay notsi
one minute	jedna minuta	yedna meenoota
half an hour	pół godziny	poowuh gojeeni
hour	godzina	gojeena

DAYS OF THE WEEK

Sunday	niedziela	n-yejela
Monday	poniedziałek	pon-yejawek
Tuesday	wtorek	vtorek
Wednesday	środa	shroda
Thursday	czwartek	chvartek
Friday	piątek	p-yAWNtek
Saturday	sobota	sobota

ACKNOWLEDGMENTS

The publisher would like to thank the following for their kind permission to reproduce their photographs:

Key: a-above; b-below/bottom; c-centre; f-far; l-left; r-right; t-top

123RF.com: Roman Babakin 152-3t; dziewul 17bl, 132-3; fazon 33br; Ievgenii Fesenko 71t; Frugo 106clb; hurricanehank 67tr; Patryk Kośmider 40br; Michał Leś 174-5t; mikolaj64 12t, 81cra; Krzysztof Nahlik 19t, 172; seregalsv 104-5b; Malgorzata Slusarczyk 51tl.

akg-images: 103tl; Henning Langenheim 56bc.

Alamy Stock Photo: AA World Travel Library 100tc, 103tr, 181tl; age fotostock / Ana Del Castillo 8-9b, / Christian Goupi 40tl, / Danuta Hyniewska 54tr; agencja FORUM 54cb, 57bl; Antiqua Print Gallery 53tl; Art Directors & TRIP / ArkReligion.com / Brian Gibbs 171cl; Norman Barrett 105tr; BE&W agencja fotograficzna Sp. z o.o. / BE&WON99 170br; Bernard Bialorucki 201br; Bildarchiv Monheim GmbH 57bc; Maurizio Biso 75cra; Michael Brooks 22bl; Inigo Bujedo Aguirre-VIEW 162t; Robert Clare 49cla; CoinUp 35cla; Maciej Czajka 199tl; Maciej Czekajewski 198b; dragoncello 103cra; Robert Dziewulski 50cl; East Images 43cl; eFesenko 131tl, 161b; Endless Travel 75tc, 92clb, 109cra, 122-3b; Europe 153br; Dmitry Evteev 115tl; Faraway Photos 34-5b; Peter Forsberg 71bc; fotolandia / Stockimo 176b; Paul Gapper 51tr; David Gee 1 189cla; Kevin George 110b; GL Archive 55bc; Janusz Gniadek 49cr, 163tr; Granger Historical Picture Archive 53bc; hemis.fr / Patrice Hauser 12clb, 18cb, 22crb, 24-5ca, 38-9t, 39br, 42-3t, 154-5, / Camille Moirenc 39cla; Heritage Image Partnership Ltd / © Fine Art Images 53tr, 54tl, 55br; imageBROKER 47cla, / Artur Cupak 168-9t, / Günter Lenz 87t; INTERFOTO 54br; Israel images 56cla; Wieslaw Jarek 51clb; John Warburton-Lee Photography / Katie Garrod 84cla; Jon Arnold Images Ltd / Neil Farrin 41crb; Huw Jones 88tr; Pawel Kazmierczak 28-9t; Brenda Kean 111tl; Linda Kennard 78-9b; Gunter Kirsch 107tr; Padraig Knudsen 102bl; Christian Kober 124b, 138t,186cr; Tetyana Kochneva 47br; Grzegorz Kozakiewicz 51cla; Torsten Krüger 48b, 68clb; Martin Lindsay 124tl; Look Studio Jerzy Ochoński / photospoland.com 37br; Marcin Łukaszewicz 191br; David Lyon 178tr; MARKA / giovanni mereghetti 27b; mauritius images GmbH / Mikolaj Gospodarek 75tr, 77tr, 194-5b; Tobias Meints 98t; John Michaels 187; mikolajn 123tr;

Roman Milert 100-1b; Krzysztof Nahlik 10-1b, 46bl; Nathaniel Noir 4, 51cra; pawlopicasso 200br; The Picture Art Collection 53cra, 146bc; Prisma Archivo 55tr, 72bl,170tl; PSI 44bl; Simon Reddy 31cl; Juergen Ritterbach 69tl, 190-1t; Robertharding / Bestravelvideo 11t, / Robert Canis 20bl, / Neil Farrin 151tr, / Chris Mouyiaris 24tl, 85b; Witold Skrypczak 122cra; Jacek Sopotnicki 56-7t; Ryszard Stelmachowicz 192t; Steve Allen Travel Photography 17tr, 118-9; Wojciech Stróżyk 57tr; Petr Svarc 140bl; James Talalay 81tl; TNT Magazine Pixate Ltd 93br; Travelimages 186crb (1944); Fabrizio Troiani 29cb; Leisa Tyler 44tc; Lucas Vallecillos 20t, 20cr, 26-7t, 38b, 65tr, 108, 136-7b, 139br; David Wootton 186cra; World History Archive 56tl; Patrizia Wyss 72cb, 72-3; Beata Zawrzel 36br; ZUMA Press; Inc. / SOPA Images / Omar Marques 50cla, 50clb, 79cra.

© Andrzej Wróblewski Foundation, www. andrzejwroblewski.pl: Poczekalnia II (Ukrzesłowienie I)/ Waiting Room I (Chairing I), 1956; olej, płótno/oil, canvas; 155 x 125 cm; Muzeum Narodowe/ National Museum, Kraków 158.

Bridgeman Images: Forum 103tc.

Conrad Festival: Edyta Dufaj 42bl.

Depositphotos Inc: Bloodua 107cra.

Dreamstime.com: Agneskantaruk 169b; Stig Alenäs 126-7; Ryhor Bruyeu 202-3; Jacek Cudak 177cr; Djw782 175bc; Darius Dzinnik 30bl; Enzodebe 18tl, 142-3; Evgeniy Fesenko 88-9b, 112t; Marcin Kadziolka 11cr; Leklek73 125tl, 150b; Liubovterletska 114b; Meinzahn 70cl; Mikolaj64 166-7t; Jaroslav Moravcik 128t; Roland Nagy 193bl; Krzysztof Nahlik 13br, 174bl, 177t, 179b, 183br; Sergiy Palamarchuk 33cla; Ryszard Parys 129br; Alexey Pevnev 163bl; Photopassjonata 22t; Janusz Pieńkowski 54bc; Yaroslava Pravedna 76bl; Peter Probst 82bc; Mariusz Prusaczyk 51crb; Pawel Przybyszewski 189tr; Aliaksei Putau 141br; Jacek Sopotnicki 6-7, 25tr, 64-5t; Studioclover 27cla; Wimalgorzata 13cr; Thomas Wyness 189tl; Zi3000 8cla.

Getty Images: ewg3D 55tl; Fine Art Images / Heritage Images 53br; Hulton Archive 189br, / Galerie Bilderwelt 186clb (1942), 186crb; Keystone 186clb; LightRocket / SOPA Images / Omar Marques 24-5t, 41tl; Pawel Litwinski 2-3; Moment / Josselin Dupont 188-9b, / Karol Majewski 196-7; Moment Open / Wendy Rauw Photography 32-3t, 44-5t, 83br; NurPhoto /